Fourth Edition

Foundation Guide
for
Religious
Grant Seekers

Kerry A. Robinson
Editor

SCHOLARS PRESS
Atlanta, Georgia

SCHOLARS PRESS
HANDBOOK SERIES

Foundation Guide for Religious Grant Seekers
Kerry A. Robinson, Editor

Table of Contents

Foundation Guide for Religious Grant Seekers
Fourth Edition

Designed and typeset by Kerry A. Robinson

Cover design by Graves Fowler Associates

Library of Congress Cataloging in Publication Data

Foundation guide for religious grant seekers / Kerry A. Robinson,
    editor. — 4th ed.
    p. cm. — (Scholars Press handbook series)
    Rev. ed. of: Foundation guide for religious grant seekers /
Francis J. Butler. 3rd ed. c1987.
    ISBN 1-55540-677-7 (alk. paper)
    1. Endowments—United States—Directories. 2. Charities—United
States—Directories. 3. Church charities—United States—
Directories. I. Robinson, Kerry A. II. Butler, Francis J.
Foundation guide for religious grant seekers. III. Series.
HV89.F68 1992
262'.0068'1—dc20   91-46752
                                                      CIP

Acknowledgements

The fourth edition of the *Foundation Guide for Religious Grant Seekers* was made possible through a grant provided by the Lilly Endowment. Since the inauguration of the *Guide* in 1979, the Endowment and FADICA have collaborated in making available a simple and comparatively inexpensive tool for the inexperienced grant seeker. Over the years the *Guide* has become an indispensable reference for thousands of religious communities, individual ministers, scholars and volunteers. This new edition is presented with particular gratitude to Mr. Fred L. Hofheinz of the Lilly Endowment, whose encouragement and initiative led to the present updating of this publication.

Research for this current edition was undertaken with the help and resources of the Foundation Center. We are grateful to the Center for its generous cooperation.

Careful research and editing was carried out by Kerry A. Robinson, Assistant Director for Communications at FADICA, with assistance rendered to this project by research intern, Amy Kroviak and FADICA staff assistant, Marie T. Beeching. We are most appreciative of the hours of painstaking research by Ms. Robinson and her colleagues and we feel confident that their labor will ease the task of the religious grant seeker immeasurably.

Dr. Francis J. Butler
President,
FADICA, Inc.

INTRODUCTION

Although religion, as a category of "charitable" activity, accounts for more than one-half of all private philanthropy in the United States, there are relatively few foundations active in the field of religion. The fact that private foundations with a genuine interest in religion are few and far between has made it difficult for religious organizations to know where to turn for help from foundations.

There has long been a need for a small, practical guide to help religious organizations (Catholic, Protestant or Jewish) locate foundations that might likely fund their projects or programs. Although there are several specialized directories for religious grant seekers today, none is as comprehensive or as inexpensive as the *Foundation Guide for Religious Grant Seekers*. This fourth edition of the *Guide* is testimony to its popularity and widespread use.

The *Guide*, however, is not a "directory" of foundations interested in religion. A directory implies a comprehensive listing of foundations with detailed information about each. While this book does contain some minimal information about 588 foundations with a history of religious grant-making, its basic function is to direct the reader to the right sources of information about these and other foundations so that he or she can undertake the necessary research to identify which ones, if any, would be interested in a particular proposal. The targeted approach is preferable (and more effective) in grant seeking than is the scattered approach. Too much precious time, money and good will are lost through the indiscriminate barrage of proposals to foundations about which little or no research has been done. The chances of obtaining a grant improve in proportion to the research effort made to pinpoint those foundations with interests and priorities corresponding to the grant seeker's.

There is no way except through careful research to know which of the more than 32,000 grant-making foundations in the nation would be willing to fund a particular project. Foundations do not keep a list of grants available for the upcoming year. Instead, most foundations make broad statements of purpose such as "to aid social, educational, charitable, religious, or other organizations serving the common welfare." Proposals from grant seekers are considered at board meetings of the foundations and then funding decisions are made. Time should be taken to investigate thoroughly the foundations to which proposals are sent. An important point in grant searching is the assurance that the foundation is interested in a specific field of endeavor. This guide will enable seekers to locate compatible foundations.

This book also intends to help answer the question: Is a foundation grant really what is needed or wanted? Not only is a foundation grant hard to get but it can, in some cases, be counterproductive. What may be needed might not be foundation support, but better support from an organization's own constituency since its long-term financial well-being lies there, not with foundations. To the extent that the prospect of foundation support distracts one from that realization, genuine harm is done.

Finally, the *Guide* may help an applicant realize that foundations have a rather limited place and role in private philanthropy in general and in religious philanthropy in particular. The *Guide*, therefore, presents a four-point plan to aid in building one's own constituency.

SECTION I

Sources Of Information Available On Foundations

The Foundation Center

The Foundation Center is the only nonprofit organization which exists solely to gather, analyze, and disseminate information on American private foundations and their grants. It was established by foundations to provide information for the grant-seeking public and is largely maintained by contributions from foundations. The Center provides (1) free library service to the walk-in public and (2) invaluable publications with information on philanthropic giving and how to determine where to apply most appropriately for funding. (See below for description of these publications.) The Center operates libraries in New York, Washington, Cleveland and San Francisco. In addition, it supplies publications and other resources to cooperating collections in over 170 public, university, government and foundation libraries in 50 states. Outside of the United States, the Foundation Center has cooperating collections in seven countries, including Australia, Canada, England, Japan, Mexico, Puerto Rico and the U.S. Virgin Islands. (See Appendix A for full listing of addresses and telephone numbers for these libraries.) The Center provides the following services at its national collections:

- Reference librarians to help visitors use resource materials
- Free weekly orientations (call for reservations)
- Special orientations arranged for groups, classes or meetings
- Microform and paper copying facilities
- Associates Program–fee services for those needing frequent or immediate access to foundation information

The cooperating libraries throughout the nation house regional collections. They contain all of the Center's reference works, recent books and information on foundations, foundation annual reports and IRS returns pertinent to those foundations within their state or region. Many have staff members who will assist the grant seeker not only in using the local resources but also in contacting the Center's national libraries for more detailed information.

The Publications of the Foundation Center

Copies of the Center's publications are available for free reference use in all of the libraries, and some may be available in other local, public and university libraries. The following publications may be purchased by writing the Center:

(1) Directories Describing Foundations

Foundation Directory. Includes entries arranged alphabetically within states for over 7,500 of the largest foundations. Contains most of the following information: name, address, statement of purpose and interest, officers, financial data, some phone numbers and some grant application guidelines. (For the latest edition, call Toll Free 1-800-424-9836.)

Source Book Profiles. Annual loose-leaf service with in-depth analyses of programs of 1,000 major foundations making annual grants of nearly $5 billion. The top 1,000 foundations are profiled on a two-year cycle with 500 new profiles issued per year and over 80 new foundations profiled every other month. Updates are issued when personnel, address, program, etc., changes occur at any foundation profiled to date.

National Data Book. Includes brief entries for over 32,000 foundations. Contains a complete list of the foundations within each state and provides complete address, contact person, and financial information on virtually all active foundations in the United States regardless of size.

Foundation Grants to Individuals. Describes programs of over 2,000 independent and corporate foundations which make grants to individuals. Subject index includes religion, religious studies, rabbinical studies, religious leadership and other appropriate subjects for the religious grant seeker.

(2) Indexes to Foundation Grants

Foundation Grants Index. Annual volume which incorporates grants of $10,000 or more of about 800 foundations.

COMSEARCH Printouts. Computer printouts listing grants and foundations making the grants in particular subject areas (See printout on Broad Topic #12 Religion, Religious Welfare and Religious Education.) Custom computer searches done on more specific topics for foundations and for subscribers to the Center's Associates Program. Searches on the Foundation Grants Index, Foundation Directory.

(3) Guides for Grant Seekers
Foundation Fundamentals, 4th edition 1991: A guide to funding research.

Internal Revenue Service Form (990-PF)

If a foundation qualifies as private, it is required to file a 990-Private Foundation Form which then becomes available to the public on the microfiche cards. The following information is found on the forms/cards:

- Name and address of the foundation
- Total assets for the year at market and book value
- Telephone numbers (sometimes just the foundation's accountant)
- Total contributions, gifts and grants received
- List of the contributions, gifts and grants paid during the year
- Principal officers, directors and trustees
- Detailed financial information

The list of grants paid is particularly useful to the grant seeker because it contains the recipients and amounts. The IRS forms are invaluable because for many of the smaller foundations they are the only source of detailed information; only the larger foundations publish printed annual reports and qualify for directories. The IRS forms are recorded on microfiche cards and complete sets on every foundation can be obtained at the Foundation Center in New York City and Washington, D.C. or from the Internal Revenue Service. Each regional collection has a full set of these cards for the foundations located in its state or region. By the fall of each year, the file should be largely complete for each preceding year.

Staff are available at the Center's libraries to assist you in your research with these IRS forms.

Completed IRS forms also put the foundations' giving patterns in perspective. The grant seeker may find a foundation described in the *Foundation Directory* as being interested in "church support," "religious associations" or "religious purposes," only to find in the IRS form that its support in the religious field was minuscule in comparison to the foundation's funding in other fields of interest.

Annual Reports Published by the Foundations

Only about ten percent of all foundations publish and distribute annual reports which serve to inform the public about their activities. Such publications are generally valuable sources of information, containing lists of grants paid and grants committed to future payment, definitions of program interests, names of officers and detailed financial statements. For the religious grant seeker, the self-description of the areas of funding interest and the lists of grants paid are useful for pointing out the extent of the foundation's interest in religion.

To find out if a foundation publishes a report, consult the *Foundation Directory*. Most of the foundations that publish annual reports are among the 7,581 major foundations listed in edition 13 of the *Foundation Directory*, and the words "report published annually" at the end of the paragraph describing the purpose and activities of the foundation will indicate which they are.

Another place to find out if a particular foundation publishes an annual report is the *Foundation Center National Data Book* available for use at the Foundation Center's national and regional libraries. This publication, previously mentioned as listing over 32,000 currently active grant-making foundations, marks with an asterisk those foundations publishing annual reports. Most foundations publishing annual reports print enough copies to fill public requests. The Foundation Center's national and regional libraries also have copies of these reports.

State Directories of Foundations

Approximately 44 states have directories listing or describing the foundations within their regional or state boundaries. These guides are important sources of information as many foundations award grants only in their locale. These state directories are available at Foundation Center libraries and at some public and university libraries. (See Appendix B for a bibliography of state foundation directories.)

Other Sources of Information

There are a number of special directories–religious and non-religious–with which the grant seeker should be familiar, as they often shed further light on perspective funding agencies. (See Appendix C for a bibliography of other useful resources.)

SECTION II

The Grant Seeking Process

Now that the resource materials have been identified you may be asking, "But how do I actually begin my search for a foundation that makes grants for religious activities?" The following steps and questions should help you get started.

(1) Use the Foundation Center library system. If you cannot travel to one of the national libraries, check your regional collection. Do not hesitate to ask the staff for help. This alone will help you avoid many problems and wrong turns.

(2) Identify foundations with a possible interest in your project by using the list in this guide and the directories and indexes described above.

(3) Research each of these foundations for answers to the following questions:

(a) Does the foundation invite applications? Some agencies have such specialized areas of interest or are so pro-active that they do not consider unsolicited appeals.

(b) What is the extent of the foundation's religious funding? Examine the IRS forms or the annual reports for the list of grants paid. Look to see what percentage of grants went to religion. Also check what type of organizations received grants.

(c) Does the foundation have geographic limitations on its grant-making? Look to see if grants were made only in the foundation's locale or on a national or international basis. It is very important to know if a foundation only funds projects in its region. The directories and annual reports contain this information. As a rule, the likelihood of getting a grant from a foundation diminishes with distance. Therefore, be sure you know all of the possibilities in your locale.

(d) Does the foundation have financial ability to respond to your request? Check the assets and the size of the average grant paid out.

(e) Does the foundation have any specific limitations or conditions on its grant awarding? Check the guidelines on what type of grants will or will not be made. For example, some foundations will not make grants to individuals, nor will they support building funds. These special limitations will be found in the directories describing the foundations.

(f) Does the foundation publish procedures by which to apply for a grant? Check the directories and annual reports for any possible deadline for submitting proposals and for the schedule of board meetings.

(4) Once you have done the appropriate research on the foundations you plan to approach, you are ready to make the initial contact. This initial contact can be by either telephone or letter to briefly describe your program and needs and to ask if the foundation would be interested in receiving a proposal. If there is interest, ask for information concerning the correct procedure, the time for applying and the possibility of a personal interview. (Often the most effective way to get a grant is through a person-to-person interview.) Contact should first be made with the appropriate person on the foundation's staff. If there is no staff, find the person who has been designated to be contacted. He or she will likely be an officer or trustee. If there is a staff, do not attempt to approach a trustee without the staff's knowing it. This would be not only poor etiquette, but also a ploy that can easily work to your detriment.

(5) The best guidelines in writing a proposal are the ones the foundation itself may provide you. If no guidelines are provided, it is up to you to state your cause as best you can in a format that seems most appropriate to your situation. Be accurate in what is said and avoid grandiose language. Make it evident that you are aware of what has been and is being done by others relative to the needs or concerns to which your proposal is addressed. Proposal writing is largely a matter of common sense and clear narrative writing. The following are certain basic elements that all proposals ought to contain.

(a) Statements of:

- Nature and purpose of your organization. (By way of introduction.)

- The problem or need.
- What you propose to do about it. (Objectives and methods of action.)
- What makes your proposal or approach distinctive from comparable requests from other institutions.
- The anticipated outcome. (What, when, and ways of measuring success.)
- Who is involved in the program and what are their qualifications (Only cite credentials pertinent to the effort to be undertaken.)
- Expected grant period. (Have you taken into account the amount of time the foundation will need to make its decision?)
- How the proposed program relates to other institutions and resources pertinent to the need described.
- Endorsements or references. (Any enclosed letters of endorsement ought to illumine the particular qualifications of the persons involved in the program and not deal with extraneous qualities.)

(b) Financial information about:

- The budget and overall financial context of the plan.
- The amount of grant support being requested.
- Other sources of support.
- Provision for ongoing support of the program. (Vague assurances are not reassuring.)
- Evidence of tax exemption.

(c) Summary:

- The highlights of the proposal ought to be summarized on one or two pages and put at the beginning along with a letter of transmittal.

Several publications designed to help the proposal writer are available through the Foundation Center and may be obtained by writing the New York office or by visiting one of their libraries.

A final reminder is in order about the importance of thoroughly researching the foundations to which you send proposals. Regardless of the effort put into it, your proposal will prove worthless if it is sent to foundations which have no interest in your area of concern.

SECTION III

The View From The Other Side Of The Desk

Foundations, and organizations which seek grants from them, have a common allegiance: both are members of what is increasingly known as the "third sector"–the world of nonprofit, private "voluntary" agencies and organizations. The other two sectors are, of course, business and government. All three provide either goods or services, but with significantly different imperatives or motives. Each is integral to American society and our system of checks and balances.

Three significant characteristics of American society largely account for the existence of the third sector: (1) the American impulse to altruism, voluntary giving of money, time and other private resources to meet the needs of others; (2) our penchant to organize ourselves into private, voluntary efforts in order to apply those resources systematically to social problem solving; and (3) our long tradition of pluralism and cultural diversity. Each of these traits also serves to explain the almost uniquely American phenomenon of private foundations.

Although private foundations fully share in the origin and experience of charitable organizations, in whatever field of endeavor– education, social welfare, the arts and sciences, conservation, religion, etc.–there is still a great deal of misunderstanding about their nature and role particularly on the part of the grant seeker.

It is hard for grant seekers to put themselves into the position of the foundation representative. Part of this difficulty is due to the failure of the foundations themselves. By and large, foundations have been reticent about explaining their problems and aspirations to the public, sometimes because of a sense of humility consistent with scriptural injunctions against the dangers of advertising one's own good deeds. More often, however, foundations are reluctant to be too visible lest their explanations about themselves invite an avalanche of requests.

Perhaps the root of the problem lies even deeper. There is almost unavoidable distance between the grant maker and the grant seeker. From the point of view of the aspiring grantee, the foundation often appears to enjoy ample resources or at least enough money to make "just this one grant." Yet, that is not how it looks from the other side of the desk. The foundation official, whether a trustee or staff member, is apt to be aware of a different kind of abundance, namely, the sheer plenitude of significant opportunities for grant-making and the relative scarcity of foundation funds to meet even a fraction of these possibilities. Where one sees abundance, the other sees scarcity.

This gap between abundance of opportunities and scarcity of available resources necessarily affects the ways in which even the most affluent foundations go about their work. While foundations react to this pressure in different ways, there are at least two contrasting tendencies in their responses.

(1) In view of the scarcity of foundation funds and the consequently increased importance of these resources, many foundations prefer to stay with the "tried and true" causes. If a foundation leans in this direction, then it will be more likely to favor support of already existing institutions and to be willing to provide a subsidy for ongoing programs or perhaps for "brick and mortar" needs. The foundation, in effect, takes its place alongside the individual donor and makes a contribution to maintain or improve the status quo. Such a donation seldom represents a risk or causes controversy except, perhaps, from those who were disappointed that this program subsidy did not go to their organization.

(2) The opposing tendency leads to a quite different response. In the judgement of some foundation representatives, the preoccupation of supporting the proven institutions and programs deflects foundations from making their most distinctive contributions. At its best American philanthropy has constituted an early warning system about the problems and possibilities that lie ahead in the future. A good grant has been one that has helped illumine the landscape of tomorrow: the needs of our society, what changes are now necessary to prepare ourselves for them, and what pitfalls to avoid as we move into the future.

Philanthropists who accept this view of foundation grant-making recognize a distinction between the role and capacities foundations can assume in our society and the role the individual donor plays.

All positive change involves risk. Foundations, unlike most donors, are uniquely prepared to assume risks in the interests of society. Their distributable funds can be "invested" in imaginative programs and projects whose chances of success are tentative and whose ability to make a "return" (least of all to the foundation) is not important. In very many such cases foundations represent the only feasible source of financial support. Foundations can also afford to live with an unpopular line of inquiry without having to worry unduly about an anxious public. These institutions can stay with issues long enough to weigh the long-term effects or to seek out alternative solutions because they can, if they will, resist the temptation to join the passing parade of fads and fancies.

Such an exploration of the future is not, of course, without its hazards. Foundations can–and do!–guess wrongly about significant issues. It is all the more important, therefore, that foundations have the freedom to admit their errors and thereby to gain the confidence and support of the community at large by searching out the most important problems of the coming years.

The role of the individual donor in private philanthropy contrasts significantly with that of foundations. It would not be overstating the matter to say that the survival of voluntary organizations depends on the continued altruism of the individual donor and not on foundations. The free will contributions of money and service by individual donors are what most private charitable organizations rely on to close the gap between operating income and actual costs. In short, the indispensable role of the individual donor in private philanthropy is subsidizing charitable institutions. The statistics bear this out.

To begin with, there are only about 32,000 private grant-making foundations in the United States, and all but about 3,000 are extremely small (with less than one million dollars each in assets). On the other hand, the number of individual donors is legion, comprising practically the whole of the adult community to some degree. (The word "donor" might be misleading in its connotation since what is being referred to is the small contributor as well as the large.)

In 1990, individual donors in the United States provided $101.8 billion, or 83.1 percent, of all private philanthropy.*

This figure does not include another $7.79 billion in bequests nor does it include the billions of hours of contributed service time. Corporations and businesses contributed an estimated $5.9 billion and foundations another $7.08 billion. Altogether, private philanthropy in the United States totaled $122.57 billion that year, only 5.8 percent of which came from foundations.

In the field of religion, the percentage contrast of total contributions made by foundations versus individuals becomes even more extreme. Less than two percent of the $65.76 billion of private philanthropy that was directed to the field of religion during 1990 came from foundations. Almost without exception, the rest came from individual donors and accounted for more than half (53.7%) of all private giving to charity of any variety!

What can be inferred from these figures in forming a realistic attitude toward foundations and private philanthropy in general when seeking financial support for religious organizations?

For one thing, we can gain a better sense of realism about the limitations of foundations as sources of financial support to religious organizations. The total amount of funds available to religious activities from foundations is infinitesimal compared to the funds contributed by individuals. There are precious few foundations active in the field of religion. In the course of preparing this guide, the authors were able to identify about 588 such foundations from the approximately 7,500 largest throughout the country, and most of these are local in their giving preferences. Moreover, the volume of requests these foundations typically receive far exceeds their available funds. In general, therefore, the chances of getting a grant from a foundation are slim and become narrower the greater the distance separating the foundation from

---

*All figures taken from the 1991 Annual Report of the American Association of Fund Raising Counsel, Inc., entitled *Giving USA*.

the organization applying for a grant. Consequently it is very important to target one's grant request as precisely as possible through careful research in identifying those foundations most likely to be able and willing to respond positively.

Second, one ought to respect the fact that foundations are a scarce source of risk capital for program areas where change and development are needed and where there is no other source of support. There are few other comparable sources of the "venture capital" available to the voluntary sector. Foundations, therefore, should not be asked to replace the private donor in subsidizing the operating and normal program expenses of charitable organizations or to aid projects whose support could come from the organization's own constituency if an adequate effort were only made. Such grants would amount to a misuse of a very limited and valuable resource for both the society and for religion in particular.

Third, it is unwise automatically to look to foundations as a solution to the financial needs or problems of your organization or program. The very existence of foundations–all that free money–engenders in too many charitable and religious organizations a reflex reaction to turn to them, the foundations, for help. In this connection, it can be parenthetically noted that grant seekers often turn to private foundations without considering the resources available for charitable purposes within grant-making religious bodies. Nearly every major denomination maintains a funding entity of some type. Many of them are significantly larger than the typical private foundation.

The prospect of foundation aid can serve to harm charitable organizations if allowed to distract them from the realization that their long term survival and well-being depends on receiving aid from their own support community. Rarely can foundations be found to be a direct part of the constituency of any one charitable or religious organization. It is a major, and sometimes fatal, error for charities to perceive foundations as such.

The fact is that the future of voluntary organizations and institutions depends almost entirely upon the extent to which they are able to develop a strong and lasting financial base from a compassionate support community. This means recognizing potential members of this community, nurturing them, and actively involving them in the life of the organization and its programs. Thus if, in responding to the imperative of raising more funds, you find yourself spending most of your time and energy trying to interest foundations in your program needs and not trying to develop your own support community, you are probably doing everybody, including yourself, a disservice. To better understand how a voluntary organization can develop a lasting financial base, the following section is provided.

SECTION IV
Building Constituency Support

A voluntary organization is wise to seek a broad base of support. Dependency on a single source of support, no matter how adequate and comfortable it may be for the time being, is almost certain to lead to severe financial problems in the future, probably the near future. Typically, a broad base of support for a volunteer organization would include all or most of the following:

(1) Fees for service, tuition or membership
(2) Endowment income
(3) Contributions
(4) Revenue from federal, state or local government agencies
(5) Sale of publications
(6) Auxiliary enterprises (housing and food services)

No matter what percent of the annual budget is derived from contributions, it is desirable to obtain gifts from a variety of sources. Here again, dependence on a single source or a very small number of donors places an organization in a high-risk position. Individuals may die, change their interests, or even become disenchanted with the organization. Foundations rarely provide extended funding. Corporations tie their giving to profits which usually fluctuate from year to year, and they generally like to spread their contributions over a rather large number of recipients. In addition, very few foundations or corporations will give to organizations that have a specific religious orientation.

Four Characteristics of Successful Fund-raising
Financial stability for most voluntary organizations requires that the fund-raising effort be successful. Success means that annual objectives for number of donors and dollars are met. There are four characteristics of successful fund-raising which are quite prominent. These will not exist to the same degree with all groups, and a single organization which is successful in fund-raising may see some variations in these characteristics from year to year.

(1) Program Worthy of Support

The first characteristic of a successful fund-raising effort is that the organization maintains a program of service which is worthy of support. It has a reputation for doing well what it purports to do. Those who know about the organization, if only slightly, believe it is doing something worthwhile. The extent to which an organization is known and truly understood will vary greatly. Some are much more adept than others at publicizing their activities. The point is, when an organization is successful in raising funds, it will be providing a service or program which any fair-minded person coming in contact with it would agree deserves support.

(2) Constituency with Ability to Provide Support

The second characteristic of a successful fund-raising effort is a constituency which has the financial ability to provide the required support. This may be a natural constituency or a developed constituency. Examples of a natural constituency would be alumni of an educational institution, former patients of a hospital, season members of a symphony orchestra or parishioners of a church. A developed constituency would include individuals, corporations and organizations which have been made aware of the voluntary organization's program and have shown a willingness to help support it. They may or may not become directly involved with the program or service of the charitable organization.

In attempting to establish a developed constituency, it is important to identify those who truly have the financial potential for providing support. Many organizations tend to look far and wide for prospects, when their best potentials may be within a few blocks or miles of the institution. As a matter of fact, most organizations which are successful in fund-raising receive significant gift dollars from board and staff members before seeking outside support.

Regular and systematic approaches need to be made to the constituents to keep them informed. It is hazardous to assume that even those who are fairly close to the work of an organization are fully aware of the program and financial situation. Newsletters, brochures, audiovisuals, and on-location visits will help interpret the organization to its natural and developed constituents.

(3) Fund-raising Plan

The third characteristic of an organization which is successful in obtaining gift support is that it has a plan for fund-raising. The plan may be a few pages in length or it may be a large and greatly detailed document. Size is not important. What is essential is that the effort be given careful thought and that it represents the commitment of the fund-raising staff, the chief executive, the administrative staff and the board of directors. Some of the elements in a typical fund-raising plan will include:

(a) Statement of organizational objectives
(b) Narrative which justifies support
(c) Detailed financial goal(s)
(d) Time schedule for each phase of the fund-raising effort
(e) Budget for fund-raising program
(f) Decision regarding personal solicitation, telephone solicitation, direct mail, benefit or special event, sale of merchandise
(g) Determination of type of gift sought outright, gifts with reservation of life income, or bequests
(h) Decision whether gift principal or income only is to be used
(i) Establishment of method of receiving gifts, gift acknowledgements, gift accounting

(4) Leadership for Fund-raising

The final characteristic of an effort which is successful in fund-raising is that there are leaders who are able to implement the fund-raising plan. Most experienced development officers would agree that this is the most important of the four characteristics cited. Why is leadership for fund-raising so important? It is rather well accepted that people give to people. The personal relationship that exists between solicitor and donor will usually be the determining factor.

Leadership for fund-raising divides into two categories–staff leadership and volunteer leadership. Both are critical if the organization hopes to obtain maximum results. Staff leadership for fund-raising begins with the chief executive. This person must give it a high priority even though he or she may spend a relatively low percent of time in fund-raising. Operating responsibility for fund-raising rests with the development officer. This person must coordinate the fund-raising activities of the chief executive and other staff members and the volunteer fund-raisers. The volunteer leadership for fund-raising usually begins with the board of directors. There may also be an advisory board or a development committee which takes primary responsibility.

Whatever the structure, organizations that achieve well in gift support have volunteers who are effective in giving and getting gifts. Conversely, most fund-raising failures can be traced to a lack of leadership for fund-raising. Experience shows that an organization will be successful in raising funds if it has a program worthy of support, identifies or develops a constituency with ability to give, prepares a plan for fund-raising, and then enlists leaders to carry out the plan.

SECTION V

Foundations With Past Interest In Funding Religious Organizations

The following list of foundations with a history of funding religious activities is not to be considered all-inclusive. It was largely compiled from the most recent IRS returns of each foundation. These were examined in the fall of 1991 to determine the actual extent of each foundation's grant-making in the field of religion. The principal researcher reviewed the entries in the third edition of the *Foundation Guide for Religious Grant Seekers* and found by checking the federal returns that substantial changes had to be made to the previous 407 entries of the third edition of the *Guide*. The current edition contains information on 588 foundations which meet the following criteria: (1) made grants to more than one religious organization (unless an unusually large amount), (2) total grants to religion were either $25,000 annually or a sizeable percent of the foundation's annual giving, and (3) grants were for religious purposes specifically and not simply for religiously-affiliated organizations such as schools and welfare groups. Using new information gathered from *COMSEARCH* printouts and the 13th edition of the *Foundation Directory* as verified by a review of IRS returns, 243 new entries were made to the present edition, while 62 previously listed entries were dropped because the foundations did not meet the above criteria.

The result is this list, which includes the largest foundations in the nation with an interest in religion, as well as some smaller foundations with an almost exclusive interest in religion. The foundations fall into three broad categories (and some overlap into more than one of these divisions):

(1) Foundations almost solely devoted to religious funding.
(2) Large foundations with a sizeable amount of funding in the religious area, although religion is only one area of interest.
(3) Foundations which fund religious activities only in their locale or as a secondary area of funding interest.

This list does not include many foundations which give grant money to religious organizations for education, health, social welfare or other "secular" programs. Those religious institutions seeking grant support for such programs are advised to consult the subject index of the *Foundation Directory*, the *National Guide to Funding in Religion*, the subject index of the *Foundation Center Source Book Profiles*, the appropriate *COMSEARCH* printout and other reference sources found at the Foundation Center libraries and cooperating libraries identified in this *Guide*.

The list also may not include the names of many small foundations which support religious activities in their own locale. These may be found in the various state directories.

Warning! Take this list for what it is–a compilation of the foundations with a past history of funding religious organizations. It should be a time saver, as it gives the grant seeker a starting place when searching for religious grants from among the 32,000 foundations. However, remember to do further research on the foundations that might fund your project. You cannot be sure until you do your homework.

PROTESTANT FOUNDATIONS

Alabama

The Baker Foundation
c/o AmSouth Bank
P.O. Box 11426
Birmingham, AL 35206
Contact: Michael W. Curl, President
Geographic Giving Pattern: Alabama
Special Interest: Christian churches and colleges; support also for education (scholarships), denominational giving, health and youth
Assets: $1,844,282
Grant Range: $100,000–$282
Limitations: No grants to individuals
Applications: Contributes to pre-selected organizations only. Applications not accepted.

The Christian Workers Foundation
3038 Bankhead Avenue
Montgomery, AL 36106
Contact: G.R. Lockhart, Trustee
Geographic Giving Pattern: National
Special Interest: Christian evangelical and mission organizations, youth agencies
Assets: $3,031,381
Grant Range: $85,500–$1,000
Limitations: No grants to individuals
Applications: Applications are by invitation only

S.E. & Margaret W. Dove Christian Foundation
1431 Kinsey Road
Dothan, AL 36302
Contact: S. Earl Dove, President
Geographic Giving Pattern: Alabama
Special Interest: Baptist church support and other religious organizations
Assets: $370,319
Grant Range: $150,000–$150
Applications: Initial approach should be by letter

The Mitchell Foundation, Inc.
2405 First National Bank Building
P.O. Box 1126
Mobile, AL 36601
(205) 432-1711
Contact: M.L. Screven, Secretary-Treasurer
Geographic Giving Pattern: Primarily Alabama
Special Interest: Secondary and higher education, social service programs, religious welfare agencies, health associations and Protestant church support
Assets: $10,760,792
Grant Range: $134,200–$1,000
Limitations: No grants to individuals
Applications: Initial approach should be by letter. There are no deadlines.

Arizona

Solheim Foundation
501 West Wakonda Lane
Phoenix, AR 85023
Contact: Louise C. Solheim, Trustee
Special Interest: Christian education, missions and other related activities
Assets: $3,423,230
Grant Range: $100,000–$20,000
Limitations: No grants to individuals
Applications: Contributes to pre-selected organizations only. Applications not accepted.

The Tell Foundation
4020 North 38th Avenue
Phoenix, AZ 85019
Contact: Ron L. Lewis, Administrator
Geographic Giving Pattern: Primarily Arizona
Special Interest: Protestant churches, church-related institutions and theological education
Assets: $1,851,674
Grant Range: $14,000–$25
Limitations: No grants to individuals
Applications: Applications are not accepted

Arkansas

The Harvey and Bernice Jones Foundation
P.O. Box 233
Springdale, AR 72765
(501) 756-0611
Contact: Mary Sellars, Director
Geographic Giving Pattern: Primarily Springdale, Arizona
Special Interest: Protestant church support, hospitals and education
Assets: $7,981,722 (Gifts received: $2,500,000)
Grant Range: $1,000,000–$30 (Grant average: $500–$50,000)
Applications: Initial approach should be by letter. An application form is required. There are no deadlines.

The Roy and Christine Sturgis Charitable and Educational Trust
P.O. Box 92
Malvern, AR 72104
(501) 332-3899
Contact: Katie Speer or Barry Findley, Trustees
Geographic Giving Pattern: Primarily Arkansas
Special Interest: Hospitals, youth and social service agencies, education and Protestant church support
Assets: $12,038,034
Grant Range: $302,500–$2,830
Limitations: No grants to individuals
Applications: Initial approach should be by letter. There are no deadlines.

California

The Ahmanson Foundation
See entry in Interfaith

Arata Brothers Trust
P.O. Box 430
Sacramento, CA 95802
Contact: Renato R. Parenti, Trustee
Geographic Giving Pattern: California
Special Interest: Hospitals, education and religion
Assets: $3,628,733
Grant Range: $50,000–$1,000
Applications: Initial approach should be by letter. There are no deadlines.

Artevel Foundation

Crocker Center I
333 South Grand Avenue, Suite 4150
Los Angeles, CA 90071
Contact: George R. Phillips, Secretary-Treasurer
Special Interest: Protestant evangelical, missionary and charitable programs
Assets: $2,067,582
Grant Range: $23,000–$500
Limitations: No grants to individuals
Applications: Contributes to pre-selected organizations only. Applications not accepted.

Atkinson Foundation

Ten West Orange Avenue
South San Francisco, CA 94080
(415) 876-1559
Contact: Norma Arlen, Administrator
Geographic Giving Pattern: Northern California and overseas
Special Interest: Support for the United Methodist Church and other church activities "to help people reach the highest potential in their spiritual and economic life." Support also for international development and relief.
Assets: $16,237,035
Grant Range: $149,506–$865 (Grant average: $2,000–$10,000)
Limitations: No support for doctoral study or elementary schools. No grants to individuals or for research or fund-raising events. No loans.
Applications: Initial approach may be by telephone, proposal or letter. There are no deadlines.

Myrtle L. Atkinson Foundation

P.O. Box 688
La Canada, CA 91011
(213) 790-7029
Contact: Elizabeth A. Whitsett, President
Geographic Giving Pattern: National, international
Special Interest: "To teach, promulgate and disseminate the gospel of Jesus Christ throughout the world and also to unite in Christian fellowship the large number of consecrated Christians in the various evangelical churches."
Assets: $19,710,911
Grant Range: $65,000–$50 (Grant average: $1,000–$10,000)

Limitations: No grants to individuals or for research, doctoral studies or continuing programs. No support for education outside of foundation's primary area of interest in Protestant denominational programs.
Applications: Initial approach should be by one-page letter. Proposals should be submitted preferably in February, early May, August or November. There is no set deadline.

The Lowell Berry Foundation
Four Orinda Way, No. 140B
Orinda, CA 94563-2513
(415) 254-1944
Contact: John C. Branagh, President
Geographic Giving Pattern: Contra Costa and northern Alameda counties, California
Special Interest: Evangelical Christian religious programs
Assets: $19,928,402
Grant Range: $346,000–$100 (Grant average: $500–$25,000)
Limitations: No grants to individuals or for building or capital funds, equipment, seed money or land acquisition.
Applications: Initial approach should be by letter. There are no deadlines. Final notification will be one to two months for religious grants.

The Henry W. Bull Foundation
c/o Santa Barbara Bank & Trust
P.O. Box 2340
Santa Barbara, CA 93120-2340
(805) 564-6211
Contact: Gary Newman, Assistant Vice-President, Santa Barbara Bank & Trust
Special Interest: Higher education, the physically impaired, health and church support
Assets: $4,997,550
Grant Range: $20,000–$500
Limitations: No grants to individuals or for building or endowment funds
Applications: Applications are not accepted

Burns-Dunphy Foundation
See entry in Interfaith

Caddock Foundation, Inc.
1793 Chicago Avenue
Riverside, CA 92507
(714) 788-1700
Contact: Richard E. Caddock, President
Special Interest: Protestant religious associations and activities, including Bible studies
Assets: $949,125
Grant Range: $20,000–$1,000
Applications: Grant proposals should be sent to the following address: 1717 Chicago Avenue, Riverside, CA 92507. There are no deadlines.

Charis Fund
Box 124
Tahoe City, CA 95730
(916) 583-4348
Contact: Paul D'Anneo, President
Geographic Giving Pattern: San Francisco Bay area, California, Washington and Oregon
Special Interest: Protestant church-related organizations, education and social service agencies
Assets: $1,049,310
Grant Range: $31,000–$2,000
Limitations: No grants to individuals
Applications: Funds are largely committed and new requests are not encouraged. Initial approach should be by letter. Six copies of grant proposal are required. There are no deadlines.

Forest Lawn Foundation
1712 South Glendale Avenue
Glendale, CA 91205
(213) 254-3131
Contact: John Llewellyn, Vice-President
Geographic Giving Pattern: Primarily California
Special Interest: Higher education, health and welfare, hospitals, youth agencies and religious institutions
Assets: $7,769,429 (Gifts received: $863,234)
Grant Range: $50,000–$250
Limitations: No grants to individuals or for endowment funds or special projects
Applications: Grants are generally initiated by the foundation. Applications are not accepted.

Earl B. Gilmore Foundation
6301 West Third Street
P.O. Box 480314
Los Angeles, CA 90036
Contact: John B. Gostovich, President
Geographic Giving Pattern: Primarily California
Special Interest: Social services, higher and secondary education,
health and youth agencies, hospitals and Protestant church support
Assets: $2,615,755
Grant Range: $7,500–$50
Applications: Contributes to pre-selected organizations only.
Applications not accepted.

The Greenville Foundation
P.O. Box 885
Pacific Palisades, CA 90272
(213) 454-0448
Contact: William Miles, Chair
Special Interest: Protestant religious programs and higher education,
including studies of world peace and hunger, environment, ecology
and community development
Assets: $2,148,972
Grant Range: $50,000–$1,000
Limitations: No grants to individuals or for operating budgets
Applications: Initial approach should be by proposal outline. Three
copies of proposal are requested. The deadline is October 1.

Helms Foundation, Inc.
25765 Quilla Road
P.O. Box 55827
Valencia, CA 91355
(805) 253-3485
Contact: William D. Manuel, Assistant Secretary
Special Interest: Religious education, health and hospitals, culture,
youth and social service organizations
Assets: $4,186,537
Grant Range: $36,000–$75
Limitations: No support for private foundations
Applications: There are no deadlines for grant proposals

J.W. and Ida M. Jameson Foundation
481 West Highland Avenue
P.O. Box 397
Sierra Madre, CA 91024
(818) 355-6973
Contact: William M. Croxton, Vice-President
Geographic Giving Pattern: Primarily California
Special Interest: Higher education including theological seminaries,
Protestant church support, hospitals and medical research, cultural
programs and youth agencies
Assets: $896,368 (Gifts received: $740,000)
Grant Total: $727,000
Limitations: No stated limitations other than geographical
Applications: There are no deadlines for grant proposals

George Frederick Jewett Foundation
See entry in Interfaith

Richard and Elizabeth Kasper Foundation
2625 West Alameda, Number 208
Burbank, CA 91505
Contact: Elizabeth H. Kasper, Trustee
Special Interest: Primarily for Christian churches, associations and
missionary programs
Assets: $90,668 (Gifts received: $79,000)
Grant Range: $25,000–$200
Limitations: No grants to individuals
Applications: Contributes to pre-selected organizations only.
Applications not accepted.

A. H. Kerr Foundation
16661 Ventura Boulevard, Suite 826
Encino, CA 91436
(818) 990-2831
Contact: William A. Kerr, Vice-President
Geographic Giving Pattern: Primarily California
Special Interest: Higher education, church support and religious
associations, including foreign missions
Assets: $8,450,099
Grant Range: $83,820–$500
Limitations: No grants to individuals or for seed money, deficit
financing or demonstration projects. No loans.
Applications: Initial approach should be by proposal. There are no
deadlines, however, the board meets in April and October.

Marin Community Foundation
See entry in Interfaith

The Marshburn Foundation
1201 South Beach Boulevard, Suite 105
La Habra, CA 90631
Contact: The Trustees
Geographic Giving Pattern: Primarily California
Special Interest: Protestant church support and higher education,
particularly religious training
Assets: $2,303,905
Grant Range: $26,000–$319
Applications: Contributes to pre-selected organizations only.
Applications not accepted.

Alfred C. Munger Foundation
355 South Grand Avenue, 35th Floor
Los Angeles, CA 90071-1560
Contact: Richard D. Ebenshade, Vice-President and Secretary
Special Interest: Education, health agencies and Protestant religious
organizations
Assets: $13,473,343
Grant Range: $251,300–$100
Applications: Contributes to pre-selected organizations only.
Applications not accepted.

Murdy Foundation
335 Centennial Way
Tustin, CA 92680
Contact: George E. Trotter, President
Geographic Giving Pattern: Primarily California
Special Interest: Higher education, Protestant church support and
cultural programs
Assets: $3,251,418
Grant Range: $41,175–$250
Applications: Contributes to pre-selected organizations only.
Applications not accepted.

Orleton Trust Fund
40 West Third Avenue, No. 904
San Mateo, CA 94402
Contact: Jean Sawyer Weaver, Trustee
Geographic Giving Pattern: Dayton, Ohio and San Mateo County,
California

Special Interest: Protestant church support, religious associations, education and welfare funds
Assets: $7,195,072
Grant Average: $500–$5,000
Limitations: No grants to individuals
Applications: Contributes to pre-selected organizations only. Applications not accepted.

Pasadena Area Residential Aid A Corporation
P.O. Box 984
Pasadena, CA 91102
(213) 681-1331
Contact: Linda M. Moore, Assistant Secretary
Geographic Giving Pattern: National
Special Interest: Higher education, cultural programs, Christian church support and social services
Assets: $2,437,261
Grant Range: $331,794–$20
Applications: Contributions initiated by donor and foundation members only. Applications not accepted.

Peery Foundation
2560 Mission College Boulevard, Suite 101
Santa Clara, CA 95050
Contact: Richard T. Peery, President
Special Interest: Mormon religious organizations; some support for youth, education and civic organizations
Assets: $6,907,708
Grant Range: $299,000–$88
Limitations: No grants to individuals
Applications: Initial approach should be by letter

The Robinson Foundation
700 South Flower Street, Suite 1122
Los Angeles, CA 90017
(213) 626-4481
Contact: C. Grant Clifford, Chair
Geographic Giving Pattern: Primarily Massachusetts
Special Interest: Primarily the First Church of Christ Scientist in Massachusetts or organizations that directly or indirectly promote and extend the religion of Christian Science.
Assets: $1,959,590 (Gifts received: $200,000)
Grant Range: $54,500–$2,000

Limitations: No grants to individuals
Applications: An application form is required. There are no deadlines.

David Claude Ryan Foundation
P.O. Box 6409
San Diego, CA 92106
(619) 291-7311
Contact: Jerome D. Ryan, President
Geographic Giving Pattern: Primarily California, with emphasis on San Diego
Special Interest: Christian religious organizations, social service and youth agencies, education and cultural programs
Assets: $2,525,638
Grant Range: $50,000–$500
Limitations: No grants to individuals
Applications: Initial approach should be by letter. There are no deadlines.

Marjorie Mosher Schmidt Foundation
2111 Palomar Airport Road, Suite 370
Carlsbad, CA 92009
(619) 438-4300
Contact: Mark F. Scudder, President
Geographic Giving Pattern: Primarily southern California
Special Interest: Christian religious organizations; also conservation, education and health
Assets: $1,845,735
Grant Average: $1,000–$5,000
Limitations: No grants to individuals
Applications: Grants are initiated by the board. Applications are not accepted.

Richard C. Seaver Charitable Trust
350 South Figueroa Street, Suite 270
Los Angeles, CA 90071
Contact: Myron E. Harpole, Trustee
Geographic Giving Pattern: National
Special Interest: Episcopal churches, a museum foundation and education
Assets: $3,607,683
Grant Range: $25,000–$1,000
Limitations: No grants to individuals
Applications: Initial approach should be by letter. There are no deadlines.

The May and Stanley Trust
49 Geary Street, Suite 244
San Francisco, CA 94108
(415) 391-0292
Contact: John P. Collins, Sr.
Geographic Giving Pattern: San Francisco area; also England, Scotland, Canada and Australia
Special Interest: Church support and religious welfare funds
Assets: $3,024,903
Grant Range: $10,000–$1,500
Limitations: No grants to individuals
Applications:

James L. Stamps Foundation, Inc.
P.O. Box 250
Downey, CA 90241
(213) 861-3112
Contact: Jolene Boutault, Manager
Geographic Giving Pattern: Primarily southern California
Special Interest: Evangelical Protestant churches, seminaries, associations and programs; also medical research and hospitals
Assets: $17,000,000
Grant Range: $25,000–$1,000
Limitations: No grants to individuals or for endowment funds, deficit financing, scholarships, publications or conferences
Applications: Initial approach should be by letter. An application form is required.

Sundean Foundation
927 Hanover Street
Santa Cruz, CA 95060
(408) 425-5927
Contact: Harold A. Sundean, President
Geographic Giving Pattern: National, with emphasis on California
Special Interest: Seventh Day Adventist churches and missionary activities, with some emphasis on Central America
Assets: $17,784,486
Grant Range: $50,000–$10
Applications: Initial approach should be by letter

Colorado

First Fruit, Inc.
7400 West 20th Avenue
Lakewood, CO 80215
(303) 232-4084
Contact: Dennis W. Thome, Secretary-Treasurer
Geographic Giving Pattern: National
Special Interest: Organizations which engage in advancing the Gospel
of Jesus Christ. Preference is given to evangelical ministries, usually
with strategic pioneering programs among peoples who have not had
repeated contact with the Gospel message.
Assets: $9,384,158 (Gifts received: $2,460,000)
Grant Range: $121,410–$3,220
Limitations: No grants to individuals
Applications: Initial approach should be by proposal letter. There are
no deadlines.

Connecticut

J. Walton Bissell Foundation
CityPlace, 25th Floor
Hartford, CT 06103
(203) 275-0100
Contact: J. Danford Anthony, Trustee
Geographic Giving Pattern: Primarily Connecticut, Massachusetts,
Vermont and New Hampshire
Special Interest: Protestant church support, higher and secondary
education, hospitals, social service organizations, arts and historic
preservation
Assets: $10,696,374
Grant Range: $50,000–$1,000
Limitations: No grants to individuals. No loans.
Applications: Initial approach should be by letter. There are no
deadlines.

Fred R. & Hazel W. Carstensen Memorial Foundation, Inc.
c/o Tellalian & Tellalian
211 State Street
Bridgeport, CT 06604
(203) 333-5566
Contact: Aram H. Tellalian, Chair
Geographic Giving Pattern: Primarily Connecticut

Special Interest: Churches and church-related activities, cultural programs, hospitals and health organizations
Assets: $2,013,372
Grant Range: $20,000–$1,000
Applications: Initial approach should be by letter. There are no deadlines.

The Sherman Fairchild Foundation, Inc.
71 Arch Street
Greenwich, CT 06830
(203) 661-9360
Contact: Patricia A. Lydon, Vice-President
Geographic Giving Pattern: No stated limits
Special Interest: Higher and theological education, arts and culture, medical research and social welfare
Assets: $204,326,334
Grant Range: $1,000,000–$11,000 (Grant average: $100,000–$800,000)
Applications: There are no deadlines for grant proposals

Wilmot Wheeler Foundation, Inc.
P.O. Box 429
Southport, CT 06490
(203) 259-1615
Contact: Wilmot F. Wheeler, President
Geographic Giving Pattern: Primarily Connecticut
Special Interest: Higher and secondary education, and Protestant church support
Assets: $1,582,651
Grant Range: $8,500–$40
Applications: Initial approach should be by letter. There are no deadlines.

Delaware

Downs Perpetual Charitable Trust
c/o Wilmington Trust Co.
GPM-21181-0
Wilmington, DE 19890
Geographic Giving Pattern: Primarily Delaware and Pennsylvania
Special Interest: Episcopal organizations, including churches, and education
Assets: $4,122,764
Grant Range: $22,578–$2,578

Limitations: No grants to individuals
Applications: Contributes to pre-selected organizations only.
Applications not accepted.

The Ada Howe Kent Foundation
1209 Orange Street
Wilmington, DE 19801
Contact: John P. Campbell, Secretary-Treasurer
Special Interest: Religious organizations carrying out studies and
practical work in comparative religions; church support; and, social
service agencies
Assets: $6,222,524
Grant Range: $25,000–$1,000
Applications: Initial approach should be by letter. There are no
deadlines.

Kent-Lucas Foundation, Inc.
101 Springer Building
3411 Silverside Road
Wilmington, DE 19810
(302) 478-4383
Contact: Elizabeth K. Van Alen, President
Geographic Giving Pattern: Primarily Philadelphia, Pennsylvania,
Maine and Florida
Special Interest: Protestant church support, cultural programs,
hospitals, education and historic preservation
Assets: $2,320,668
Grant Range: $100,000–$25 (Grant average: $100–$5,000)
Limitations: No grants to individuals or for endowment funds
Applications: Initial approach should be by letter. There are no
deadlines. The mailing address is as follows: P.O. Box 7048,
Wilmington, DE 19803.

The Lovett Foundation, Inc.
82 Governor Printz Boulevard
Claymont, DE 19703
(302) 798-6604
Contact: Michael J. Robinson, Vice-President
Geographic Giving Pattern: Wilmington, Delaware and Philadelphia,
Pennsylvania
Special Interest: Protestant church support, hospitals, education and
social service agencies
Assets: $2,925,138

Grant Range: $20,000–$19
Limitations: No grants to individuals
Applications: Initial approach should be by letter. Grant proposals should be submitted before March 15.

District of Columbia

The Appleby Foundation
c/o Crestar Bank, N.A., Trust Division
1445 New York Avenue, N.W.
Washington, D.C. 20005
(202) 879-6341
Contact: Virginia M. Herrin, Vice-President, Crestar Bank, N.A.
Geographic Giving Pattern: Washington, D.C., Florida and Georgia
Special Interest: Higher education, Protestant church support, youth agencies, music, cultural programs and hospitals
Assets: $7,013,029
Grant Average: $15,000
Applications: Initial approach should be by letter. There are no deadlines.

Thomas and Frances McGregor Foundation
See entry in Interfaith

Florida

Norris & Margaret Aldeen Charitable Foundation
6554 Ridgewood Drive
Naples, FL 33963
Contact: Margaret Aldeen, Trustee
Geographic Giving Pattern: Primarily Rockford, Illinois
Special Interest: Christian education; some support for churches and hospitals
Assets: $3,203,672
Grant Range: $36,000–$500
Applications: Initial approach should be by letter. There are no deadlines.

The Aurora Foundation
P.O. Box 1848
Bradenton, FL 33506
(813) 748-4100

Contact: Anthony T. Rossi, Chair
Special Interest: Missionary work, church support, religious associations, education and scholarships for religious studies
Assets: $59,231,775
Grant Range: $1,179,954–$350 (Grant average: $3,000–$65,000)
Limitations: No support for building funds of schools and colleges and no professorships offered
Applications: The foundation reports that no new requests are currently being considered

John E. and Nellie J. Bastien Memorial Foundation
See entry in Interfaith

Bible Alliance, Inc.
P.O. Box 1894
Bradenton, FL 33506
(813) 748-4100
Contact: Anthony T. Rossi, President
Geographic Giving Pattern: No stated limitations
Special Interest: Production and distribution of recorded portions of the Bible and religious messages on cassette tapes in various languages for use for missionary outreach, particularly regarding the visually impaired and those in prisons
Assets: $1,836,995 (Gifts received: $1,179,959)
Limitations: Generally no cash grants
Applications: No application form is required. Certification of blindness is requested, when pertinent. There are no deadlines.

The Chatlos Foundation, Inc.
P.O. Box 915048
Longwood, FL 32791-5048
(407) 862-5077
Contact: William J. Chatlos, President
Geographic Giving Pattern: National
Special Interest: Higher education including religious education, religious associations, hospitals, health agencies, social services, international relief and child welfare
Assets: $72,932,792
Grant Range: $100,000–$175 (Grant average: $5,000–$25,000)
Limitations: No support for the arts. No grants to individuals or for seed money, deficit financing, building or endowment funds, research or conferences. No loans. Only one grant per organization per 12-month period.
Applications: Initial approach should be by letter at any time

The Raymond E. and Ellen F. Crane Foundation

P.O. Box 25427
Tamarac, FL 33320
Contact: George A. Owen, Manager
Geographic Giving Pattern: Primarily the southeastern states
Special Interest: Higher education and community funds; also cultural programs, health and Protestant church support
Assets: $3,210,246
Grant Range: $5,000–$500
Limitations: No grants to individuals
Applications: Contributes to pre-selected organizations only. Applications not accepted.

The Arthur Vining Davis Foundations

See entry in Interfaith

The Tine W. Davis Family–W.D. Charities, Inc.

4190 Belfort Road, Suite 240
Jacksonville, FL 32216
Contact: Charitable Grants Committee
Geographic Giving Pattern: Primarily the Southeast
Special Interest: Higher education, church support, youth agencies, medical research, health and social service agencies
Assets: $14,351,241
Grant Range: $100,000–$10 (Grant average: $1,000–$5,000)
Limitations: No grants to individuals
Applications: Initial approach should be by letter at any time

Jessie Ball duPont Religious, Charitable and Educational Fund

See entry in Interfaith

Horatio B. Ebert Charitable Foundation

P.O. Box 2058
Marco Island, FL 33969
Contact: Robert O. Ebert, Trustee
Geographic Giving Pattern: Primarily North Carolina, Ohio, Kentucky and Florida
Special Interest: Hospitals, higher education, child welfare and Christian churches and organizations
Assets: $5,812,610
Grant Range: $90,000–$2,000
Applications: Initial approach should be by letter at any time

Jefferson Lee Ford III Memorial Foundation, Inc.
c/o Sun Bank Miami
9600 Collins Avenue
P.O. Box 546487
Bal Harbour, FL 33154
(305) 868-2630
Contact: Herbert L. Kurras, Director
Geographic Giving Pattern: Primarily Florida
Special Interest: Health agencies, education, medical research, disabled children, hospitals and religious institutions
Assets: $2,198,355
Grant Range: $15,000–$1,000
Applications: Initial approach should be by letter. There are no deadlines.

The John E. & Aliese Price Foundation, Inc.
1279 Lavin Lane
P.O. Box 4607
North Fort Myers, FL 33918-4607
(813) 656-0196
Contact: T. Wainwright Miller, President
Geographic Giving Pattern: Primarily southwest Florida
Special Interest: Protestant church support and religious associations, including missionary work
Assets: $11,654,789
Grant Range: $151,500–$150 (Grant average: $1,000–$5,000)
Limitations: No grants to individuals
Applications: Initial approach should be by telephone. Grant proposals should be submitted preferably in July, however there is no set deadline.

Festus Stacy Foundation II
c/o McMillan, Unruh & Davis
1941 West Oakland Park Boulevard
Fort Lauderdale, FL 33311-1572
Contact: Festus Stacy, Trustee
Geographic Giving Pattern: National
Special Interest: Christian missionary efforts, evangelism, churches and social service programs
Assets: $3,927,378
Grant Range: $25,000–$1,000
Limitations: No grants to individuals

Applications: Contributes to pre-selected organizations only. Applications not accepted.

Samuel E. & Mary W. Thatcher Foundation, Inc.
3030 N.E. Second Avenue
Miami, FL 33137
Contact: John W. Thatcher, President and Treasurer
Geographic Giving Pattern: International
Special Interest: Primarily religious ministries, particularly those which involve youth
Assets: $10,400,732 (Gifts received: $2,700,000)
Grant Range: $50,000–$500
Applications: Initial approach should be by letter

Edna Sproull Williams Foundation
1500 Independent Square
Jacksonville, FL 32202
Contact: J.W. Burke, Trustee
Geographic Giving Pattern: Primarily Florida
Special Interest: Youth agencies, Protestant religious organizations, higher education, hospitals and social services
Assets: $13,894,291
Grant Range: $50,000–$1,000
Applications: Contributes to pre-selected organizations only. Applications not accepted.

Georgia

Bradley-Turner Foundation
P.O. Box 140
Columbus, GA 31902
(404) 571-6040
Contact: Stephen T. Butler, Chair
Geographic Giving Pattern: Primarily Georgia, with emphasis on Columbus
Special Interest: Higher education, religious associations, youth and social service agencies
Assets: $37,031,428
Grant Range: $1,250,000–$400 (Grant average: $2,000–$65,000)
Limitations: No grants to individuals
Applications: Initial approach should be by letter. Two copies of grant proposal are requested. There are no deadlines.

Callaway Foundation, Inc.
209 Broome Street
P.O. Box 790
LaGrange, GA 30241
(404) 884-7348
Contact: J.T. Gresham, President
Geographic Giving Pattern: Primarily Georgia, with emphasis on the city of LaGrange and Troup County, Georgia
Special Interest: Education, community funds and development, hospitals, care for the aged, historic preservation and church support
Assets: $145,416,275
Grant Range: $3,575,000–$200 (Grant average: $1,000–$100,000)
Limitations: No grants to individuals or for endowment funds, operating expenses, deficit financing, scholarships or fellowships. No loans.
Applications: Initial approach should be by letter. Grant proposals should be sent by the end of March, June, September or December.

Fuller E. Callaway Foundation
209 Broome Street
P.O. Box 790
LaGrange, GA 30241
(404) 884-7348
Contact: J.T. Gresham, President
Geographic Giving Pattern: Primarily the city of LaGrange and Troup County, Georgia
Special Interest: Religious, charitable and educational organizations. Scholarships for worthy students.
Assets: $27,135,276
Grant Range: $500,000–$250 (Grant average: $250–$10,000) (Scholarship average: $900–$3,000)
Limitations: No support for endowment funds. No loans.
Applications: No application form is required for organizations. Deadlines are the end of each month preceding board meetings. Board meetings fall in January, April, July and October. There is an application form for scholarships which should be submitted by February 15 for college students.

J. Bulow Campbell Foundation
1401 Trust Company Tower
25 Park Place, N.E.
Atlanta, GA 30303
(404) 658-9066
Contact: John W. Stephenson, Executive Director

Geographic Giving Pattern: Primarily Georgia; limited giving in Alabama, Florida, North Carolina, South Carolina and Tennessee
Special Interest: Protestant church-related agencies, especially Presbyterian; support also for education, human welfare, youth development and the arts
Assets: $123,125,861
Grant Range: $500,000–$25,000 (Grant average: $100,000–$200,000)
Limitations: No grants to local church congregations. No grants to individuals or for research, special projects or operating budgets. No loans.
Applications: Submit a one-page proposal and three copies of tax information. Deadlines are January 15, April 15, July 15 and October 15.

Cecil B. Day Foundation, Inc.
4725 Peachtree Corners Circle, Suite 300
Norcross, GA 30092
(404) 446-1500
Contact: Edward L. White, President
Geographic Giving Pattern: Primarily the New England states. Also Georgia, especially the metropolitan Atlanta area.
Special Interest: Grants to Christian churches for evangelism, missions and discipleships and for Pastor's Leadership Training
Assets: $22,556,319
Grant Range: $100,000–$100 (Grant average: $500–$10,000)
Limitations: No grants to individuals or for deficit financing, endowment funds, scholarships or fellowships
Applications: Initial approach should be by letter requesting program brochure. There are no deadlines.

Philip and Irene Toll Gage Foundation
c/o Citizens & Southern Trust Co.
P.O. Box 4446
Atlanta, GA 30302
(404) 897-3222
Contact: Larry B. Hooks, Senior Vice-President, Citizens & Southern Trust Co.
Geographic Giving Pattern: Primarily Atlanta, Georgia
Special Interest: Education, culture, hospitals, health services and Protestant giving
Assets: $4,545,825
Grant Range: $20,000–$100
Limitations: No grants to individuals or for endowment programs

Applications: Two copies of grant proposal should be submitted preferably in August or September. The deadline is October 15.

J.K. Gholston Trust
c/o Citizens & Southern National Bank
P.O. Box 992
Athens, GA 30613
(404) 549-8700
Contact: Janey Cooley, Trust Officer
Geographic Giving Pattern: Limited to the Comer, Georgia area
Special Interest: Education including scholarship funds, and Baptist church support
Assets: $3,481,593
Grant Range: $220,846–$100
Applications: An application form is required. There are no deadlines.

A. and M.L. Illges Memorial Foundation, Inc.
1224 Peacock Avenue
P.O. Box 103
Columbus, GA 31902
(404) 323-5342
Contact: Howell Hollis, President
Geographic Giving Pattern: Primarily Georgia
Special Interest: Higher education including scholarship funds, hospitals, church support and cultural programs
Assets: $2,953,318
Grant Range: $10,000–$100
Applications: No application forms required. There are no deadlines for grant proposals.

Ruth T. Jinks Foundation
P.O. Box 375
Colquitt, GA 31737
Contact: G.C. Jinks, Sr., Chair and President
Geographic Giving Pattern: Primarily Georgia
Special Interest: Christian religious organizations and churches, higher education and social services
Assets: $5,042,372
Grant Range: $15,500–$100
Applications: Initial approach should be by letter

Mattie H. Marshall Foundation

c/o Trust Co. Bank
P.O. Box 4655
Atlanta, GA 30302-4655
Contact: Martha M. Dykes, Director
Geographic Giving Pattern: Primarily Georgia
Special Interest: Higher education; support also for churches and hospitals
Assets: $1,685,736
Grant Range: $22,500–$1,500
Applications: Initial approach should be by letter. There are no deadlines.

Patterson-Barclay Memorial Foundation, Inc.

1020 Spring Street, N.W.
Atlanta, GA 30309
(404) 876-1022
Contact: Lee Barclay Patterson Allen, Trustee
Geographic Giving Pattern: Atlanta, Georgia metropolitan area
Special Interest: Christian organizations, hospitals, education, health, social services, youth agencies, arts and culture, and the environment
Assets: $5,418,358
Grant Average: $1,000–$5,000
Limitations: No grants to individuals
Applications: Contributes to pre-selected organizations only. Applications not accepted.

William I.H. and Lula E. Pitts Foundation

c/o Trust Co. Bank
P.O. Box 4655
Atlanta, GA 30302
(404) 588-8544
Contact: Clare Ranney, Secretary
Geographic Giving Pattern: Limited to Georgia
Special Interest: Methodist church-related institutions
Assets: $13,889,650
Grant Range: $47,000–$100 (Grant average: $5,000–$47,000)
Limitations: No grants to individuals or for endowment funds, scholarships, fellowships or research. No loans or matching gifts.
Applications: Initial approach should be by letter. There are no deadlines.

Ragan and King Charitable Foundation

c/o First Wachovia Charitable Funds Management
First National Bank of Atlanta
Two Peachtree Street, N.W., Suite 705
Atlanta, GA 30383
(404) 332-6586
Contact: Charles Buchholz
Geographic Giving Pattern: Limited to Georgia
Special Interest: Support for Baptist organizations only, including churches, religious organizations and theological seminaries
Assets: $2,495,374
Grant Range: $67,000–$4,000 (Grant average: $15,000)
Limitations: No grants to individuals
Applications: Initial approach should be by letter. There are no deadlines.

Rainbow Fund

P.O. Box 937
Fort Valley, GA 31030
(912) 825-2021
Contact: Albert L. Luce, Treasurer
Special Interest: Higher education, Protestant church support, religious organizations, missionary programs and theological education
Assets: $481 (Gifts received: $1,240,220)
Grant Range: $345,000–$250 (Grant average: $1,000–$5,000)
Applications: Applications are not accepted

Rutland Foundation, Inc.

215 Church Street
Decatur, GA 30030
Contact: Marie Rutland, President
Geographic Giving Pattern: Primarily Georgia
Special Interest: Baptist church support
Assets: $1,679,041 (Gifts received: $1,100,000)
Grant Range: $50,000–$100
Applications: Initial approach should be by letter

Warren P. and Ava F. Sewell Foundation

P.O. Drawer 645
Bremen, GA 30110
Contact: Guy Darnell

Geographic Giving Pattern: Primarily Haralson and Carroll counties, Georgia and Randolph and Cleburne counties, Alabama
Special Interest: Protestant churches, secondary and elementary education, health and child development agencies
Assets: $4,884,165
Grant Average: $1,000–$10,000
Applications: Initial approach should be by letter. There are no deadlines.

Loyd Strickland Foundation, Inc.
P.O. Box 7181
Chestnut Mountain, GA 30502
(404) 967-6152
Contact: Ben H. Lancaster, Secretary-Treasurer
Geographic Giving Pattern: Primarily Tennessee and Georgia
Special Interest: To promote the cause of the Christian faith, education and human welfare
Assets: $1,603,510
Grant Range: $56,400–$200
Applications: Initial approach should be a two to three-page letter

Watkins Christian Foundation, Inc.
1946 Monroe Drive, N.E.
Atlanta, GA 30324
Contact: Bill Watkins, President
Special Interest: Evangelism, churches, ministries and a variety of religious organizations
Assets: $3,915,545 (Gifts received: $725,058)
Grant Range: $50,000–$100
Applications: Contributes to pre-selected organizations only. Applications not accepted.

The Frances Wood Wilson Foundation, Inc.
1549 Clairmont Road, Suite 104
Decatur, GA 30033
(404) 634-3363
Contact: Emory K. Crenshaw, President
Geographic Giving Pattern: Primarily Georgia
Special Interest: Child welfare and religious, civic, health and higher education organizations
Assets: $29,458,515
Grant Range: $205,000–$500

Limitations: No grants to individuals or for endowment funds. No loans.
Applications: There are no deadlines. Grant proposals should be sent to the following address: P.O. Box 33188, Decatur, GA 30033

Hawaii

Atherton Family Foundation
c/o Hawaiian Trust Co., Ltd.
P.O. Box 3170
Honolulu, HI 96802
Contact: Jeanne Corrigan (grants)
Caroline Sherman (scholarships)
Geographic Giving Pattern: Limited to Hawaii
Special Interest: General charitable purposes, Protestant church support and scholarships for Protestant ministers' children and for theological education
Assets: $42,491,262
Grant Average: $2,500–$25,000 (organizations)
$1,000–$3,000 (individuals)
Limitations: No grants to organizations who will distribute grants to organizations of their own choosing
Applications: Initial approach for all grants should be by telephone or letter. Six copies of grant proposal must be sent. The deadline for scholarship requests is March 1 and an application form is required for scholarships. The application address is as follows: c/o Hawaii Community Foundation, 222 Merchant Street, 2nd Floor, Honolulu, HI 96813
Tel.: (808) 537-6333 (grants to organizations)
Tel.: (808) 536-8839 (scholarships)

Samuel N. and Mary Castle Foundation
c/o Hawaii Community Foundation
222 Merchant Street, 2nd Floor
Honolulu, HI 96813
(808) 537-6333
Contact: Jane R. Smith, Grants Administrator
Geographic Giving Pattern: Limited to Hawaii
Special Interest: Higher and secondary education, cultural programs, human service organizations, community funds and denominational giving
Assets: $18,708,253
Grant Range: $70,000–$1,000 (Grant average: $3,000–$25,000)

Limitations: No grants to individuals or for continuing support, endowment funds or scholarships. Generally no support for research. No loans.
Applications: Initial approach should be by telephone or written proposal. Seven copies of an executive summary should be submitted with grant proposal. Deadlines are January 1, April 1, May 1 and October 1.

G.N. Wilcox Trust
c/o Bishop Trust Co., Ltd.
1000 Bishop Street
Honolulu, HI 96813-2390
(808) 523-2233
Contact: Lois C. Loomis, Vice-President and Corporate Secretary, Bishop Trust Co., Ltd.
Geographic Giving Pattern: Hawaii, particularly the island of Kauai
Special Interest: Education and child welfare, general charitable purposes and Protestant church support
Assets: $13,646,780
Grant Range: $50,000–$500 (Grant average: $1,000–$10,000)
Limitations: No support for government agencies, individuals, endowment funds, research, publications or deficit financing. No loans.
Applications: Initial approach should be by telephone or grant proposal. Six copies of grant proposal are required. The deadlines are January 15, April 15, July 15 and October 15. Send proposals to the following address: c/o Bishop Trust Co., Ltd, P.O. Box 2390, Honolulu, HI 96804-2390

Illinois

Bere Foundation, Inc.
641 South Elm Street
Hinsdale, IL 60521
Contact: James F. Bere, President
Geographic Giving Pattern: Primarily the greater Chicago, Illinois metropolitan area
Special Interest: Churches and religious groups; some support for cultural programs
Assets: $4,136,899
Grant Range: $31,000–$250
Applications: Contributes to pre-selected organizations only. Applications not accepted.

Bjorkman Foundation
923 South Bruner Street
Hinsdale, IL 60521
(312) 654-3661
Contact: Glenn Bjorkman
Special Interest: Denominational giving, including churches,
Protestant welfare and Christian campaigns; some support for
hospitals, housing and hunger
Assets: $1,609,575
Grant Range: $20,500–$250
Applications: Applications are not accepted

Chapin-May Foundation of Illinois
c/o The Northern Trust Co.
50 South LaSalle Street
Chicago, IL 60675
(312) 630-6000
Contact: Michael E. Reed
Geographic Giving Pattern: Primarily Chicago, Illinois
Special Interest: Religious organizations, higher education, social
services and hospitals
Assets: $1,511,312
Grant Average: $800–$6,000
Limitations: No grants to individuals
Applications: Letter and grant proposal should be sent to the
following address: Vedder, Price, Kaufman & Kamholz, 222 North
LaSalle Street, Suite 2600, Chicago, IL 60601. Tel. (312) 609-7640.
Deadlines are March and September.

Henry P. Crowell and Susan C. Crowell Trust
Lock Box 442
Chicago, IL 60690
(312) 372-5202
Contact: Lowell L. Kline, Executive Director
Geographic Giving Pattern: National and international
Special Interest: To aid evangelical Christianity
Assets: $36,911,401
Grant Range: $350,000–$3,000 (Grant average: $10,000–$25,000)
Limitations: No grants to individuals or for endowment funds or
research. No loans.
Applications: The deadlines for grant proposals are April 1 and
October 1

Epaphroditus Foundation
650 Devon Avenue, Suite 160
Itasca, IL 60143
Contact: K.E. Gundersen, President
Geographic Giving Pattern: National
Special Interest: Religious purposes and programs for the disadvantaged
Assets: $1,814,329
Grant Range: $15,000–$1,000
Applications: Contributes to pre-selected organizations only. Applications not accepted.

Eben W. Erickson Charitable Fund
c/o The Northern Trust Co.
50 South LaSalle Street
Chicago, IL 60675
(312) 630-6000
Contact: Eben W. Erickson, The Northern Trust Co.
Geographic Giving Pattern: National
Special Interest: Youth, social service agencies, education, religious education, churches and other religious organizations
Assets: $7,018,113
Grant Total: $348,996
Applications: There are no deadlines for grant proposals

Hales Charitable Fund, Inc.
120 West Madison Street, Suite 700-E
Chicago, IL 60602
(312) 641-7016
Contact: William M. Hales, President
Geographic Giving Pattern: Primarily Illinois
Special Interest: Protestant church organizations, health agencies and higher education
Assets: $5,847,897
Grant Range: $150,000–$100
Limitations: No grants to individuals or for deficit financing, seed money, land acquisition, equipment, publications, conferences or renovations. No loans or matching gifts.
Applications: Generally funds pre-selected organizations

Philip S. Harper Foundation
c/o Harper-Wyman Co.
930 North York Road, Suite 204
Hinsdale, IL 60521
Contact: Philip S. Harper, Jr., President
Special Interest: Protestant church support and general charitable purposes
Assets: $4,710,435
Grant Range: $9,000–$250

The H. Earl Hoover Foundation
1801 Green Bay Road
P.O. Box 330
Glencoe, IL 60022
(312) 835-3350
Contact: Robert L. Foote or Miriam W. Hoover, Trustees
Geographic Giving Pattern: Primarily Illinois
Special Interest: Youth agencies, hospitals, social welfare agencies, cultural organizations and Protestant church support
Assets: $2,655,226
Grant Range: $75,000–$250
Applications: Initial approach should be by letter. There are no deadlines.

Irvin E. Houck Charitable Trust
c/o First United Trust Co.
Village Mall Plaza
Oak Park, IL 60301-1194
Contact: Margaret R. Houck, Trustee
Geographic Giving Pattern: Primarily Illinois
Special Interest: Churches and other Christian organizations, social welfare, the environment, culture and education
Assets: $1,000,412
Grant Range: $15,000–$100
Limitations: No grants to individuals
Applications: Initial approach should be by letter. There are no deadlines.

Jennie Huizenga Foundation
200 North LaSalle Street, Suite 3000
Chicago, IL 60601-1083
(312) 323-6310
Contact: Janet Evenhouse, President

Geographic Giving Pattern: Primarily Illinois
Special Interest: Giving limited to organizations "involved in the service of Our Lord Jesus Christ"
Assets: $2,458,179
Grant Range: $110,000–$1,000
Limitations: No grants to individuals
Applications: Written grant proposal letters should be sent by November 1. The application address is as follows: 105051 Corraine Drive, Hinsdale, IL 60521.

Thomas M. & Mary M. Owens Foundation
10336 Cook Avenue
Oak Lawn, IL 60453
(312) 424-3374
Contact: Mary M. Owens, President and Secretary
Geographic Giving Pattern: Primarily Chicago, Illinois
Special Interest: Primarily for religious purposes, especially missionary activity; support also for secondary education and social services
Assets: $1,892,696 (Gifts received: $1,470,000)
Grant Range: $40,000–$300
Applications: Contributes to pre-selected organizations only. Applications not accepted.

Luther I. Replogle Foundation
5744 South Blackstone Avenue
Chicago, IL 60637-1824
Contact: Gwenn Gebhard
Geographic Giving Pattern: Primarily Chicago, Illinois
Special Interest: Museums, churches and other Protestant organizations, hospitals, clinics and higher education
Assets: $7,276,399
Grant Range: $31,000–$35
Applications: Initial approach should be by letter sent to the following address: 726 Fifth Street, N.E., Washington, D.C. 20002. Tel. (202) 544-2355. There are no deadlines.

The Retirement Research Foundation
See entry in Interfaith

Otto L. and Hazel T. Rhoades Fund
6106 North Landers
Chicago, IL 60646
(312) 775-2257

Contact: Harry M. Coffman, Vice-President
Geographic Giving Pattern: Primarily Illinois
Special Interest: Religious support and Christian communications organizations, higher education, health and social services
Assets: $2,002,744
Grant Range: $30,000–$1,500
Applications: Initial approach should be by letter

William E. Schmidt Charitable Foundation
Two Larkspur
Belleville, IL 62221
Contact: Lucille Barton, Director
Special Interest: Primarily religious organizations, higher education and health services
Assets: $4,462,691 (Gifts received: $1,404,975)
Grant Range: $10,000–$1,000
Applications: Contributes to pre-selected organizations only. Applications not accepted.

Solo Cup Foundation
See entry in Interfaith

Thomas & Gertrude Tibstra Charitable Foundation
119 South Old Creek Road
Palos Park, IL 60464
Contact: Thomas Tibstra, President
Geographic Giving Pattern: Primarily Michigan and Illinois
Special Interest: Christian education and religious programs
Assets: $2,853,756
Grant Range: $20,000–$4,000
Limitations: No grants to individuals
Applications: Contributes to pre-selected organizations only. Applications not accepted.

Tyndal House Foundation
336 Gundersen Drive, Box 80
Wheaton, IL 60187
(312) 668-8300
Contact: Mary Kleine Yehling, Executive Director
Geographic Giving Pattern: National and international
Special Interest: Missions, evangelical organizations, Christian literature projects and Bible translation
Assets: $199,910 (Gifts received: $761,697)

Grant Total: $776,750
Limitations: No support for libraries. No grants to individuals or for building or endowment funds, scholarships, fellowships or personnel support.
Applications: New grants awarded on a limited basis. Initial approach should be by letter or telephone. Ten copies of the grant proposal are required. The deadline is the middle of August.

Clara and Spencer Werner Foundation, Inc.
616 South Jefferson Street
Paris, IL 61944
Contact: W. Frank Wiggins, President
Geographic Giving Pattern: Primarily Illinois and surrounding states, including Missouri and Indiana
Special Interest: Lutheran programs including theological education
Assets: $11,077,807
Grant Range: $2,227,860–$4,500
Limitations: No support for individual churches, congregations or parochial schools. No grants to individuals.
Applications: Initial approach should be by letter and proposal

Indiana

Ball Brothers Foundation
222 South Mulberry Street
P.O. Box 1408
Muncie, IN 47308
(317) 741-5500
Contact: Douglas A. Bakken, Executive Director
Geographic Giving Pattern: Limited to Indiana
Special Interest: Educational, cultural and religious organizations
Assets: $77,478,000
Grant Range: $1,500,000–$1,000 (Grant average: $1,000–$50,000)
Limitations: No grants to individuals
Applications: There are no set deadlines, however the foundation prefers to receive grant proposals before June

Bierhaus Foundation, Inc.
P.O. Box 538
Vincennes, IN 47591
(812) 882-0990
Contact: Robert V. Bierhaus, Secretary
Geographic Giving Pattern: Primarily Indiana

Special Interest: Protestant churches, higher education and youth
Assets: $2,068,472
Grant Range: $50,100–$50
Applications: Initial approach should be by letter or telephone. There are no deadlines.

English-Bonter-Mitchell Foundation
900 Fort Wayne National Bank Building
Fort Wayne, IN 46802
Contact: Mary E. Mitchell, Board Member
Geographic Giving Pattern: Primarily Fort Wayne, Indiana
Special Interest: Cultural programs and programs for youth; support also for higher education, hospitals, churches and religious organizations, social services, health and community development
Assets: $37,416,157
Grant Range: $155,000–$1,000
Applications: Initial approach should be by letter

John A. Hillenbrand Foundation
See entry in Interfaith

Irwin-Sweeney-Miller Foundation
See entry in Interfaith

Lilly Endowment, Inc.
See entry in Interfaith

Ober Foundation
38 North Pennsylvania Street, Room 200
Indianapolis, IN 46204
Contact: C.S. Ober, Trustee
Geographic Giving Pattern: Primarily Indiana
Special Interest: Protestant churches and organizations; support also for higher and secondary education and social services
Assets: $1,070,053
Grant Range: $40,000–$15
Applications: Initial approach should be by letter

Frank L. and Laura L. Smock Foundation
c/o Lincoln National Bank and Trust Co.
P.O. Box 9340
Fort Wayne, IN 46899
(219) 461-6451

Contact: Alice Kopfer, Vice-President, Lincoln National Bank and Trust Co.
Geographic Giving Pattern: Limited to Indiana
Special Interest: Presbyterian churches and to "promote the health, welfare and happiness of ailing or needy or crippled or blind or elderly and aged men and women of the Presbyterian faith throughout the state of Indiana"
Assets: $7,070,725
Grant Range: $30,454–$140 (organizations) and $24,783–$108 (individuals)
Limitations: No grants for general or operating support, capital campaigns, building or endowment funds. No loans or matching gifts.
Applications: Initial approach should be by letter. An application form is required. There are no deadlines.

Thrush-Thompson Foundation, Inc.
P.O. Box 185
Peru, IN 46970
Contact: Robert L. Thompson, Secretary
Geographic Giving Pattern: Primarily Indiana
Special Interest: Protestant church support; also higher education, health agencies, cultural programs and youth agencies
Assets: $3,422,082
Grant Range: $23,600–$100
Applications: Initial approach should be by letter

Iowa

The Barzillai Foundation
Two Ruan Center, Suite 1100
601 Locust Street
Des Moines, IA 50309
(515) 283-2076
Contact: Marvin Winick
Geographic Giving Pattern: National
Special Interest: Christian organizations including missionary programs, churches and evangelism
Assets: $1,684,708
Grant Range: $24,100–$1,000
Limitations: No grants to individuals
Applications: An application form is required. Initial approach should be by letter. There are no deadlines.

E & M Charities
2610 Park Avenue
P.O. Box 209
Muscatine, IA 52761
(319) 264-8342
Contact: Linda A. Thompson, Executive Secretary
Geographic Giving Pattern: National
Special Interest: Christian-related projects, churches, church-related independent colleges, community charitable and educational projects and prevention of world hunger
Assets: $23,821,011
Grant Range: $350,000–$100 (Grant average: $2,000–$50,000)
Limitations: No support for private foundations. No grants to individuals or for research.
Applications: Initial approach should be by letter. There are no deadlines.

Peter H. and E. Lucille Gaass Kuyper Foundation
c/o Rolscreen Co.
Pella, IA 50219
(515) 628-1000
Contact: Joan Kuyper Farver, President
Geographic Giving Pattern: Primarily Pella, Iowa
Special Interest: Christian welfare funds, hospitals, civic affairs and a college
Assets: $11,196,609
Grant Range: $250,000–$500
Applications: Initial approach should be by letter. There are no deadlines.

Vermeer Charitable Foundation, Inc.
c/o Vermeer Manufacturing Co.
P.O. Box 200
Pella, IA 50219
(515) 628-3141
Contact: Mary Andringa, Director
Geographic Giving Pattern: Primarily Pella, Iowa
Special Interest: Christian religious organizations, higher education and care of the elderly
Assets: $3,686,248 (Gifts received: $771,212)
Grant Range: $50,000–$310 (Grant average: $10,000)
Limitations: No grants to individuals or for endowment funds, scholarships or fellowships. No matching gifts or loans.

Applications: An application form is required. Initial approach should be by letter with two copies of grant proposal.

Kansas

DeVore Foundation, Inc.
P.O. Box 118
Wichita, KS 67201
(316) 267-3211
Contact: Richard A. DeVore, President
Geographic Giving Pattern: Primarily Wichita, Kansas
Special Interest: Youth agencies, Protestant church support, arts and culture, higher education and health and social services
Assets: $2,491,670
Grant Range: $135,200–$40
Applications: Initial approach should be by proposal letter. There are no deadlines.

W.J. & Irene Hupfer Foundation
c/o Russell State Bank
507 Main
Russell, KS 67665
Contact: John T. Harrell, Trustee
Geographic Giving Pattern: Primarily Russell, Kansas
Special Interest: Methodist churches and organizations, higher education and a senior citizens' center
Assets: $1,279,963
Grant Range: $18,517–$926
Limitations: No grants to individuals
Applications: Contributes to pre-selected organizations only. Applications are rarely accepted.

The Powell Family Foundation
10990 Roe Avenue
P.O. Box 7270
Shawnee Mission, KS 66207
(913) 345-3000
Contact: Marjorie P. Allen, President
Geographic Giving Pattern: Primarily Kansas City
Special Interest: Education, religion (particularly Christian Scientist churches), civic affairs and social service and youth agencies
Assets: $56,154,381
Grant Range: $707,566–$100 (Grant average: $1,000–$50,000)

Limitations: No grants to individuals or for building or endowment funds
Applications: Two copies of a three to five-page grant proposal are requested. The deadline is thirty days preceding board meeting. Board meetings are usually held in January, April, July and October.

Kentucky

V.V. Cooke Foundation Corporation
The Summit
4350 Brownsboro Road, Suite 110
Louisville, KY 40207-1681
(502) 893-4598
Contact: John B. Gray, Executive Director
Geographic Giving Pattern: Primarily Kentucky
Special Interest: Baptist church and school support and higher education, including medical education
Assets: $4,918,711
Grant Range: $60,000–$50
Limitations: No grants to individuals or for general endowment funds, research, scholarships or fellowships. No loans.
Applications: The foundation does not conduct personal interviews. Initial approach should be by proposal. There are no deadlines.

Ervin G. Houchens Foundation, Inc.
900 Church Street
Bowling Green, KY 42101
(502) 843-3252
Contact: Ervin D. Houchens, President
Geographic Giving Pattern: Southwest Kentucky
Special Interest: Baptist and Methodist church support, generally in the form of loans
Assets: $3,685,632
Loan Range: $145,000–$125
Applications: Initial approach should be by proposal letter with comprehensive details. There are no deadlines.

Ralph E. Mills Foundation
c/o Drawer M
Frankfort, KY 40601
Contact: Ralph E. Mills, President
Geographic Giving Pattern: Primarily Kentucky

Special Interest: Higher education, hospitals, Christian churches and social services
Assets: $11,523,687
Grant Range: $100,000–$500
Limitations: No grants to individuals
Applications: Initial approach should be by letter

Al J. Schneider Foundation Corporation
3720 Seventh Street Road
Louisville, KY 40216
Contact: Al J. Schneider, President
Geographic Giving Pattern: Primarily Kentucky
Special Interest: Church support, health, cultural programs, youth agencies and education
Assets: $1,387,317 (Gifts received: $477,000)
Grant Range: $50,000–$25
Applications: Initial approach should be by letter

Louisiana

Charles T. Beaird Foundation
P.O. Box 31110
Shreveport, LA 71130
(318) 459-3242
Contact: Charles T. Beaird, President
Geographic Giving Pattern: Primarily Shreveport, Louisiana
Special Interest: Higher education including theological seminaries, Protestant welfare, social services for women and youth organizations
Assets: $2,178,724
Grant Range: $25,000–$200
Applications: Initial approach should be by letter. Deadlines are June 1, August 15 and November 15.

Coughlin-Saunders Foundation, Inc.
1412 Centre Court, Suite 202
Alexandria, LA 71301-3406
(318) 442-9642
Contact: R.R. Saunders, President
Geographic Giving Pattern: Primarily central Louisiana
Special Interest: Higher education and church support. Preference is given to organizations that have received grants between 1949-1983.
Assets: $6,806,326

Grant Range: $184,380–$50
Limitations: No grants to individuals or for matching gifts
Applications: Initial approach should be by letter. Grant proposals
should be submitted preferably in January or February. The deadline
is March 15.

Frazier Foundation, Inc.
P.O. Box 1175
Minden, LA 71055-1175
(318) 377-0182
Contact: James Walter Frazier, President
Special Interest: Church of Christ, Christian religious organizations
and educational institutions
Assets: $11,706,642
Grant Range: $155,500–$2,500 (Grant average: $5,000–$20,000)
Limitations: No grants to individuals or for endowment funds. No
loans.
Applications: Four copies of grant proposal should be sent preferably
in April or October. Deadlines are May 1 and November 1.

Libby-Dufour Fund
See entry in Interfaith

J. Edgar Monroe Foundation (1976)
228 St. Charles Street, Suite 1402
New Orleans, LA 70130
(504) 529-3539
Contact: Robert J. Monroe, Trustee
Geographic Giving Pattern: Primarily Louisiana
Special Interest: Higher education, social services, Christian
organizations, hospitals, hospices, the arts and historic preservation
Assets: $7,500,000
rant Range: $75,000–$25
Applications: Initial approach should be by letter

The Wheless Foundation
c/o Commercial National Bank in Shreveport
P.O. Box 21119
Shreveport, LA 71152
(318) 429-1704
Contact: Bobby L. Miller, Trust Officer, Commercial National Bank in
Shreveport
Geographic Giving Pattern: Primarily Louisiana

Special Interest: Higher education, church support, community funds and youth agencies
Assets: $2,898,836
Grant Range: $51,025–$100
Applications: There are no deadlines for applications

Maine

The Clarence E. Mulford Trust
Eight Portland Street
Fryeburg, ME 04037
(207) 935-2061
Contact: David R. Hastings, Trustee
Geographic Giving Pattern: Primarily Fryeburg, Maine and neighboring towns
Special Interest: Schools, church support, community services, welfare programs and youth services
Assets: $4,758,263
Grant Total: $259,299
Limitations: No grants to individuals or for building or endowment funds, scholarships or fellowships. No matching gifts and no loans.
Applications: Initial approach should be by letter. Three copies of grant proposal should be submitted preferably in June or December.

Maryland

Clark-Winchcole Foundation
Air Rights Building
4550 Montgomery Avenue, Suite 345N
Bethesda, MD 20814
(301) 654-3607
Contact: Laura E. Phillips, President
Geographic Giving Pattern: Primarily the Washington, D.C. area
Special Interest: Higher education, health and youth agencies, medical research and hospitals, Protestant church support, cultural programs and social service agencies
Assets: $36,747,927
Grant Range: $200,000–$1,000 (Grant average: $30,000–$50,000)
Applications: Initial approach should be by letter. Proposal letters should be sent during the first six months of the calendar year.

The M.E. Foundation
Two West Rolling Crossroads, Suite 207
Baltimore, MD 21228-6201
(301) 944-8676
Contact: F. Carroll Brown, Vice-President
or Margaret Brown Trimble, President
Geographic Giving Pattern: National, international
Special Interest: Protestant evangelical missionary work and Bible studies
Assets: $11,936,972
Grant Range: $60,000–$300
Applications: There are no deadlines for written grant requests

Vincent Mulford Foundation
c/o Mercantile Safe Deposit & Trust Co.
Two Hopkins Plaza
Baltimore, MD 21201
(301) 237-5416
Contact: Lloyd Batzler
Geographic Giving Pattern: Primarily New York, New Jersey and Connecticut
Special Interest: The arts, higher and secondary education, Protestant church support and social service agencies
Assets: $2,038,120
Grant Range: $14,000–$250
Applications: Initial approach should be by letter or grant proposal. There are no deadlines.

Three Swallows Foundation
See entry in Interfaith

Marcia Brady Tucker Foundation
11 South Washington Street
Easton, MD 21601
(301) 822-3155
Contact: Luther Tucker, President
Special Interest: Education, conservation and medical, welfare, religious and cultural institutions
Assets: $8,354,869
Grant Range: $42,500–$150
Limitations: No grants to individuals
Applications: Initial approach should be by letter or proposal. There are no deadlines.

Massachusetts

Aimee M.L. Becker Foundation
c/o The Massachusetts Co., Inc.
99 High Street
Boston, MA 02110
Contact: Maurice F. Lesses, Vice-President
Geographic Giving Pattern: Primarily Missouri
Special Interest: Lutheran churches and organizations; some support for higher education
Assets: $2,673,971
Grant Range: $42,085–$9,018
Limitations: No grants to individuals
Applications: Contributes to pre-selected organizations only. Applications not accepted.

The Howard Johnson Foundation
See entry in Interfaith

The Rogers Family Foundation
P.O. Box 100
Lawrence, MA 01842
(508) 685-1000
Contact: Irving E. Rogers, Trustee
Geographic Giving Pattern: Limited to the greater Lawrence, Massachusetts area, including Methuen, Andover and Haverhill, Massachusetts and southeastern New Hampshire
Special Interest: Hospitals, higher and secondary education, Protestant giving and community funds
Assets: $7,117,643 (Gifts received: $853,840)
Grant Range: $50,000–$300
Limitations: No grants to individuals or for endowment funds, research, scholarships or fellowships. No matching gifts or loans.
Applications: Initial approach should be by letter. Funds are, however, largely committed. There are no deadlines.

Michigan

Wallace and Irene Bronner Family Charitable Trust
625 East Tuscola
Frankenmuth, MI 48734-1717
(517) 652-6723
Contact: Wallace J. Bronner, Trustee

Geographic Giving Pattern: Primarily Frankenmuth and Saginaw, Michigan
Special Interest: Lutheran organizations, including churches and a theological institute
Assets: $1,102,280
Grant Range: $11,250–$100
Applications: Applications are not accepted

Gerald W. Chamberlin Foundation, Inc.
21 Kercheval Street, Suite 270
Grosse Pointe, MI 48236
Contact: Donald F. Chamberlin, President
Geographic Giving Pattern: Primarily Michigan
Special Interest: Protestant church support, youth agencies, higher and secondary education, and cultural programs
Assets: $2,314,918
Grant Range: $10,000–$100
Applications: Contributes to pre-selected organizations only. Applications not accepted.

Opal Dancey Memorial Foundation
c/o Manufacturers National Bank of Detroit
100 Renaissance Center
Detroit, MI 48243
Contact: Rev. Gary Imms, Chair
Geographic Giving Pattern: Primarily the Midwest
Special Interest: Limited to seminaries and schools of theology
Assets: $1,008,002
Grant Average: $700–$12,500
Applications: An application form is required. The deadline is June 15. Applicants should write to the following address: 28400 Evergreen Avenue, Flat Rock, MI 48134.

The Richard and Helen DeVos Foundation
7575 East Fulton Road
Ada, MI 49355
(616) 676-6222
Contact: Richard M. DeVos, President
Special Interest: Religious programs and associations, church support, music and the performing arts, higher education and social welfare
Assets: $18,688,415 (Gifts received: $6,000,000)
Grant Range: $316,500–$21 (Grant average: $1,000–$25,000)
Limitations: No stated limitations
Applications: Initial approach should be by letter

Walter and Josephine Ford Fund
100 Renaissance Center, 34th Floor
Detroit, MI 48243
(313) 259-7777
Contact: Pierre V. Heftler, Secretary
Geographic Giving Pattern: Primarily Michigan
Special Interest: Education, community funds, arts, hospitals,
Protestant church support, medical research and youth and social
agencies
Assets: $6,886,763 (Gifts received: $1,191,216)
Grant Range: $200,000–$50
Limitations: No grants to individuals
Applications: Initial approach should be by letter. There are no
deadlines.

The Rollin M. Gerstacker Foundation
P.O. Box 1945
Midland, MI 48640
(517) 631-6097
Contact: E.N. Brandt, Vice-President
Geographic Giving Pattern: Primarily Michigan and Ohio
Special Interest: Community projects with emphasis on the aged and
youth, higher education (including seminaries) and healthcare
Assets: $86,325,247
Grant Range: $3,639,906–$1,000 (Grant average: $5,000–$25,000)
Limitations: No grants to individuals or for scholarships or
fellowships. No loans.
Applications: Initial approach should be by letter. Grant proposal
letters should be sent by May 15 or November 15.

Charles Stewart Harding Foundation
1802 Genesee Towers
Flint, MI 48502
(313) 767-0136
Contact: C. Edward White, Secretary
Special Interest: Primarily Christian Scientist organizations and
theological education
Assets: $6,154,440
Grant Range: $300,000–$250
Limitations: No grants to individuals
Applications: Initial approach should be by letter. There are no
deadlines.

Herrick Foundation
2500 Comerica Building
Detroit, MI 48226
(313) 963-6420
Contact: Kenneth G. Herrick, President
Geographic Giving Pattern: Primarily Michigan
Special Interest: Higher and secondary education, hospitals, health
and welfare agencies, and Protestant church support
Assets: $210,459,774
Grant Range: $1,000,000–$500 (Grant average: $5,000–$100,000)
Limitations: No grants to individuals
Applications: Initial approach should be by letter. There are no
deadlines.

Orville D. & Ruth A. Merillat Foundation
P.O. Box 1946
Adrian, MI 49221
Contact: Orville D. Merillat, President
Geographic Giving Pattern: Primarily Michigan
Special Interest: Churches and religious welfare
Assets: $64,695,846
Grant Average: $1,000–$100,000
Applications: Contributes to pre-selected organizations only.
Application not accepted.

Roy G. Michell Charitable Foundation and Trust
c/o Janz & Knight
1100 North Woodward
Birmingham, MI 48011
(313) 646-9666
Contact: The Trustees
Special Interest: Protestant giving, higher education and social services
Assets: $1,896,514
Grant Range: $30,000–$500
Limitations: No stated limitations
Applications: Initial approach should be by letter

William M. and Mary E. Pagel Trust
c/o National Bank of Detroit
611 Woodward Avenue
Detroit, MI 48226
(313) 225-3124
Contact: Therese M. Thorn, Second Vice-President, National Bank of
Detroit

Geographic Giving Pattern: Primarily Michigan, with emphasis on the Detroit metropolitan tri-county area
Special Interest: Health and hospitals, the aged, child welfare, rehabilitation, the disabled and Protestant church support
Assets: $6,720,170
Grant Range: $45,000–$1,000
Limitations: No grants to individuals
Applications: Grant proposal letter should be sent by October 30 to the following address: c/o National Bank of Detroit, P.O. Box 222, Detroit, MI 48232.

Prince Foundation
1057 South Shore Drive
Holland, MI 49423
Contact: Edgar D. Prince, President
Geographic Giving Pattern: Primarily Michigan
Special Interest: Christian organizations, churches and schools
Assets: $9,876,597 (Gifts received: $5,725,000)
Grant Range: $1,702,750–$150
Limitations: No stated limitations
Applications: Initial approach should be by letter

Jay and Betty VanAndel Foundation
7186 Windy Hill Road, S.E.
Grand Rapids, MI 49506
Contact: Jay VanAndel, President
Geographic Giving Pattern: Michigan
Special Interest: Christian religious activities, including higher and secondary education
Assets: $8,540,753
Grant Range: $125,000–$100
Applications: Initial approach should be by letter

Samuel L. Westerman Foundation
See entry in Interfaith

Word Investments, Inc.
3366 Burton Street, S.E.
Grand Rapids, MI 49546
Contact: Clare De Graaf, President
Geographic Giving Pattern: Primarily Michigan
Special Interest: Christian missionary programs and education
Assets: $6,349,368

Grant Range: $86,497–$800
Limitations: No grants to individuals
Applications: Applications are not accepted

Minnesota

Athwin Foundation
1420 Midwest Plaza West
Minneapolis, MN 55402
(612) 340-3618
Contact: Henry H. Nowicki, Managing Director
Geographic Giving Pattern: Primarily the Minneapolis-St. Paul,
Minnesota area. Some grants awarded in Claremont, California and
Phoenix, Arizona.
Special Interest: Educational, cultural, religious and community
welfare programs
Assets: $3,930,564
Grant Range: $500,000–$35 (Grant average: $1,000–$5,000)
Limitations: No grants to individuals or for scholarships or
fellowships. No loans.
Applications: Five copies of grant proposal should be sent to the
following address: 801 Nicollet Mall, Suite 1420, Minneapolis, MN
55402. Tel. (612) 340-3616. There are no deadlines.

Bayport Foundation, Inc.
287 Central Avenue
Bayport, MN 55003
(612) 439-1557
Contact: Katherine B. Andersen, Trustee
Geographic Giving Pattern: Primarily Minnesota
Special Interest: Hospitals, medical research, community projects,
youth agencies and religious organizations
Assets: $18,639,584 (Gifts received: $1,000,000)
Grant Range: $71,000–$131
Limitations: No grants to individuals
Applications: Initial approach should be by letter. There are no
deadlines.

Otto Bremer Foundation
See entry in Interfaith

Getsch Family Foundation Trust
c/o First National Bank of Minneapolis
120 South Sixth Street
Minneapolis, MN 55480
(612) 540-6207
Contact: Paul Schliesman, Vice-President, First National Bank of Minneapolis
Geographic Giving Pattern: Primarily Minnesota and Wisconsin
Special Interest: General charitable giving, with emphasis on higher education, youth agencies and Protestant church support
Assets: $2,366,209
Grant Range: $55,000–$500
Limitations: No grants to individuals or for endowment funds
Applications: Applications are not accepted

Lutheran Brotherhood Foundation
625 Fourth Avenue South
Minneapolis, MN 55415
(612) 340-5821
Contact: Turi Whiting
Geographic Giving Pattern: National
Special Interest: Lutheran churches, schools and other religious organizations only
Assets: $31,256,000 (Gifts received: $8,000,000)
Grant Range: $80,000–$2,000 (Grant average: $25,000–$35,000)
Limitations: No grants to individuals or for operating budgets, continuing support, annual campaigns, emergency funds, deficit financing, building funds, equipment, land acquisition, renovation projects, endowments, scholarships, research or publications. No loans.
Applications: Initial approach should be by telephone or letter of not more than three typewritten pages. There are no deadlines. An application form is required.

Onan Family Foundation
435 Ford Road, Suite 310
Minneapolis, MN 55426
(612) 544-4702
Contact: David W. Onan, President
Geographic Giving Pattern: Primarily the Twin Cities, Minnesota metropolitan area
Special Interest: To improve the physical, cultural, educational condition of mankind, giving primarily to Protestant churches, social

welfare agencies, cultural and civic organizations and educational institutions
Assets: $4,997,434
Grant Range: $28,000–$1,500 (Grant average: $1,500–$10,000)
Limitations: No grants to individuals or for capital or endowment funds, research, scholarships or political campaigns. No matching gifts and no loans.
Applications: A letter and grant proposal should be submitted in April or September.

Margaret Rivers Fund
See entry in Interfaith

Sundet Foundation
2791 Pheasant Road
Excelsior, MN 55331-9572
Contact: Leland N. Sundet, President
Geographic Giving Pattern: Primarily Minnesota
Special Interest: Community and social services, higher and secondary education, Protestant churches and organizations, and medical research
Assets: $2,504,588
Grant Range: $15,800–$100
Applications: The deadline for grant proposals is January 15

Mississippi

The Community Foundation, Inc.
P.O. Box 924
Jackson, MS 39205-0924
(601) 372-2227
Contact: W.K. Paine, President
Geographic Giving Pattern: Primarily Mississippi
Special Interest: Protestant religious associations, higher education and social service agencies
Assets: $4,476,902
Grant Range: $50,000–$1,000
Limitations: No grants to individuals
Applications: Contributes to pre-selected organizations only. Applications not accepted.

Elizabeth M. Irby Foundation
P.O. Box 1819
Jackson, MS 39215-1819
(601) 969-1811
Contact: Stuart M. Irby, Vice-President
Geographic Giving Pattern: Primarily Mississippi
Special Interest: Higher education including a theological seminary, Protestant church support and religious organizations
Assets: $1,601,717
Grant Range: $38,000–$50
Limitations: No grants to individuals
Applications: Initial approach should be by letter. There are no deadlines.

Missouri

The Catherine Manley Gaylord Foundation
See entry in Interfaith

Herschend Family Foundation
Silver Dollar City Inc.
Branson, MO 65616
(417) 338-2611
Contact: Jack R. Herschend, Director
Geographic Giving Pattern: Primarily Missouri
Special Interest: Protestant organizations including churches and ministries; support also for family and social services
Assets: $2,247,671 (Gifts received: $952,500)
Grant Range: $25,000–$2,500
Applications: Initial approach should be by letter. There are no deadlines for grant proposals.

Herschend Foundation
2512 South Campbell
Springfield, MO 65807
(417) 883-9970
Contact: Don G. Smillie, Manager
Special Interest: Christian projects, including missions and Episcopal churches
Assets: $1,491,375 (Gifts received: $1,460,174)
Grant Range: $43,080–$500
Limitations: No grants to individuals or for medical expenses
Applications: Initial approach should be by proposal. There are no deadlines.

Oscar C. Hirsch Foundation

P.O. Box 611
Cape Girardeau, MO 63702-0611
(314) 334-2555
Contact: James F. Hirsch, Trustee
Special Interest: Primarily Protestant church support; some giving for youth programs, education and social service agencies
Assets: $1,054,997
Grant Range: $15,100–$200
Applications: Initial approach should be by letter. There are no deadlines.

David B. Lichtenstein Foundation

P.O. Box 19740
St. Louis, MO 63144
Contact: Daniel B. Lichtenstein, Manager
Geographic Giving Pattern: Limited to Missouri
Special Interest: Protestant religious and charitable organizations
Assets: $6,130,274 (Gifts received: $1,813,742)
Grant Range: $55,140–$100
Applications: Initial approach should be by letter. There are no deadlines.

The Pillsbury Foundation

Six Oakleigh Lane
St. Louis, MO 63124
Contact: Joyce S. Pillsbury, President
Geographic Giving Pattern: Primarily Missouri, with emphasis on St. Louis
Special Interest: Education, Baptist church support, religious associations and social service agencies
Assets: $16,044,673
Grant Range: $281,790–$100 (Grant average: $100–$10,000)
Limitations: No grants to individuals. No loans.
Applications: Applications are not accepted

Robert W. Plaster Foundation, Inc.

P.O. Box 129
Lebanon, MO 65536-0129
Contact: Robert W. Plaster, President and Treasurer
Geographic Giving Pattern: Primarily Missouri
Special Interest: Protestant organizations including churches and educational institutions

Assets: $2,996,352 (Gifts received: $525,000)
Grant Range: $15,000–$5,000
Limitations: No grants to individuals
Applications: Contributes to pre-selected organizations only. Applications not accepted.

The George Herbert Walker Foundation
500 North Broadway, Suite 1700
St. Louis, MO 63102
(314) 342-2109
Contact: George H. Walker, Trustee
Geographic Giving Pattern: Primarily Missouri and Connecticut
Special Interest: Higher and secondary education and Protestant church support
Assets: $1,461,131
Grant Range: $20,000–$250
Limitations: No grants to individuals
Applications: Contributes to pre-selected organizations only. Applications not accepted.

Montana

Charles M. Bair Memorial Trust
c/o First Trust Co. of Montana
P.O. Box 30678
Billings, MT 59115
(406) 657-8122
Contact: Alberta M. Bair, First Trust Co. of Montana
Geographic Giving Pattern: Primarily Montana
Special Interest: Hospitals and Protestant churches
Assets: $18,847,092
Grant Range: $300,000–$10,000
Applications: An application form is required. The deadline is usually set early and normally falls in April.

Nebraska

Thomas D. Buckley Trust
See entry in Interfaith

The Faith Charitable Trust

10315 Rockbrook Road
Omaha, NE 68124
Contact: Marshall E. Faith, Manager
Geographic Giving Pattern: Primarily Omaha, Nebraska
Special Interest: Christian organizations, churches and higher education
Assets: $1,670,984
Grant Total: $180,797
Applications: Contributes to pre-selected organizations only. Applications not accepted.

Lincoln Family Foundation

P.O. Box 80269
Lincoln, NE 68501
Contact: George A. Lincoln, President
Geographic Giving Pattern: Primarily Nebraska and Kansas
Special Interest: Higher education and Protestant church support
Assets: $2,031,991
Grant Range: $125,000–$25
Limitations: No loans

New Jersey

Harris Brothers Foundation

Stonewyck 156B Sutton Road
Lebanon, NJ 08833
(201) 832-2671
Contact: Barbara L. Harris, Secretary-Treasurer
Geographic Giving Pattern: New Jersey
Special Interest: Local Protestant church support
Assets: $1,902,224
Grant Range: $50,000–$500
Applications: There are no deadlines for grant proposals

F.M. Kirby Foundation, Inc.

17 DeHart Street
P.O. Box 151
Morristown, NJ 07963-0151
(201) 538-4800
Contact: F.M. Kirby, President
Geographic Giving Pattern: Primarily New York, New Jersey, Pennsylvania and Virginia

Special Interest: Higher and secondary education, church support and church-related organizations, social service and conservation
Assets: $200,000,000
Grant Range: $570,000–$150 (Grant average: $15,000–$25,000)
Limitations: No grants to individuals or for fund-raising campaigns. No loans or pledges. Grants are almost entirely limited to organizations associated with personal interests of present or former foundation directors.
Applications: Grant proposal with cover letter should be sent to the foundation contact before October 31. Final notification for positive responses only will be made by December 31. No telephone solicitations are accepted.

The Magowan Family Foundation, Inc.
See entry in Interfaith

The Harold B. and Dorothy A. Snyder Foundation
See entry in Interfaith

The Willits Foundation
731 Central Avenue
Murray Hill, NJ 07974
(201) 277-8259
Contact: Emily D. Lawrence, Secretary-Treasurer
Geographic Giving Pattern: Primarily New Jersey
Special Interest: Higher education, Protestant church support, religious activities, schools, social service agencies and hospitals
Assets: $4,179,851
Grant Range: $10,000–$200
Limitations: No grants to individuals
Applications: Grant proposals should be submitted preferably between August and October

New York

The Baird Foundation
122 Huntington Court
P.O. Box 514
Williamsville, NY 14221
(716) 633-5588
Contact: Carl E. Gruber, Manager
Geographic Giving Pattern: Primarily Erie County, New York

Special Interest: Higher education, church support, hospitals and cultural programs
Assets: $7,003,987
Grant Range: $14,000–$500
Limitations: No grants to individuals. No loans.
Applications: Grant proposals are accepted at any time. Final notification will be three months after receipt of proposal.

Booth Ferris Foundation
See entry in Interfaith

James J. Colt Foundation, Inc.
See entry in Interfaith

Constans Culver Foundation
See entry in Interfaith

The Dewar Foundation, Inc.
c/o Rutson R. Henderson
16 Dietz Street
Oneonta, NY 13820
(607) 432-3530
Contact: Frank W. Getman, President
Geographic Giving Pattern: Primarily the greater Oneonta, New York area
Special Interest: Civic and charitable organizations, Protestant churches, education, child welfare and youth agencies
Assets: $14,112,012
Grant Range: $335,000–$500 (Grant average: $2,000–$10,000)
Limitations: No grants to individuals
Applications: Initial approach should be by letter. There are no deadlines.

The Caleb C. and Julia W. Dula Educational and Charitable Foundation
See entry in Interfaith

The Goodman Family Foundation
See entry in Interfaith

The William Randolph Hearst Foundation, Inc.
See entry in Interfaith

Virginia Hunt Trust for Episcopal Charitable Institutions
c/o Chemical Bank Corp.
270 Park Avenue
New York, NY 10017
Contact: J.J. Kindred, Vice-President
Geographic Giving Pattern: Primarily New York and Vermont
Special Interest: Limited to Episcopal charitable institutions including a diocese, churches, a convent and a hospital
Assets: $2,429,563
Grant Range: $48,500–$5,000
Limitations: No grants to individuals
Applications: Initial approach should be by letter. There are no deadlines.

The Conrad and Virginia Klee Foundation, Inc.
700 Security Mutual Building
80 Exchange Street
Binghamton, NY 13901
(607) 723-5341
Contact: Clayton M. Axtell, President
Geographic Giving Pattern: Primarily New York, especially Broome County and Guilford
Special Interest: Community funds, Protestant church support and higher education
Assets: $6,196,205 Gifts received: $899,765)
Grant Range: $77,000–$1,500
Limitations: No grants to individuals
Applications: Initial approach should be by letter. There are no deadlines.

Knox Family Foundation
P.O. Box 387
Johnstown, NY 12095
Contact: Eleanor G. Nalle, President and Treasurer
Special Interest: Higher and secondary education, hospitals, Protestant church support and social services
Assets: $4,370,304
Grant Range: $13,550–$50
Limitations: No grants to individuals
Applications: Contributes to pre-selected organizations only. Applications not accepted.

The Henry Luce Foundation, Inc.
See entry in Interfaith

James J. McCann Charitable Trust and McCann Foundation, Inc.
See entry in Interfaith

Mostyn Foundation, Inc.
c/o James C. Edwards & Co.
805 Third Avenue, 8th Floor
New York, NY 10022
Contact: Arthur B. Choate, President
Special Interest: Protestant church support and religious associations; also, social service agencies, higher education, health agencies, hospitals and youth agencies
Assets: $2,574,224
Grant Range: $25,000–$1,000
Limitations: No grants to individuals
Applications: Contributes to pre-selected organizations only. Applications not accepted.

The Francis Asbury Palmer Fund
c/o U.S. Trust Co. of New York
45 Wall Street
New York, NY 10005
Contact: The Directors
Special Interest: Support for home missions, educational institutions and Christian ministers and workers. Support also for needy persons desiring to become Christian ministers, teachers or workers and for placing Bible teachers and lecturers in colleges and schools.
Assets: $2,466,679
Grant Range: $12,000–$9,000
Limitations: No grants to individuals
Applications: Applications are not accepted

The Perrin Foundation
72 Reade Street
New York, NY 10007
Contact: John G. Jeffers, President and Treasurer
Special Interest: Christian organizations including churches, missionary programs and schools
Assets: $668,472
Grant Range: $81,600–$300

Limitations: No grants to individuals
Applications: There are no deadlines for grant proposals. Requests should be sent to the following address: 926 Coolidge Street, Westfield, NJ 07090 Tel: (201) 295-5944.

The Margaret L. Wendt Foundation
1325 Liberty Building
Buffalo, NY 14202
(716) 855-2146
Contact: Robert J. Kresse, Secretary
Geographic Giving Pattern: Primarily western New York, especially Buffalo
Special Interest: Education, the arts and social services; also churches, religious organizations and health organizations
Assets: $41,280,939
Grant Range: $80,000–$200 (Grant average: $5,000–$15,000)
Limitations: No grants to individuals or for scholarships
Applications: Letter and four copies of grant proposal should be sent one month prior to quarterly board meetings

Fred & Floy Willmott Foundation
c/o Marine Midland Bank
P.O. Box 4203
Buffalo, NY 14240
Geographic Giving Pattern: Primarily New York
Special Interest: Protestant churches and other religious organizations, education and social services
Assets: $4,417,882
Grant Range: $25,000–$50
Limitations: No grants to individuals
Applications: Contributes to pre-selected organizations only. Applications not accepted.

North Carolina

Robert C. and Sadie G. Anderson Foundation
c/o NCNB National Bank Trust Group
One NCNB Plaza T09-1
Charlotte, NC 28255
(704) 374-5731
Contact: The Manager, Institutional Services
Geographic Giving Pattern: Primarily North Carolina and Virginia, with preference for the former

Special Interest: Support only for Presbyterian causes or institutions
Assets: $2,159,421
Grant Range: $64,000–$1,500
Limitations: No grants to individuals or for operating budgets, building or endowment funds. No matching gifts or loans.
Applications: Contributes to pre-selected organizations only. Applications not accepted.

The Blumenthal Foundation
See entry in Interfaith

The Cannon Foundation, Inc.
P.O. Box 548
Concord, NC 28026-0548
(704) 786-8216
Contact: Dan L. Gray, Executive Director
Geographic Giving Pattern: Primarily North Carolina, especially the Cabarrus County area
Special Interest: Hospitals, higher and secondary education, cultural programs and Protestant church support
Assets: $97,652,868
Grant Range: $800,000–$125
Limitations: No grants to individuals or for operating budgets, seed money, emergency funds, deficit financing, land acquisition, endowment funds, research, conferences, publications or scholarships. No loans.
Applications: Letter and grant proposal should be sent by January 15, April 15, July 15 or October 15. An application form is required.

The Chapin Foundation of Myrtle Beach, South Carolina
c/o NCNB National Bank of North Carolina, T11-5
Charlotte, NC 28255
(704) 386-7749
Contact: Harold D. Clardy, Chair
Geographic Giving Pattern: Limited to Myrtle Beach, South Carolina area
Special Interest: Local Protestant churches and libraries
Assets: $8,036,756
Grant Range: $100,000–$570
Applications: Initial approach should be by letter or proposal sent to the following address: P.O. Box 2568, Myrtle Beach, SC 29577. There are no deadlines.

Christian Training Foundation
2004 Valencia Terrace
Charlotte, NC 28226
Contact: C. Wilbur Peters, President
Special Interest: Protestant organizations with emphasis on religious studies
Assets: $12,049,781
Grant Range: $73,893–$38
Limitations: No grants to individuals
Applications: Contributes to pre-selected organizations only. Applications not accepted.

The Dover Foundation, Inc.
P.O. Box 208
Shelby, NC 28150
(704) 847-2000
Contact: Hoyt Q. Bailey, President
Geographic Giving Pattern: Primarily North Carolina
Special Interest: Education, museums, church support, health services and social service agencies
Assets: $13,000,000
Grant Range: $250,000–$100
Applications: Proposal letter should be sent by July.

The Duke Endowment
200 South Tryon Street, Suite 1100
Charlotte, NC 28202
(704) 376-0291
Contact: Billy G. McCall, Executive Director or Jere W. Witherspoon, Deputy Executive Director
Geographic Giving Pattern: Primarily North Carolina and South Carolina
Special Interest: "To make provision in some measure for the needs of mankind along physical, mental and spiritual lines." Support is for hospitals and child care institutions, rural United Methodist churches and retired ministers in North Carolina and their dependents, and local universities.
Assets: $990,835,850
Grant Total: $45,940,739
Limitations: No support for deficit financing. No loans.
Applications: Initial approach should be by letter. There are no deadlines. The board meets monthly.

Kirkland S. and Rena B. Lamb Foundation, Inc.

c/o Parks N. Austin
901 Greentree Drive
Charlotte, NC 28211
Contact: Lillian L. Williams, Vice-President
Special Interest: Protestant church support, theological studies and evangelical activities
Assets: $8,937,159
Grant Range: $215,506–$1,260
Limitations: Applicants must subscribe to doctrinal position of the foundation
Applications: Initial approach should be by letter. Organizations should write to contact at the following address: 1312 Eckles Drive, Tampa, FL 33612. The scholarship application address is as follows: c/o Martha L. Johnston, Secretary, 3213 Milton, Dallas, TX 75205. The deadline for all applications is September.

Magee Christian Education Foundation

P.O. Box 754
Lake Junaluska, NC 28745
(704) 452-5427
Contact: Edward L. Tullis, Secretary-Treasurer
Geographic Giving Pattern: National
Special Interest: Giving only for scholarship programs for students studying for a full-time church-related vocation
Assets: $2,024,328
Grant Range: $25,000–$1,000
Limitations: No grants to individuals
Applications: An application form is required. Initial approach should be by letter requesting this form. The deadline is September 1.

The Morgan Trust for Charity, Religion, and Education

Old Wire Road
Laurel Hill, NC 28351
(919) 462-2016
Contact: James L. Morgan, Chair
Geographic Giving Pattern: Primarily North Carolina
Special Interest: Higher education, a theological seminary and Protestant church support
Assets: $7,162,348
Grant Range: $175,000–$50
Limitations: No grants to individuals or for scholarships or fellowships. No loans. Generally no grants for operating budgets.

Applications: Initial approach should be by letter. There are no deadlines.

E.A. Morris Charitable Foundation
c/o Duke University Medical Center
2200 West Main Street, Suite 1040
Durham, NC 27705
(919) 684-5332
Contact: John S. Thomas, Vice-President and Executive Director
Special Interest: Christian missionary organizations, education and churches
Assets: $4,791,254
Grant Average: $5,000–$20,000
Limitations: No stated limitations
Applications: Initial approach should be by letter. There are no deadlines.

The Mary Lynn Richardson Fund
P.O. Box 20124
Greensboro, NC 27420
(919) 274-5471
Contact: Adele Richardson Ray, Trustee
Geographic Giving Pattern: International; domestic grants are limited to North Carolina
Special Interest: Support for organizations which aid the needy and foreign Presbyterian causes
Assets: $4,760,144
Grant Range: $15,000–$750
Limitations: No grants to individuals or for building funds, research programs or matching gifts. No loans.
Applications: Grant proposals should be sent preferably between January and March. Deadlines are April 1 and October 1.

Robert Lee Stowe, Jr. Foundation, Inc.
100 North Main Street
P.O. Box 351
Belmont, NC 28012
(704) 825-5314
Contact: Daniel Harding Stowe, President
Geographic Giving Pattern: Primarily North Carolina
Special Interest: Church support, child welfare and higher education
Assets: $2,391,392
Grant Range: $30,000–$100
Applications: Initial approach should be by letter. There are no deadlines.

Ohio

The Austin Memorial Foundation
Aurora Commons Office Building, Suite 230
Aurora, OH 44202
(216) 562-5515
Contact: Donald G. Austin, Jr., President
Geographic Giving Pattern: Limited to U.S. and its possessions
Special Interest: Education, hospitals, social services and Protestant
church support
Assets: $5,397,124
Grant Range: $47,540–$200
Limitations: No grants to individuals
Applications: Contributes to pre-selected organizations only.
Applications not accepted.

The Leon A. Beeghly Fund
c/o Bank One, Youngstown N.A.
Six Federal Plaza West
Younstown, OH 44503
(216) 743-3151
Contact: James L. Beeghly, Executive Secretary
Geographic Giving Pattern: Primarily Youngstown, Ohio metropolitan
area and western Pennsylvania
Special Interest: Protestant church support and religious associations,
higher education, cultural programs and community development
Assets: $3,733,732
Grant Average: $5,000–$10,000
Limitations: No grants to individuals or for research, special projects,
publications or conferences. No loans.
Applications: There are no deadlines for grant proposals. The mailing
address is as follows: 808 Stambaugh Building, Youngstown, OH
44503.

William Dauch Foundation
1570 Dutch Hollow Road
P.O. Box 3175
Elida, OH 45807-1803
(419) 339-4441
Contact: Thomas E. Brown, President
Geographic Giving Pattern: National and international
Special Interest: Organizations and individuals promoting Christian
knowledge and disseminating the Gospel

Assets: $4,221,427
Grant Range: $184,000–$1,000
Limitations: No stated limitations
Applications: There are no deadlines for grant proposal letters

The Generation Trust
c/o Society Bank & Trust
P.O. Box 10099
Toledo, OH 43699-0099
Contact: J. Philip Ruyle, Trust Officer, Society Bank & Trust
Geographic Giving Pattern: National and international
Special Interest: Support limited to "organizations with a Christian purpose," including churches and ministries
Assets: $7,610,362
Grant Range: $82,000–$2,500
Limitations: No grants to individuals
Applications: There are no deadlines for grant proposal letters

MLM Charitable Foundation
410 United Savings Building
Toledo, OH 43604
(419) 255-0500
Contact: Charles A. McKenny, Treasurer
Geographic Giving Pattern: Ohio and New York
Special Interest: Higher education and Protestant church support
Assets: $1,047,600
Grant Range: $30,000–$100
Limitations: No grants to individuals
Applications: Contributes to pre-selected organizations only. Applications not accepted.

The Harry C. Moores Foundation
3010 Hayden Road
Columbus, OH 43235
(614) 764-8999
Contact: David L. Fenner, Secretary
Geographic Giving Pattern: Columbus, Ohio
Special Interest: Protestant church support, rehabilitation of the disabled, hospitals, higher education and cultural programs
Assets: $18,159,045
Grant Range: $200,000–$1,000 (Grant average: $1,000–$20,000)
Limitations: No support for private foundations. No grants to individuals or for endowment funds. No matching gifts or loans.

Applications: Applications are seldom accepted. Proposal in letter form should be sent between October and July. The deadline is August 1.

The Murphy Family Foundation
See entry in Interfaith

R.C. Musson and Katherine M. Musson Charitable Foundation
1188 Greenvale Avenue
Akron, OH 44313
(216) 864-5515
Contact: Irvin J. Musson, Trustee
Geographic Giving Pattern: Primarily Summit County, Ohio
Special Interest: Social services and Protestant churches
Assets: $3,451,668
Grant Average: $1,000–$10,000
Limitations: No stated limitations
Applications: There are no deadlines for grant proposals

Paulstan, Inc.
P.O. Box 921
Cuyahoga Falls, OH 44223
Contact: Stanley D. Myers, President
Special Interest: Religious organizations and missionary programs
Assets: $649,167
Grant Range: $485,007–$250
Limitations: No grants to individuals
Applications: Contributes to pre-selected organizations only. Applications not accepted.

Paul P. Tell Foundation
1105 TransOhio Building
156 South Main Street
Akron, OH 44308
(216) 434-8355
Contact: David J. Schipper, Executive Director
Special Interest: The furtherance of evangelical Christianity. Grants primarily for foreign missions and church-related educational institutions.
Assets: $3,072,601
Grant Range: $34,500–$100

Limitations: No grants to individuals or for building or endowment funds, scholarships, fellowships or matching gifts. No loans.
Applications: Applications are not accepted

Van Dorn Foundation
See entry in Interfaith

The I.J. Van Huffel Foundation
See entry in Interfaith

Oklahoma

Broadhurst Foundation
401 South Boston, Suite 100
Tulsa, OK 74103
(918) 584-0661
Contact: Ann Shannon Cassidy, Chair
Geographic Giving Pattern: Primarily the Midwest, especially Oklahoma
Special Interest: Support for scholarship funds at institutions selected by the foundation, specifically for students training for the Christian ministry. Grants also to educational and religious institutions. Loans to churches for building projects.
Assets: $5,362,885
Grant Range: $40,000–$20
Limitations: No grants directly to individuals or for scholarship funds except at the 31 schools the foundation already supports.
Applications: Initial approach may be by letter or grant proposal. There are no deadlines.

The J.E. and L.E. Mabee Foundation, Inc.
3000 Mid-Continent Tower
401 South Boston
Tulsa, OK 74103
(918) 584-4286
Contact: John H. Conway, Vice-Chair
Geographic Giving Pattern: Limited to Oklahoma, Texas, Kansas, Arkansas, Missouri and New Mexico
Special Interest: To aid Christian religious organizations, charitable organizations and institutions of higher learning
Assets: $494,281,654
Grant Range: $1,250,000–$600 (Grant average: $100,000–$500,000)

Limitations: No support for secondary or elementary education or tax-supported institutions. No grants to individuals. No support for research, endowment funds, scholarships, fellowships or operating expenses. No loans.
Applications: Grant proposals should be sent by March 1, June 1, September 1 or December 1.

Tulsa Royalties Company
3229-A South Harvard Avenue
Tulsa, OK 74135
(918) 747-5638
Contact: Lawrence A. Peitz, President
Geographic Giving Pattern: Primarily Oklahoma
Special Interest: Higher education, hospitals, social service agencies and Protestant church support
Assets: $3,966,951
Grant Range: $30,000–$25
Limitations: No grants to individuals. No matching gifts or loans.
Applications: Funds are largely committed

The R.A. Young Foundation
6401 North Pennsylvania Avenue, Suite 209
Oklahoma City, OK 73116
(405) 840-4444
Contact: Raymond A. Young, President
Geographic Giving Pattern: Primarily Oklahoma
Special Interest: Protestant church support and religious service associations, higher education and arts and culture
Assets: $3,123,632
Grant Range: $60,000–$100
Limitations: No grants to individuals
Applications: There are no deadlines for grant proposal letters

Pennsylvania

Asplundh Foundation
Blair Mill Road
Willow Grove, PA 19090
(215) 784-4200
Contact: E. Boyd Asplundh, Secretary
Geographic Giving Pattern: Primarily Pennsylvania
Special Interest: Protestant church support
Assets: $3,973,445

Grant Range: $110,000–$100
Limitations: No grants to individuals
Applications: Initial approach should be by letter. There are no deadlines.

Earle M. Craig and Margaret Peters Craig Trust
c/o Mellon Bank, N.A.
P.O. Box 185
Pittsburgh, PA 15230
(412) 234-5784
Contact: Barbara K. Robinson, Assistant Vice-President, Mellon Bank, N.A.
Geographic Giving Pattern: Primarily Pennsylvania; also Texas, New York, New England and Maine
Special Interest: Higher education, private secondary schools, hospitals, Protestant churches, religious organizations, arts, public policy research and social service agencies
Assets: $1,279,723
Grant Range: $100,000–$1,000 (Grant average: $1,000–$20,000)
Limitations: No grants to individuals or for deficit financing, scholarships, fellowships or demonstration projects. No matching gifts and no loans.
Applications: The family directs the distribution of funds. Applications are not accepted.

E.R. Crawford Estate
Trust Fund A
P.O. Box 487
McKeesport, PA 15134
Contact: Francis E. Neish, Trustee
Geographic Giving Pattern: Primarily Pennsylvania with emphasis on Allegheny County
Special Interest: Protestant church support, hospitals, higher education, youth and community agencies
Assets: $5,430,167
Grant Range: $40,000–$500
Limitations: No grants to individuals except former employees of the McKeesport Tin Plate Company
Applications: There are no deadlines for grant proposals

The Henry L. Hillman Foundation
2000 Grant Building
Pittsburgh, PA 15219
(412) 338-3466

Contact: Ronald W. Wertz, Executive Director and Secretary
Geographic Giving Pattern: Primarily Pittsburgh and southwestern Pennsylvania
Special Interest: Arts and culture, youth, conservation, civic affairs, community development, church support, education, social services and hospitals
Assets: $14,330,556
Grant Range: $381,950–$250 (Grant average: $1,000–$5,000)
Limitations: No grants to individuals or for deficit financing, land acquisition, endowment funds, research, publications or conferences. No loans.
Applications: Initial approach should be by letter. There are no deadlines.

The Huston Foundation
P.O. Box 139
Gladwyne, PA 19035
(215) 527-4371
Contact: Dorothy C. Hamilton, Officer
Geographic Giving Pattern: Primarily southeastern Pennsylvania
Special Interest: Social services and Protestant missionary programs
Assets: $20,452,974
Grant Range: $50,000–$500
Limitations: No grants to individuals or for research programs or fellowships. No loans.
Applications: An application form is required. Submit applications preferably between March and April or September and October. Deadlines are April 1 and October 1 of each year.

Massey Charitable Trust
See entry in Interfaith

The Charles F. Peters Foundation
2008 Duquesne Avenue
McKeesport, PA 15132
Contact: J. Charles Peterson, Administrator
Geographic Giving Pattern: Limited to the McKeesport, Pennsylvania area
Special Interest: Protestant church support, youth agencies and community services
Assets: $2,003,483
Grant Range: $5,000–$250
Limitations: No grants to individuals

Applications: Initial approach should be by letter or proposal. There are no deadlines. The board meets monthly.

The Pew Charitable Trusts
See entry in Interfaith

South Carolina

Belk-Simpson Foundation
P.O. Box 528
Greenville, SC 29602
Contact: Willou R. Bichel, Trustee
Geographic Giving Pattern: Primarily South Carolina
Special Interest: Protestant church support and social service agencies
Assets: $3,352,178
Grant Range: $7,500–$100
Limitations: No grants to individuals
Applications: Initial approach should be by letter. The board meets in May and November.

The Simpson Foundation
P.O. Box 528
Greenville, SC 29602
(803) 297-3451
Contact: W.H.B. Simpson
Geographic Giving Pattern: Primarily North Carolina and South Carolina
Special Interest: Protestant church support, religious organizations and social services
Assets: $3,245,806
Grant Range: $7,500–$100
Applications: Initial approach should be by letter. Application proposals should be submitted prior to November 1 or May 1 board meetings.

John T. Stevens Foundation
P.O. Box 158
Kershaw, SC 29067
Contact: John S. Davidson, President and Secretary-Treasurer
Geographic Giving Pattern: Primarily South Carolina
Special Interest: Protestant church support, medical and secondary education and youth agencies
Assets: $3,699,360

Grant Range: $31,010–$500
Applications: Initial approach should be by letter

Tennessee

The Dora Maclellan Brown Charitable Trust
1001 McCallie Avenue
Chattanooga, TN 37403
(615) 266-4574
Contact: Henry A. Henegar, President
Geographic Giving Pattern: Primarily the Chattanooga, Tennessee area
Special Interest: To promote the work of the Christian church through scholarships to schools, colleges and theological seminaries and grants to evangelical ministries
Assets: $10,562,381
Grant Range: $36,000–$262
Limitations: Scholarships limited to residents of Chattanooga, Tennessee. No support for secular education. No grants to individuals or for seed money, emergency funds, deficit financing, capital funds, endowment funds, equipment, land acquisition, renovations, research or publications. No loans.
Applications: An application form is required for scholarships to seminaries only. Initial approach should be by letter. Eight copies of proposal are required. Deadline is prior to second week of any month.

J. R. Hyde Foundation, Inc.
3030 Poplar Avenue
Memphis, TN 38111
(901) 325-4245
Contact: Margaret R. Hyde, President
Geographic Giving Pattern: Primarily the Midsouth
Special Interest: Protestant church support, education, cultural programs, community funds and social service and youth agencies
Assets: $14,688,291 (Gifts received: $750,000)
Grant Range: $50,000–$600
Limitations: No grants to individuals. No general support, or grants for capital or endowment funds or research. No loans or matching gifts.
Applications: There is no deadline for grant proposals

The Maclellan Foundation, Inc.
Provident Building, Suite 501
Chattanooga, TN 37402
(615) 755-1366
Contact: Hugh O. Maclellan, Jr., President
Geographic Giving Pattern: Primarily Chattanooga, Tennessee
Special Interest: Protestant missions and religious associations, youth
agencies, social services and higher education
Assets: $129,235,513
Grant Range: $475,000–$330 (Grant average: $50,000–$150,000)
Limitations: No grants to individuals or for emergency funds, deficit
financing, land acquisition, renovations, endowment funds, research,
demonstration projects, publications or conferences
Applications: Initial approach should be by letter. The deadline is
three weeks prior to board meetings. Board meetings are the last
Tuesday of each month except January and November.

Washington Foundation
3815 Cleghorn Avenue
P.O. Box 159057
Nashville, TN 37215
(615) 244-0600
Contact: Paul A. Hargis, President
Geographic Giving Pattern: Limited to the U.S.
Special Interest: Church of Christ-related organizations including
churches, schools and colleges
Assets: $11,892,278
Grant Range: $65,000–$200
Limitations: No grants to individuals
Applications: The deadline for grant proposals is December 1

Texas

Abell-Hanger Foundation
See entry in Interfaith

The Allbritton Foundation
5615 Kirby Drive, Suite 310
Houston, TX 77005
Contact: Joe L. Allbritton, President
Special Interest: Christian religious organizations, education and
cultural programs

Assets: $6,206 (Gifts received: $315,000)
Grant Range: $75,000–$250
Applications: There are no deadlines for grant proposals

Bell Trust
10726 Plano Road
Dallas, TX 75238
(214) 349-0060
Contact: H.L. Packer, Trustee
Special Interest: Exclusively to the Church of Christ
Assets: $7,292,604
Grant Range: $6,800–$400
Limitations: No grants to individuals or for building or endowment funds. No loans or matching gifts.
Applications: There are no deadlines for grant proposals

M.K. Brown Foundation, Inc.
P.O. Box 662
Pampa, TX 79066-0662
(806) 669-6851
Contact: Bill W. Waters, Chair
Geographic Giving Pattern: Panhandle area of Texas with emphasis on Pampa and Gray County
Special Interest: Christian church support, youth agencies, community projects and social service agencies
Assets: $3,503,974
Grant Range: $110,000–$1,000
Limitations: No grants to individuals
Applications: Grant proposals should be sent before July 1 or December 1.

C.I.O.S
315 Washington Avenue
Waco, TX 76701
(817) 752-5551
Contact: Paul P. Piper, Trustee
Special Interest: Protestant church support and religious programs, including Christian education, evangelism, welfare and support for foreign missions
Assets: $58,695,588
Grant Range: $93,334–$500
Applications: Initial approach should be by letter or proposal. The deadline is June.

Community Hospital Foundation, Inc.
P.O. Box 24185
Houston, TX 77229
(713) 450-3457
Contact: Dr. Loren Rohr, President
Geographic Giving Pattern: Primarily Texas
Special Interest: Higher education and Protestant churches
Assets: $4,443,082
Grant Range: $35,000–$500
Limitations: No religious grants to individuals
Applications: There are no deadlines for grant proposals

The R.W. Fair Foundation
P.O. Box 689
Tyler, TX 75710
(214) 592-3811
Contact: Wilton H. Fair, President
Geographic Giving Pattern: Primarily the Southwest, with emphasis on Texas
Special Interest: Protestant church support and church-related programs, education and social service agencies
Assets: $15,192,264
Grant Range: $197,500–$200 (Grant average: $1,000–$20,000)
Limitations: No grants to individuals or for operating budgets
Applications: Initial approach should be by letter. An application form is required. Deadlines are March 1, June 1, September 1 and December 1.

The Fleming Foundation
500 West 7th Street, Suite 1007
Fort Worth, TX 76102
(817) 335-3741
Contact: G. Malcolm Louden, Assistant Secretary
Geographic Giving Pattern: Primarily Texas, with emphasis on Fort Worth
Special Interest: Protestant church support, church-related activities and cultural programs
Assets: $12,858,902
Grant Range: $600,000–$200 (Grant average: $1,000–$10,000)
Limitations: No grants to individuals or for deficit financing, building or endowment funds, land acquisition, scholarships, publications or conferences. No loans or matching gifts.

Applications: Initial approach should be by letter. There are no deadlines. Applications are accepted for single-year grant requests only.

Robert and Ruth Glaze Foundation
2001 Bryan Tower, Suite 3131
Dallas, TX 75201
(214) 969-5595
Contact: Robert E. Glaze, President
Geographic Giving Pattern: Primarily Dallas, Texas
Special Interest: Religious organizations, particularly a Baptist church and groups promoting Christian ministry
Assets: $2,941,632
Grant Range: $108,000–$100
Limitations: No stated limitations
Applications: There are no deadlines for grant proposal letters

Ed and Mary Heath Foundation
P.O. Box 338
Tyler, TX 75710
(214) 597-7436
Contact: W.R. Smith, Chair
Geographic Giving Pattern: Limited to Texas, particularly Smith County
Special Interest: Protestant church support, youth agencies, recreation and health services
Assets: $2,142,207
Grant Total: $94,250
Limitations: No grants to individuals or for endowment funds
Applications: Initial approach should be by letter. There are no deadlines.

J.A. Leppard Foundation Trust
2519 Waterford
San Antonio, TX 78217
(512) 824-2148
Contact: Harry J. Fraser
Geographic Giving Pattern: Primarily Texas
Special Interest: Christian churches, missions and schools
Assets: $1,631,080
Grant Range: $32,600–$600
Limitations: No grants to individuals. The Independent Branch of Christian Churches and their related organizations only are eligible.
Applications: There are no deadlines for grant proposal letters

The LeTourneau Foundation
P.O. Box 489
Rockwall, TX 75087
Contact: Roy S. LeTourneau, President
Geographic Giving Pattern: Primarily Texas
Special Interest: Evangelical Christian activities in foreign missions, evangelism and education
Assets: $5,466,440
Grant Range: $160,000–$100
Applications: All funds are presently committed. Applications are not accepted.

Sollie & Lilla McCreless Foundation for Christian Evangelism, Christian Missions, and Christian Education
P.O. Box 2341
San Antonio, TX 78298
(512) 736-6767
Contact: G. Richard Ferdinandtsen, Secretary-Treasurer
Special Interest: Christian education, missions and evangelical organizations
Assets: $2,322,215
Grant Range: $50,000–$65
Limitations: No grants to individuals. No loans.
Applications: Initial approach should be by letter. There are no deadlines.

Bruce McMillan, Jr. Foundation, Inc.
P.O. Box 9
Overton, TX 75684
(214) 834-3148
Contact: Ralph Ward, President
Geographic Giving Pattern: Eastern Texas
Special Interest: Higher education, health agencies, church support and social service and youth agencies
Assets: $15,043,219
Grant Range: $99,606–$500 (Grant average: $1,000–$40,000)
Applications: An application form is required. The deadline for receipt of applications is May 15.

Oldham Little Church Foundation
5177 Richmond Avenue, Suite 1068
Houston, TX 77056-6701
(713) 621-4190
Contact: Louis E. Finlay, Executive Director

Special Interest: Aid for small Protestant churches and religious educational institutions
Assets: $19,000,000
Grant Range: $5,000–$1,000
Limitations: No grants to individuals or for operating budgets, endowment funds or deficit financing
Applications: An application form is required. There are no deadlines.

The Trull Foundation
404 Fourth Street
Palacios, TX 77465
(512) 972-5241
Contact: Colleen Claybourn, Executive Director
Geographic Giving Pattern: Primarily southern Texas
Special Interest: Protestant church support and welfare programs, education, youth agencies and Hispanic concerns
Assets: $14,003,918
Grant Range: $15,000–$50 (Grant average: $5,000)
Limitations: No grants to individuals. There is rarely support for building or endowment funds. No loans.
Applications: Initial approach should be by letter. There are no deadlines.

Virginia

The Elmer Bisbee Foundation
P.O. Box 7332
Arlington, VA 22207-0332
Contact: Helga B. Henry, Chair and President
Geographic Giving Pattern: National and international
Special Interest: Evangelical Christian religious organizations, missionaries and schools
Assets: $1,446,740
Grant Range: $5,000–$1,000
Applications: Contributes to pre-selected organizations only. Applications not accepted.

The English Foundation-Trust
1522 Main Street
Altavista, VA 24517
(804) 369-4771
Contact: E.R. English, Sr., Trustee
Geographic Giving Pattern: Campbell County, Virginia

Special Interest: Civic affairs and community development; Protestant religious organizations and church support; and higher education, including scholarships
Assets: $1,462,899
Grant Range: $26,000–$50
Applications: Initial approach should be by letter. An application form is required for scholarships.

Elis Olsson Memorial Foundation
c/o McGuire, Woods, Battle & Boothe
P.O. Box 397
Richmond, VA 23203
(804) 644-4131
Contact: Carle E. Davis, Secretary
Geographic Giving Pattern: Virginia
Special Interest: Education and Protestant church support
Assets: $11,856,145 (Gifts received: $520,287)
Grant Range: $125,000–$100
Limitations: No grants to individuals
Applications: Initial approach should be by letter. There are no deadlines.

The Titmus Foundation, Inc.
P.O. Box 10
Sutherland, VA 23885-0010
(804) 265-5834
Contact: Edward B. Titmus, President
Geographic Giving Pattern: Virginia
Special Interest: Emphasis on Baptist church support and religious organizations; also higher education, health, cancer research and child welfare
Assets: $10,535,891
Grant Range: $140,200–$98
Limitations: No grants to individuals
Applications: Application proposals should be sent to the foundation contact at the following address: Route 1, Box 358, Sutherland, VA 23885. There are no deadlines.

The J. Edwin Treakle Foundation, Inc.
P.O. Box 1157
Gloucester, VA 23061
(804) 693-3101
Contact: John Warren Cooke, Treasurer
Geographic Giving Pattern: Virginia

Special Interest: Emphasis on Protestant church support; also community development, youth agencies, higher education, hospitals, cancer research and cultural organizations
Assets: $3,719,036
Grant Range: $20,000–$300
Limitations: No grants to individuals
Applications: An application form is required and should be submitted between January 1 and April 30

Washington Forrest Foundation
See entry in Interfaith

Washington

Anderson Foundation
4755 First Avenue South
Seattle, WA 98134
(206) 762-0600
Contact: Charles M. Anderson, President
Geographic Giving Pattern: Pacific Northwest, particularly Washington
Special Interest: Protestant church support, higher education and social services
Assets: $2,441,248
Limitations: No grants to individuals or for endowment funds or matching gifts. No loans.
Applications: Applications are not accepted.

Robert G. Hemingway Foundation
c/o Seattle First National Bank
P.O. Box 24565
Seattle, WA 98124
Contact: Susan G. Hemingway
Geographic Giving Pattern: Idaho and Washington
Special Interest: Higher education, hospitals, medical research, social services and Episcopal churches
Assets: $4,026,480
Grant Range: $90,000–$1,000
Limitations: No grants to individuals
Applications: Initial approach should be by letter. The prefered deadline is March 1. The application address is as follows: 1301 Spring Street, Unit 203, Seattle, WA 98104.

The Stewardship Foundation
Tacoma Financial Center, Suite 1500
1145 Broadway Plaza
Tacoma, WA 98402
(206) 272-8336
Contact: C. Davis Weyerhaeuser, Trustee or George S. Kovats,
Executive Director
Geographic Giving Pattern: International, national, Pacific Northwest
Special Interest: At least 85 percent of funds are to support evangelical
religious organizations whose ministries reach beyond the local
community. Grants primarily are for Christian colleges, universities
and seminaries, international development organizations, foreign
missions and youth ministries.
Assets: $70,541,530
Grant Range: $390,000–$1,000 (Grant average: $5,000–$25,000)
Limitations: No support for churches. Religious support only to
Christian parachurch organizations. No grants to individuals or for
endowment funds, deficit financing, research or fellowships. No
loans.
Applications: Send letter and two copies of grant proposal to the
foundation contact at the following address: P.O. Box 1278, Tacoma,
WA 98401. There are no deadlines.

Wisconsin

Patrick and Anna M. Cudahy Fund
See entry in Interfaith

Kurth Religious Trust
141 North Main, Suite 207
West Bend, WI 53095
Contact: Katherine Kurth, Trustee
Special Interest: Religious and charitable purposes. Grants largely for
Lutheran church support, religious associations and welfare funds.
Some support for higher education.
Assets: $4,301,203
Grant Range: $35,000–$75
Limitations: No grants to individuals
Applications: Initial approach should be by letter. There are no
deadlines.

Hamilton Roddis Foundation, Inc.
1108 East Fourth Street
Marshfield, WI 54449
Contact: Augusta D. Roddis, Secretary-Treasurer
Special Interest: Episcopal church support and religious education;
also social services, medical research, educational organizations,
historic preservation and local associations
Assets: $3,087,094
Grant Range: $17,500–$100
Limitations: No grants to individuals
Applications: Contributes to pre-selected organizations only.
Applications not accepted.

Roehl Foundation, Inc.
P.O. Box 168
Oconomowoc, WI 53066-0168
(414) 569-3000
Contact: Peter Roehl, Vice-President
Geographic Giving Pattern: Primarily Wisconsin
Special Interest: Lutheran churches and welfare organizations,
education, hospitals and medical research
Assets: $2,139,822
Grant Range: $8,000–$50
Limitations: No grants to individuals
Applications: Initial approach should be by grant proposal. There are
no deadlines.

Siebert Lutheran Foundation, Inc.
2600 North Mayfair Road, Suite 390
Wauwatosa, WI 53226
(414) 257-2656
Contact: Jack S. Harris, President
Geographic Giving Pattern: Wisconsin
Special Interest: Support is limited to Lutheran churches and other
Lutheran institutions, including colleges, schools, programs for the
aged and religious welfare agencies
Assets: $53,108,719
Grant Range: $300,000–$100 (Grant average: $2,500–$10,000)
Limitations: No grants to individuals or for endowment funds,
scholarships or fellowships. No loans.
Applications: Initial approach should be by telephone or letter. Grant
proposals should be sent by March 15, June 15, September 15 or
December 15. Grantees are required to sign Grant Agreement Form.

Irvin L. Young Foundation, Inc.
Snow Valley Ranch
Palmyra, WI 53156
(414) 495-2568
Contact: Fern D. Young, President
Special Interest: Grants largely for Protestant medical missionary programs in Africa, including the training of African medical workers
Assets: $8,035,749
Grant Range: $525,000–$500
Limitations: No grants to individuals
Applications: Initial approach should be by letter. Grant proposal should be submitted in October or November.

CATHOLIC FOUNDATIONS

Arizona

Elizabeth Ann Parkman Foundation
1840 East River Road, Suite 302
Tucson, AZ 85718
Contact: James M. Murphy, Trustee
Geographic Giving Pattern: National
Special Interest: Christian institutions, hospitals, medical research, community projects and education
Assets: $1,114,757
Grant Range: $7,500–$10
Limitations: No stated limitations
Applications: Initial approach should be by letter

Arkansas

The Wrape Family Charitable Trust
P.O. Box 412
Little Rock, AR 72203
(501) 663-1551
Contact: A.J. Wrape, Jr., Manager
Geographic Giving Pattern: Arkansas
Special Interest: Roman Catholic educational and religious organizations
Assets: $4,150,423
Grant Range: $32,250–$100
Applications: Initial approach should be by letter. There are no deadlines.

California

Fritz B. Burns Foundation
4001 West Alameda Avenue, Suite 203
Burbank, CA 91505
(818) 840-8802
Contact: Joseph E. Rawlinson, President
Geographic Giving Pattern: Primarily the Provo, Utah and Los Angeles, California areas

Special Interest: Education, hospitals, medical research and Roman Catholic religious associations and church support
Assets: $138,492,443
Grant Range: $500,000–$300 (Grant average: $1,000–$100,000)
Limitations: No grants to individuals or to private foundations
Applications: Initial approach should be by letter. There are no deadlines.

Burns-Dunphy Foundation
See entry in Interfaith

The Callison Foundation
1319 Rosita Road
Pacifica, CA 94104
(415) 359-2105
Contact: Dorothy J. Sola, Secretary
Geographic Giving Pattern: Primarily San Francisco, California
Special Interest: Roman Catholic religious organizations, social welfare organizations, higher education, hospitals, youth and cultural organizations
Assets: $4,439,364
Grant Range: $25,000–$5,000
Limitations: No grants to individuals
Applications: There are no deadlines for grant proposals

Francis H. Clougherty Charitable Trust
P.O. Box 93490
Pasadena, CA 91109-3490
Contact: Patrick F. Collins
Geographic Giving Pattern: Southern California
Special Interest: Higher and secondary education, Catholic churches and hospitals
Assets: $5,986,703
Grant Range: $150,000–$2,000
Limitations: No grants to individuals
Applications: Contributes to pre-selected organizations only. Applications not accepted.

Louise M. Davies Foundation
580 California Street, Suite 1800
San Francisco, CA 94104
(415) 765-4400
Contact: Donald D. Crawford

Special Interest: Education, youth, social services and Catholic church support
Assets: $1,204,650
Grant Range: $25,000–$100
Applications: Contributes to pre-selected organizations only. Applications not accepted.

Frank C. Diener Foundation
P.O. Box 278
Five Points, CA 93624
Contact: Marie C. Demera, Vice-President
Geographic Giving Pattern: Limited to Fresno County, California
Special Interest: Catholic welfare only, especially mission work and general church funds
Assets: $1,652,782
Grant Range: $52,500–$500
Applications: No new applications accepted

Carrie Estelle Doheny Foundation
911 Wilshire Boulevard, Suite 1750
Los Angeles, CA 90017
(213) 488-1122
Contact: Robert A. Smith, President, Carrie Estelle Doheny Foundation Corporation
Geographic Giving Pattern: Primarily the Los Angeles, California area
Special Interest: Roman Catholic churches and church-related organizations, hospitals, ophthalmological research, child welfare, education and community funds
Assets: $75,938,492
Grant Range: $1,000,000–$750 (Grant average: $3,000–$25,000)
Limitations: No grants to individuals or for endowment funds, publications, travel, advertising or radio and television programs
Applications: Initial approach should be by letter. There are no deadlines.

The Drum Foundation
c/o Northern Trust of California, N.A.
580 California Street, Suite 1800
San Francisco, CA 94104
Contact: Philip Hudner, President
Geographic Giving Pattern: Primarily the San Francisco, California area
Special Interest: Roman Catholic church-related educational and charitable organizations

Assets: $5,315,963
Grant Range: $25,000–$500 (Grant average: $1,000–$50,000)
Limitations: No grants to individuals or for endowment funds. No matching gifts.
Applications: Contributes to pre-selected organizations only. Applications not accepted.

Edwin M. & Gertrude S. Eaton Foundation
440 Davis Court, No. 1711
San Francisco, CA 94111
Contact: Evelyn T. Eaton, President
Geographic Giving Pattern: Primarily California, especially San Francisco, and France
Special Interest: Catholic organizations including churches and missions, and a French social service organization
Assets: $105,765 (Gifts received: $2,683,188)
Grant Total: $2,753,773
Limitations: No grants to individuals
Applications: Contributes to pre-selected organizations only. Applications not accepted.

The Julio R. Gallo Foundation
P.O. Box 1130
Modesto, CA 95353
(209) 579-3373
Contact: Robert J. Gallo, Vice-President
Geographic Giving Pattern: Primarily California
Special Interest: Education and Roman Catholic church support and religious associations
Assets: $5,382,884 (Gifts received: $350,000)
Grant Range: $66,000–$500
Limitations: No grants to individuals
Applications: Initial approach should be by letter. There are no deadlines.

Silvio and Mary Garaventa Family Foundation
4080 Mallard Drive
Concord, CA 94520
Contact: Silvio Garaventa, Manager
Special Interest: Medical research and healthcare, Catholic religious and educational institutions
Assets: $457,363 (Gifts received: $290,451)
Grant Range: $15,000–$5,000

Applications: Contributes to pre-selected organizations only.
Applications not accepted.

The Carl Gellert Foundation
2222 19th Avenue
San Francisco, CA 94116
(415) 566-4420
Contact: Peter J. Brusati, Secretary
Geographic Giving Pattern: Primarily the San Francisco Bay area
Special Interest: The aged and hospitals; also Roman Catholic church
support, higher and secondary education, medical research, drug
abuse programs, community development, and social service
agencies
Assets: $7,535,654
Grant Range: $100,000–$1,000 (Grant average: $1,000–$10,000)
Limitations: No grants to individuals or for seed money, emergency
funds, land acquisition, or conferences. No loans or matching gifts.
Applications: Five copies of grant proposal are requested. Proposals
should be submitted preferably in August or September; the deadline
is October 1.

James Gleason Foundation
Hearst Building, Suite 1200
Third and Market Streets
San Francisco, CA 94103
Contact: Walter M. Gleason, President, Treasurer and Manager
Special Interest: Roman Catholic welfare agencies, church support and
a university
Assets: $1,805,584
Grant Range: $15,000–$1,000
Applications: Initial approach should be by letter

Katherine Gleason Foundation
Hearst Building, Suite 1200
Third and Market Streets
San Francisco, CA 94103
Contact: Walter M. Gleason, President and Treasurer
Special Interest: Roman Catholic religious and welfare associations,
secondary schools and a college
Assets: $3,237,115
Grant Range: $25,000–$1,000
Applications: Initial approach should be by letter

Crescent Porter Hale Foundation
220 Bush Street, Suite 1069
San Francisco, CA 94104
(415) 986-5177
Contact: Ulla Davis, Consultant
Geographic Giving Pattern: Primarily the San Francisco Bay area
Special Interest: Roman Catholic organizations, education, hospitals, disadvantaged youth and the elderly
Assets: $17,887,457
Grant Range: $25,000–$1,000 (Grant average: $10,000)
Limitations: No grants to individuals
Applications: Initial approach should be by letter of intent. Eleven copies of grant proposal are requested. The deadlines are February, July and October.

William H. Hannon Foundation
8055 West Manchester Boulevard, Number 400
Playa Del Rey, CA 90293-7990
Contact: William H. Hannon, President
Geographic Giving Pattern: Primarily the Playa Del Rey, California area
Special Interest: Higher education, Roman Catholic churches, medical research and hospitals
Assets: $2,633,883
Grant Range: $156,825–$75
Limitations: No grants to individuals
Applications: Initial approach should be by letter

William R. & Virginia Hayden Foundation
110 West Las Tunas Drive, Suite A
San Gabriel, CA 91776
Contact: Stanley D. Hayden, President
Geographic Giving Pattern: Primarily California
Special Interest: Roman Catholic religious and social service organizations and church support
Assets: $8,121,674 (Gifts received: $1,562,500)
Grant Range: $89,000–$50
Limitations: No grants to individuals
Applications: Contributes to pre-selected organizations only. Applications not accepted.

Conrad N. Hilton Fund for Sisters
10100 Santa Monica Boulevard, Suite 740
Los Angeles, CA 90067-4011
(213) 785-0746
Contact: Sister Mary Ewens, OP, Executive Director
Geographic Giving Pattern: National and international
Special Interest: Direct services of Roman Catholic sisters among the poor
Assets: $1,425,589
Grant Average: $10,000
Limitations: No grants to individuals. No support for construction, purchase of land, debt retirement, endowment funds, fund-raising campaigns, programs in spirituality, tuition scholarships or for internal needs of religious congregations. Does not support programs which are the direct responsibility of U.S. arch/dioceses.
Applications: Initial approach should be by letter. An application form is required.

George Frederick Jewett Foundation
See entry in Interfaith

Komes Foundation
1801 Van Ness Avenue, Suite 300
San Francisco, CA 94109
(415) 441-6462
Contact: J.W. Komes, President
Geographic Giving Pattern: Primarily northern California
Special Interest: Health agencies and hospitals, education, cultural programs, Christian giving and welfare organizations
Assets: $2,667,000
Grant Range: $25,000–$250
Limitations: No support for literary publications. No grants to individuals or for budget deficits, conferences or travel.
Applications: Initial approach should be by proposal letter. There are no deadlines.

Walter & Francine Laband Foundation
3311 East Cameron Avenue
West Covina, CA 91791
Contact: Francine Laband, President
Geographic Giving Pattern: California
Special Interest: Catholic social service and religious organizations; support also for hospitals
Assets: $45,709 (Gifts received: $85,616)

Grant Range: $19,780–$25
Applications: Contributes to pre-selected organizations only. Applications not accepted.

Thomas and Dorothy Leavey Foundation
4680 Wilshire Boulevard
Los Angeles, CA 90010
(213) 930-4252
Contact: J. Thomas McCarthy, Trustee
Geographic Giving Pattern: Primarily southern California
Special Interest: Hospitals, medical research, higher and secondary education and Catholic church groups
Assets: $85,984,845
Grant Average: $10,000–$25,000
Limitations: No stated limitations
Applications: Initial approach should be by letter. There are no deadlines.

Leonardt Foundation
1801 Avenue of the Stars, # 811
Los Angeles, CA 90067
(213) 556-3932
Contact: Felix S. McGinnis, President
Special Interest: Roman Catholic church support, welfare funds, higher and secondary education, hospitals and health agencies
Assets: $2,730,695
Grant Range: $26,000–$100
Limitations: No grants to individuals
Applications: Initial approach should be by letter

Marin Community Foundation
See entry in Interfaith

Marini Family Trust
c/o Wells Fargo Bank, N.A.
420 Montgomery Street, 5th Floor
San Francisco, CA 94163
(415) 396-3215
Contact: Eugene Ranghiasci, Vice-President, Wells Fargo Bank, N.A.
Geographic Giving Pattern: Limited to the San Francisco Bay area
Special Interest: Roman Catholic church support, education and social services
Assets: $3,496,568

Grant Range: $48,000–$500 (Grant average: $5,000–$15,000)
Limitations: No grants to individuals
Applications: Contributes to pre-selected organizations only.
Applications not accepted.

Muller Foundation
11357 Pala Loma Drive
Valley Center, CA 92082-3114
(213) 463-8176
Contact: Walter Muller, Treasurer
Geographic Giving Pattern: Primarily California
Special Interest: Higher and secondary education, social services,
Roman Catholic church support, hospitals and cultural programs
Assets: $6,086,560
Grant Range: $25,000–$100
Limitations: No grants to individuals
Applications: Initial approach should be by letter. There are no
deadlines.

Dan Murphy Foundation
P.O. Box 76026
Los Angeles, CA 90076
(213) 623-3120
Contact: Grace Robinson
Geographic Giving Pattern: Primarily Los Angeles, California
Special Interest: Support for activities and charities of the Roman
Catholic Church in the Archdiocese of Los Angeles, individual
religious orders, education, social service and medical institutions
Assets: $174,061,302
Grant Range: $2,544,400–$1,000 (Grant average: $1,000–$100,000)
Limitations: No stated limitations
Applications: Grants generally initiated by the trustees. Applications
are not accepted.

Pacific Western Foundation
8344 East Florence, Suite E
Downey, CA 90240
Contact: Charles F. Bannan, President
Geographic Giving Pattern: Primarily California
Special Interest: Higher and secondary education, Roman Catholic
church support, hospitals and medical research
Assets: $3,563,426
Grant Range: $80,000–$50

Applications: Initial approach should be by proposal letter. There are no deadlines.

Warren P. Powers Foundation
7711 East Margaret Drive
Anaheim Hills, CA 92808-1801
(714) 283-2842
Contact: Patrick D. Powers, Chair
Special Interest: Vocations, ministry to the disabled, care of retired clergy and religious, homelessness
Assets: $6,000,000
Grant Range: $100,000–$1,000
Limitations: Awards grants only within the Catholic Dioceses of Orange, Salt Lake City, Kansas City, Kansas, Atlanta and St. Augustine
Applications: Initial approach should be by letter

The Richard & Jill Riordan Foundation
300 South Grand Avenue
29th Floor
Los Angeles, CA 90071
(213) 629-4824
Contact: Mary Odell, President
Geographic Giving Pattern: Primarily California
Special Interest: Early childhood education; some Catholic support
Assets: $15,451,011
Grant Range: $204,562–$81
Limitations: No grants to individuals
Applications: Contributes to pre-selected organizations only. Applications not accepted.

The Shea Foundation
655 Brea Canyon Road
Walnut, CA 91789-0489
(714) 594-9500
Contact: Rudy Magallanes
Geographic Giving Pattern: Primarily California
Special Interest: Roman Catholic church support and religious associations, secondary education and the disabled
Assets: $3,358,824
Grant Range: $14,000–$200
Applications: Initial approach should be by letter

Trust Funds, Inc.
100 Broadway, Third Floor
San Francisco, CA 94111
(415) 434-3323
Contact: Albert J. Steiss, President
Geographic Giving Pattern: Limited to the San Francisco Bay area or to projects of national or global scope
Special Interest: Roman Catholic institutions and projects which promote the religious, educational and social welfare of all people
Assets: $3,713,131
Grant Range: $15,000–$300 (Grant average: $5,000)
Limitations: No grants for capital or endowment funds or annual campaigns. No loans. No support for organizations that draw substantial public support.
Applications: Initial approach should be by letter. Two copies of grant proposal are requested. There are no deadlines.

Wayne & Gladys Valley Foundation
4000 Executive Parkway, Suite 535
San Ramon, CA 94583
(415) 275-9300
Contact: Paul D. O'Connor, President and Executive Director
Geographic Giving Pattern: Primarily Alameda, Contra Costa and Santa Clara counties, California
Special Interest: Roman Catholic giving, including Catholic welfare and schools; support also for hospitals and recreation
Assets: $70,159,697 (Gifts received: $31,295,000)
Grant Range: $500,000–$500
Applications: Initial approach should be by letter. An application form is required. There are no deadlines.

Von der Ahe Foundation
4605 Lankershim Boulevard, Suite 707
North Hollywood, CA 91602
(213) 579-1400
Contact: Wilfred L. Von der Ahe, President
Geographic Giving Pattern: Primarily California
Special Interest: Roman Catholic religious institutions, health and welfare services and higher education
Assets: $4,272,737
Grant Range: $50,000–$250
Limitations: No grants to individuals
Applications: Due to funding limitations, the trustees prefer to initiate grants

Colorado

The J.K. Mullen Foundation
1640 Logan Street
Denver, CO 80203
(303) 893-3151
Contact: John F. Malo, Secretary
Geographic Giving Pattern: Primarily Denver, Colorado
Special Interest: Higher and secondary education, hospitals and Roman Catholic-affiliated organizations
Assets: $3,953,468
Grant Range: $25,000–$2,000
Limitations: No grants to individuals
Applications: Initial approach should be by letter. The deadline is September 1.

Eleanore Mullen Weckbaugh Foundation
13064 Parkview Drive
Aurora, CO 80011
(303) 367-1545
Contact: Edward J. Limes, President
Geographic Giving Pattern: Primarily Colorado
Special Interest: Roman Catholic church support, welfare funds, education, missionary programs, performing arts and health institutions
Assets: $6,251,619
Grant Range: $30,000–$2,000
Limitations: No grants to individuals
Applications: Application proposals and initial letter should be sent to: P.O. Box 31678, Aurora, CO 80041. There are no deadlines.

Connecticut

John P. & Margaret Mary Brogan Family Foundation
289 Greenwich Avenue
Greenwich, CT 06830-6542
Contact: John P. Brogan or Margaret M. Brogan, Trustees
Geographic Giving Pattern: Connecticut, New York and Massachusetts
Special Interest: Catholic organizations, including higher educational organizations and a convent
Assets: $389,688
Grant Range: $25,000–$100
Limitations: No grants to individuals

Applications: Contributes to pre-selected organizations only.
Applications not accepted.

The Hazel Dell Foundation
c/o Carroll & Lane
P.O. Box 771
Norwalk, CT 06852
(203) 853-6565
Contact: June M. Powers, President
Special Interest: Roman Catholic church support, hospitals, education
and aid to the disabled
Assets: $2,474,711
Grant Range: $12,000–$100
Limitations: No support for individuals
Applications: There are no deadlines for grant proposals

The Huisking Foundation, Inc.
P.O. Box 353
Botsford, CT 06404-0353
Contact: Frank R. Huisking, Treasurer
Special Interest: Catholic higher and secondary education, church
support, welfare funds, hospitals and related associations
Assets: $4,812,029
Grant Range: $55,000–$100
Limitations: No grants to individuals
Applications: Grant proposal letters should be sent in February or
August to: Plumtree Road (R.R. No.1) Newtown, CT 06470

John Jay Mann Foundation, Inc.
c/o Whitman and Ransom
P.O. Box 2250
Greenwich, CT 06836-2250
Contact: John Jay Mann, President
Geographic Giving Pattern: Connecticut, New York and Florida
Special Interest: Churches and hospitals
Assets: $1,758,758
Grant Range: $20,000–$100
Applications: Grant proposals should be sent to the following address:
Lucille Drive, Fort Lauderdale, FL 33316. There are no deadlines.

Lucien B. and Katherine E. Price Foundation, Inc.
896 Main Street
P.O. Box 790
Manchester, CT 06040
(203) 643-4129
Contact: Rt. Rev. Msgr. Edward J. Reardon, President
Geographic Giving Pattern: National
Special Interest: Roman Catholic church support, religious associations
and church-related schools, colleges and hospitals
Assets: $2,385,169
Grant Range: $16,000–$300
Applications: Initial approach should be by letter

Ray H. & Pauline Sullivan Foundation
c/o Connecticut National Bank
777 Main Street
Hartford, CT 06115
Contact: John J. Curtin
Geographic Giving Pattern: Primarily the Diocese of Norwich,
Connecticut
Special Interest: Roman Catholic charities and educational institutions;
some support for scholarships
Assets: $8,541,566
Grant Range: $20,000–$500
Limitations: There are no stated limitations other than geographical.
See above.
Applications: An application form is required. The deadline is May 1.

Delaware

Arguild Foundation
1220 Market Street, 10th Floor
Wilmington, DE 19801
(302) 658-9141
Contact: Arthur G. Connolly, President
Special Interest: Education, welfare funds and Roman Catholic
organizations
Assets: $1,053,781
Grant Range: $5,500–$100
Limitations: No grants to individuals
Applications: Initial approach should be by letter. There are no
deadlines.

Laffey-McHugh Foundation
1220 Market Building
P.O. Box 2207
Wilmington, DE 19899
(302) 658-9141
Contact: Arthur G. Connolly, President
Geographic Giving Pattern: Primarily Delaware, with emphasis on Wilmington
Special Interest: Roman Catholic church support and church-related institutions including schools, welfare agencies, religious associations and child welfare agencies
Assets: $38,302,040
Grant Range: $183,333–$1,000 (Grant average: $5,000–$50,000)
Limitations: No grants to individuals or for operating budgets, endowment funds, research or conferences. No loans.
Applications: Proposal letters should be sent in April or October

Raskob Foundation for Catholic Activities, Inc.
P.O. Box 4019
Wilmington, DE 19807
(302) 655-4440
Contact: Gerard S. Garey, President
Geographic Giving Pattern: National and international
Special Interest: Institutions and organizations identified with the Roman Catholic Church
Assets: $64,787,954
Grant Range: $250,000–$100 (Grant average: $5,000–$15,000)
Limitations: No grants to individuals or for endowment funds, deficit financing, continuing support, annual campaigns, tuition, scholarships or building projects prior to the start or after the completion of construction
Applications: An application form is required. Applications are accepted from June 15–August 15 and from December 15–February 15.

District of Columbia

Mary and Daniel Loughran Foundation, Inc.
c/o American Security & Trust Co.
15th Street & Pennsylvania Avenue, N.W.
Washington, DC 20013
(202) 624-4283
Contact: Tim Talley, Assistant Administrator

Geographic Giving Pattern: District of Columbia, Virginia and Maryland
Special Interest: Religious institutions, education, youth and social service agencies
Assets: $14,398,132
Grant Range: $60,000–$1,000
Limitations: No grants to individuals or for capital or endowment funds. No loans.
Applications: Grant proposals should be submitted between January and May. The deadline is June 1.

The Loyola Foundation, Inc.
308 C Street N.E.
Washington, DC 20002
(202) 546-9400
Contact: Albert G. McCarthy III, Secretary-Treasurer
Geographic Giving Pattern: National and international, primarily in developing nations. Grants made in the U.S. only to institutions or organizations of special interest to the trustees.
Special Interest: Roman Catholic missionary work and other Catholic activities of interest to the trustees
Assets: $6,368,793
Grant Range: $108,600–$100 (Grant average: $500–$15,000)
Limitations: No grants to individuals or for endowment funds, emergency funds, research, continuing support, deficit financing, annual budgets, scholarships, publications or conferences.
Applications: Submit grant proposals preferably in April or October. Deadlines are May 1 and November 1. An application form is required.

Thomas and Frances McGregor Foundation
See entry in Interfaith

Florida

Anthony R. Abraham Foundation, Inc.
6600 S.W. 57th Avenue
Miami, FL 33143
(305) 665-2222
Contact: Thomas G. Abraham, Secretary
Geographic Giving Pattern: National

Special Interest: Catholic giving, education, health and social services
Assets: $5,569,431
Grant Range: $25,245–$50
Applications: Initial approach should be by letter. There are no deadlines.

The Amaturo Foundation, Inc.
2929 East Commercial Boulevard, PH-C
Fort Lauderdale, FL 33308
(305) 776-7815
Contact: Cara E. Cameron, Manager
Geographic Giving Pattern: New York and Florida
Special Interest: Catholic charities, education, child welfare and a medical center
Assets: $1,000,752
Grant Range: $23,000–$750
Applications: There are no deadlines for grant proposals

John E. and Nellie J. Bastien Memorial Foundation
See entry in Interfaith

Chadbourne Foundation, Inc.
4375 McCoy Drive
Pensacola, FL 32501
(904) 433-3001
Contact: Edward M. Chadbourne, Jr., President
Geographic Giving Pattern: Primarily Pensacola, Florida
Special Interest: Catholic churches and parishes; support also for social services and health associations
Assets: $2,111,243
Grant Range: $25,000–$125
Limitations: No grants to individuals
Applications: Initial approach should be by letter. There are no deadlines.

The Arthur Vining Davis Foundations
See entry in Interfaith

Jessie Ball duPont Religious, Charitable and Educational Fund
See entry in Interfaith

The Fortin Foundation of Florida, Inc.

c/o First National in Palm Beach Trust Department
255 South County Road
Palm Beach, FL 33480-4113
(407) 655-9500
Contact: Mary Alice Fortin, President
Geographic Giving Pattern: Florida and Montana
Special Interest: Social service and youth agencies, Catholic churches and a diocese
Assets: $9,400,411
Grant Range: $50,000–$25
Limitations: No grants to individuals
Applications: Initial approach should be by letter. There are no deadlines.

Alma Jennings Foundation, Inc.

2222 Ponce de Leon Boulevard
Coral Gables, FL 33134
Contact: The Directors
Geographic Giving Pattern: Florida
Special Interest: Higher education, health and Catholic support
Assets: $4,312,994 (Gifts received: $2,054,933)
Grant Range: $15,000–$375
Applications: Applications are not accepted

Koch Foundation, Inc.

2830 N.W. 41st Street, Suite H
Gainseville, FL 32606
(904) 373-7491
Contact: Richard A. DeGraff, Executive Director
Geographic Giving Pattern: National and international
Special Interest: Roman Catholic religious organizations that propagate the faith
Assets: $90,184,795
Grant Range: $200,000–$1,500 (Grant average: $4,000–$50,000)
Limitations: No grants to individuals or for endowment funds, deficit financing, emergency funds, scholarships or fellowships. No loans.
Applications: Initial approach should be by letter. An application form is required. The deadline is December 1. Proposals are considered at the February meeting.

Jacob & Sophie Rice Family Foundation, Inc.

c/o Hamilton & Co.
P.O. Box 6370
Vero Beach, FL 32961
Contact: Richard G. Keneven, Trustee
Geographic Giving Pattern: Primarily New York
Special Interest: Hospitals and Roman Catholic welfare funds; some support for higher education
Assets: $1,741,326
Grant Range: $50,000–$1,000 (Grant average: $2,000–$10,000)
Applications: Initial approach should be by letter

Saint Gerard Foundation

3041 Braeloch Circle East
Clearwater, FL 34621-2708
Contact: Elizabeth C. Mooney, Vice-President
Special Interest: Conservative public policy organizations and Roman Catholic church support, including groups concerned with social issues; support also for education
Assets: $3,010,097 (Gifts received: $616,555)
Grant Range: $100,000–$10
Limitations: No grants to individuals
Applications: Contributes to pre-selected organizations only. Applications not accepted.

Georgia

Mary Ryan & Henry G. Kuhrt Foundation

c/o Trust Co. Bank
P.O. Box 4655
Atlanta, GA 30302-4655
(404) 588-7356
Contact: Brenda Rambeau
Geographic Giving Pattern: Limited to Georgia, with emphasis on Atlanta
Special Interest: Primarily for a Catholic hospital, monasteries, convents and schools
Assets: $1,419,436
Grant Range: $23,209–$1,000
Applications: Initial approach should be by letter. Grant proposal deadline is November 1.

St. Joseph Foundation, Inc.
8980 Huntcliff Trace
Atlanta, GA 30350
(404) 993-2776
Contact: William A. Chesney, Trustee
Special Interest: Catholic giving and Catholic welfare
Assets: $77,107 (Gifts received: $85,700)
Grant Range: $83,000–$25
Applications: Initial approach should be by letter. There are no deadlines.

Illinois

Ralph J. Baudhuin Foundation
501 Seventh Street
Rockford, IL 61101
(815) 399-3148
Contact: Fran Baudhuin
Geographic Giving Pattern: Primarily Fort Lauderdale, Florida and Rockford, Illinois
Special Interest: Roman Catholic churches; also universities and health organizations
Assets: $1,263,889
Grant Range: $6,000–$100
Applications: Initial approach should be by letter sent to the following address: 4109 Rural Street, Rockford, IL 61101. There are no deadlines.

The Alvin H. Baum Family Fund
See entry in Interfaith

The Ambrose and Gladys Bowyer Foundation
175 West Jackson Boulevard, Suite 909
Chicago, IL 60604
Contact: D.T. Hutchison, President
Geographic Giving Pattern: Primarily Illinois
Special Interest: Higher education, hospitals and welfare funds; some Catholic church support
Assets: $2,238,784
Grant Range: $53,000–$1,000
Limitations: No stated limitations
Applications: Contributes to pre-selected organizations only. Applications not accepted.

Christiana Foundation, Inc.
c/o Hinshaw, Culbertson, Moelmann, Hoban and Fuller
222 North LaSalle Street, Suite 300
Chicago, IL 60601-1081
Contact: Jerome A. Frazel, President
Geographic Giving Pattern: Primarily Illinois
Special Interest: Roman Catholic community welfare organizations,
secondary and higher education
Assets: $1,176,073
Grant Range: $20,000–$250
Limitations: No grants to individuals
Applications: No application form is required. There are no deadlines.
Initial approach should be by letter.

The Cottrell Foundation
c/o Carleton M. Tower & Co.
33 North Dearborn Street, Suite 2020
Chicago, IL 60602
Contact: Joseph J. Cottrell, Sr., Trustee
Geographic Giving Pattern: National
Special Interest: Catholic-affiliated schools, churches and
organizations, including missionaries in Africa and Asia
Assets: $1,649,888
Grant Range: $10,000–$100
Limitations: No grants to individuals
Applications: Initial approach should be by letter. Application address
is the following: 296 Alexander Palm Road, Boca Raton, FL 33432.
There are no deadlines.

The Cuneo Foundation
9101 Greenwood Avenue, Suite 210
Niles, IL 60648-1466
Contact: John F. Cuneo, President
Geographic Giving Pattern: Primarily the Chicago metropolitan area
Special Interest: Roman Catholic church support, church related-
organizations, religious associations, welfare funds and hospitals
Assets: $15,385,335
Grant Range: $31,413–$50
Limitations: No grants to individuals or for scholarship, fellowship or
research funds. No loans.
Applications: There are no deadlines for grant proposals

Thomas W. Dower Foundation

c/o John M. Hartigan
9730 South Western Avenue, Suite 206
Evergreen Park, IL 60642-2814
Contact: Daniel J. O'Shaughnessy, Executive Director
Geographic Giving Pattern: Primarily Illinois
Special Interest: Education, welfare, health, hospitals and Christian organizations
Assets: $3,906,413
Grant Range: $35,471–$50 (Grant average: less than $10,000)
Applications: Initial approach should be by letter

Father James M. Fitzgerald Scholarship Trust

c/o Commercial National Bank of Peoria
301 South West Adams Street
Peoria, IL 61631
(309) 655-5322
Contact: Rev. William C. Feeney, Trustee
Geographic Giving Pattern: Limited to residents of Illinois
Special Interest: Scholarships restricted to Illinois residents who are studying for the priesthood and attending a Catholic university or college
Assets: $1,430,753
Grant Total: $86,671 (individuals)
Limitations: No support for general purposes, capital or endowment funds, research, publications or conferences. No loans or matching gifts.
Applications: An application form is not required. Initial approach should be by letter. There are no deadlines.

Robert W. Galvin Foundation

1303 East Algonquin Road
Schaumburg, IL 60196
(312) 576-5300
Contact: Robert W. Galvin, President
Geographic Giving Pattern: Primarily Illinois
Special Interest: Higher and secondary education, the disabled, hospitals and church support
Assets: $7,593,535 (Gifts received: $643,875)
Grant Range: $100,000–$15
Limitations: No grants to individuals
Applications: Initial approach should be by letter

Paul V. Galvin Trust
c/o Harris Trust & Savings Bank
111 West Monroe Street
Chicago, IL 60603
Contact: Lisa R. Curcio
Special Interest: Roman Catholic religious organizations and church support
Assets: $849,761
Grant Range: $250,000–$2,000
Applications: There are no deadlines for grant proposals. Proposals should be sent to the following address: Harris Trust & Savings Bank, 7E, P.O. Box 755, Chicago, IL 60690 Tel. (312) 461-2613.

Lawrence & Ada Hickory Foundation
615 Woodland Lane
Northfield, IL 60093
Contact: Lawrence Hickey, President
Geographic Giving Pattern: Primarily Illinois
Special Interest: Catholic churches and Catholic organizations
Assets: $1,423,389
Grant Range: $50,000–$100
Limitations: No grants to individuals
Applications: Contributes to pre-selected organizations only. Applications not accepted.

Frank J. Lewis Foundation
Three First National Plaza, Suite 1950
Chicago, IL 60602
Contact: The Trustees
Geographic Giving Pattern: National
Special Interest: To foster, preserve and extend the Roman Catholic faith. Contributes to educational institutions, church support, religious orders and church-sponsored programs.
Assets: $17,132,707
Grant Range: $110,000–$100 (Grant average: $1,000–$15,000)
Limitations: No grants to individuals or for endowment funds
Applications: Contributes to pre-selected organizations only. Applications not accepted.

Mazza Foundation
225 West Washington Street, Suite 1300
Chicago, IL 60606-3405
(312) 444-9300

Contact: Joseph O. Rubinelli, Secretary-Treasurer
Geographic Giving Pattern: Primarily Chicago, Illinois
Special Interest: Churches, religious organizations, social service
agencies, hospitals; some support for education
Assets: $37,922,994 (Gifts received: $925,978)
Grant Range: $100,000–$500
Applications: There are no deadlines for grant proposals

McIntosh Foundation, Inc.
c/o Salomon Brothers, Inc.
8700 Sears Tower
Chicago, IL 60606
Contact: William A, McIntosh, President and Treasurer
Geographic Giving Pattern: Primarily Chicago, Illinois
Special Interest: Primarily for programs of the Archdiocese of Chicago
and other Catholic parishes, schools and charities
Assets: $4,726,121
Grant Range: $150,000–$100
Limitations: No grants to individuals
Applications: Contributes to pre-selected organizations only.
Applications not accepted.

Merrion Foundation
10321 South Maplewood
Chicago, IL 60655
Contact: The Directors
Special Interest: Catholic organizations, education and social services
Assets: $2,156,288
Grant Range: $20,000–$50
Applications: Contributes to pre-selected organizations only.
Applications not accepted.

Virginia G. Piper Foundation
Three First National Plaza, Suite 1950
Chicago, IL 60603
Contact: Virginia G. Piper, President
Geographic Giving Pattern: National
Special Interest: Social services, the arts, higher education, hospitals,
Catholic churches and Catholic religious orders
Assets: $2,106,048
Grant Range: $25,000–$1,000
Applications: Contributes to pre-selected organizations only.
Applications not accepted.

James M. Ragen, Jr. Memorial Fund Trust No. 1.
30 North Michigan Avenue
Chicago, IL 60602-3402
Geographic Giving Pattern: National
Special Interest: Catholic churches, social services and education
Assets: $2,249,055
Grant Range: $36,000–$1,000
Applications: There are no deadlines for grant proposals

The Retirement Research Foundation
See entry in Interfaith

Arthur J. Schmitt Foundation
Two North LaSalle Street, Suite 2010
Chicago, IL 60602
(312) 236-5089
Contact: John A. Donahue, Executive Director
Geographic Giving Pattern: Primarily the Chicago metropolitan area
Special Interest: Roman Catholic educational and religious institutions
Assets: $15,526,204
Grant Range: $100,000–$100 (Grant average: $2,000–$50,000)
Limitations: No grants to individuals. No support for research, capital or building funds. No loans or matching gifts.
Applications: Submit three copies of grant proposal preferably in July, October, January or April

Fred B. Snite Foundation
550 Frontage Road, Suite 3082
North Field, IL 60093
(312) 446-7705
Contact: Terrance J. Dillon, President
Special Interest: Roman Catholic church support and church-related educational institutions
Assets: $8,034,473
Grant Total: $288,800
Applications: There are no deadlines for grant proposals

Solo Cup Foundation
See entry in Interfaith

Indiana

Arnold F. Habig Foundation, Inc.
1301 St. Charles Street
Jasper, IN 47546
(812) 634-1010
Contact: Arnold F. Habig, President
Geographic Giving Pattern: Primarily Indiana
Special Interest: Education and Roman Catholic religious organizations
Assets: $2,604,533
Grant Range: $40,150–$10
Limitations: No grants to individuals
Applications: Initial approach should be by letter sent to the following address: 1500 Main Street, Jasper, IN 47546. There are no deadlines.

John A. Hillenbrand Foundation, Inc.
See entry in Interfaith

Indiana Chemical Trust
c/o The Merchants National Bank of Terre Haute
701 Wabash Avenue
Terre Haute, IN 47808
(812) 234-5571
Contact: John F. Sweet, Trust Officer, The Merchants National Bank of Terre Haute
Geographic Giving Pattern: Primarily Vigo County, Indiana
Special Interest: Civic, charitable, youth and educational institutions and Catholic church support, including monasteries
Assets: $5,171,156
Grant Range: $25,000–$1,000
Applications: There are no deadlines for grant proposals

Irwin-Sweeney-Miller Foundation
See entry in Interfaith

Lilly Endowment, Inc.
See entry in Interfaith

Our Sunday Visitor, Inc.
200 Noll Plaza
Huntington, IN 46750
(219) 356-8400
Contact: Robert Lockwood, President

Geographic Giving Pattern: National
Special Interest: Roman Catholic church support and religious organizations
Grant Range: $60,000–$1,000
Limitations: No grants to individuals. Grant recipients must be registered in the *Official Catholic Directory.*
Applications: Initial approach should be by letter

M.E. Raker Foundation
3242 Mallard Cove Lane
Fort Wayne, IN 46804
(219) 436-2182
Contact: John E. Hogan, President
Special Interest: Catholic secondary and higher education and youth; some support for churches
Assets: $6,392,330
Grant Range: $50,000–$500
Limitations: No support for the arts. No grants to individuals.
Applications: An application form is required. Initial approach should be by written proposal.

Louisiana

The Azby Fund
635 Gravier Whitney Bank Building, Room 1311
New Orleans, LA 70130-2613
Contact: Thomas Lemann, Secretary-Treasurer
Special Interest: Catholic giving, higher education and medical sciences
Assets: $9,034,264 (Gifts received: $1,429,155)
Grant Range: $78,672–$100
Applications: Contributes to pre-selected organizations only. Applications not accepted.

Libby-Dufour Fund
See entry in Interfaith

Maryland

The Marion I. and Henry J. Knott Foundation, Inc.
3904 Hickory Avenue
Baltimore, MD 21211
(301) 235-7068

Contact: Ann von Lossberg, Administrator
Geographic Giving Pattern: Limited to the greater Baltimore, Maryland area
Special Interest: Roman Catholic activities and other charitable, cultural, educational and health and human service organizations
Assets: $23,496,526
Grant Range: $164,000–$1,000 (Grant average: $10,000–$30,000)
Limitations: No support for pro-abortion causes or public education. No grants to individuals. No support for scholarship funds or annual giving appeals.
Applications: Two copies of grant proposal should be sent by February 1 or August 1

The Thomas F. and Clementine L. Mullan Foundation, Inc.
2330 West Joppa Road, Suite 210
Lutherville, MD 21093
(301) 494-9200
Contact: Thomas F. Mullan, President
Geographic Giving Pattern: Primarily Baltimore, Maryland
Special Interest: Hospitals and health agencies, higher and secondary education, Roman Catholic church support and social services
Assets: $3,505,731
Grant Range: $25,200–$100
Applications: Contributes to pre-selected organizations only. Applications not accepted.

The W. O'Neil Foundation
5454 Wisconsin Avenue, No. 750
Chevy Chase, MD 20815
(301) 656-3442
Contact: Holly Buchanan, Vice-President
Special Interest: Roman Catholic church support and church-related institutions, particularly basic needs programs
Assets: $30,179,730
Grant Range: $500,000–$3,500 (Grant average: $5,000–$12,500)
Limitations: There are no stated limitations
Applications: Initial approach should be by letter with proposal. There are no deadlines.

Massachusetts

Birmingham Foundation
10 Post Office Square, #600 South
Boston, MA 02109
(617) 439-9065
Contact: Paul J. Birmingham, Trustee
Special Interest: Roman Catholic welfare funds, education and social
service agencies
Assets: $5,210,770
Grant Range: $150,000–$2,000
Applications: Initial approach should be by letter. Proposals should be
sent by the end of the third quarter.

Irene E. and George A. Davis Foundation
American Saw and Manufacturing Co.
301 Chestnut Street
East Longmeadow, MA 01028
(413) 525-3961
Contact: James E. Davis, Trustee
Geographic Giving Pattern: Primarily Massachusetts
Special Interest: Higher education and Roman Catholic institutions,
including churches; support also for social services, hospitals and
community funds
Assets: $17,185,146 (Gifts received: $2,000,000)
Grant Range: $55,000–$100
Limitations: No grants to individuals or for deficit financing,
equipment, endowment funds, scholarships, research, publications or
conferences. No matching gifts or loans.
Applications: Contributes to pre-selected organizations only.
Applications not accepted.

The Howard Johnson Foundation
See entry in Interfaith

Norman Knight Charitable Foundation
63 Bay State Road
Boston, MA 02215-1892
(617) 262-1950
Contact: Norman Knight, Trustee
Geographic Giving Pattern: Massachusetts, New Hampshire and
Vermont

Special Interest: Community funds and development, performing arts, museums, hospitals and health associations, education, social services and Catholic church support
Assets: $308,979
Grant Range: $15,000–$100
Applications: There are no deadlines for grant proposal letters

Leclerc Charity Fund
1045 Oak Hill Road
Fitchburg, MA 01420-4819
Contact: Raymond Leclerc, Manager
Special Interest: Catholic religious organizations and churches; support also for schools for the deaf and blind
Assets: $1,203,422
Grant Range: $15,000–$100
Applications: Contributes to pre-selected organizations only. Applications not accepted.

Perini Memorial Foundation, Inc.
73 Mount Wayte Avenue
Framingham, MA 01701
(617) 875-6171
Contact: Bart W. Perini, Treasurer
Geographic Giving Pattern: Primarily Massachusetts
Special Interest: Higher education, Roman Catholic church support and religious associations, and hospitals
Assets: $5,648,855
Grant Range: $32,500–$70
Limitations: No grants to individuals (except employee-related scholarships) or for research, scholarships or fellowships. No matching gifts and no loans.
Applications: Initial approach should be by grant proposal letter

Sawyer Charitable Foundation
See entry in Interfaith

Blanche M. Walsh Charity Trust
174 Central Street, Suite 329
Lowell, MA 01852
(617) 454-5654
Contact: Robert F. Murphy, Trustee
Special Interest: Giving limited to Roman Catholic organizations, including educational institutions and welfare organizations

Assets: $2,532,507
Grant Range: $11,000–$500
Limitations: No grants to individuals or for endowment funds, continuing support, annual campaigns, deficit financing or matching gifts. No loans.
Applications: Initial approach should be by letter. An application form is required. The deadline for grant applications is November 10.

Michigan

Deseranno Educational Foundation, Inc.
4600 Bellevue
Detroit, MI 48207
Contact: The Rt. Rev. Ferdinand DeCheudt
Special Interest: Catholic organizations and scholarships to a Catholic college
Assets: $5,497,838 (Gifts received: $1,214,056)
Grant Range: $60,000–$500
Applications: Initial approach should be by letter. There are no deadlines.

Myrtle E. & William C. Hess Charitable Trust
c/o National Bank of Detroit, Trust Division
611 Woodward Avenue
Detroit, MI 48226
(313) 225-3124
Contact: Therese M. Thorn, Second Vice-President, National Bank of Detroit
Geographic Giving Pattern: Primarily Michigan
Special Interest: Catholic churches, religious orders and welfare; support also for education, religious schools, social services, youth programs, religious welfare organizations and hospitals
Assets: $6,908,708
Grant Range: $115,000–$1,000
Applications: Initial approach should be by grant proposal. There are no deadlines.

Molloy Foundation, Inc.
P.O. Box 200
St. Clair Shores, MI 48080
Contact: Therese M. Molloy, President
Geographic Giving Pattern: Primarily Michigan

Special Interest: Education, religion, hospitals and social services
Assets: $1,189,750
Grant Range: $25,000–$100 (Religious grant average: $200–$6,125)
Applications: Initial approach should be by letter. There are no deadlines.

Sage Foundation
150 West Jefferson, Suite 2500
Detroit, MI 48226
(313) 963-6420
Contact: Dolores deGakeford, Trustee
Geographic Giving Pattern: Primarily Michigan
Special Interest: Emphasis on higher and secondary education and hospitals. Grants also for aid to the disabled, Roman Catholic religious and charitable organizations, church support, and cultural programs.
Assets: $51,373,554
Grant Range: $200,000–$500 (Grant average: $1,000–$15,000)
Applications: Initial approach should be by letter. There are no deadlines.

Sehn Foundation
23874 Kean Avenue
Dearborn, MI 48124
Contact: Francis J. Sehn, President
Geographic Giving Pattern: Primarily Detroit, Michigan
Special Interest: Roman Catholic organizations; some support for health, social services and education
Assets: $3,176,105
Grant Range: $110,448–$100
Applications: Contributes to pre-selected organizations only. Applications not accepted.

Seymour and Troester Foundation
21500 Harper Avenue
St. Clair Shores, MI 48080
Contact: B.A. Seymour, President and Treasurer
Special Interest: Grants largely for higher and secondary educational institutions and Roman Catholic and charitable organizations
Assets: $3,150,866
Grant Range: $37,000–$500
Limitations: No grants to individuals
Applications: Contributes to pre-selected organizations only. Applications not accepted.

Emmet and Frances Tracy Fund
400 Renaissance Center, 35th Floor
Detroit, MI 48243
(313) 881-5007
Contact: Emmet E. Tracy, President
Geographic Giving Pattern: Primarily Michigan, especially Detroit
Special Interest: Roman Catholic religious organizations and missionary groups. Grants also for social services, education and health agencies.
Assets: $1,531,669 (Gifts received: $1,050,000)
Grant Range: $100,000–$100 (Grant average: $1,000–$30,000)
Applications: There are no deadlines

Vlasic Foundation
200 Town Center, Suite 900
Southfield, MI 48075
Contact: Robert J. Vlasic, President
Special Interest: Cultural programs, health agencies, hospitals, social services and Roman Catholic organizations
Assets: $1,656,198
Grant Range: $20,000–$100
Applications: Applications are not accepted

Minnesota

Otto Bremer Foundation
See entry in Interfaith

John & Clara Dolan Foundation
15608 Willowwood Drive
Minnetonka, MN 55345
(612) 934-9706
Contact: John F. Dolan, President
Special Interest: Catholic organizations
Assets: $95,486 (Gifts received: $50,000)
Grant Range: $10,000–$250
Limitations: No stated limitations
Applications: Initial approach should be by letter. There are no deadlines.

Kasal Charitable Trust
c/o Minnesota Trust Co.
107 West Oakland Avenue
P.O. Box 463
Austin, MN 55912
(507) 437-3231
Contact: Warren F. Plunkett, President
Geographic Giving Pattern: National
Special Interest: Catholic charities in the U.S. and education of young men and women for religious life
Assets: $1,630,301
Grant Range: $10,000–$500
Limitations: No support for education below college level, building or endowment funds, or research. No loans. No grants to individuals.
Applications: An application form is required. Initial approach should be by letter. Two copies of proposal are required. Deadlines are January 10, April 10 and July 10.

The Casey Albert T. O'Neil Foundation
c/o First Trust, N.A.
P.O. Box 64704
St. Paul, MN 55164-0704
(612) 291-6240
Contact: Sally A. Mullen
Geographic Giving Pattern: St. Paul metropolitan area
Special Interest: Emphasis on Roman Catholic religious associations and missions, health agencies and aid to disabled children
Assets: $8,374,354
Grant Range: $35,000–$500 (Grant average: $2,000–$20,000)
Limitations: No grants to individuals or for deficit financing, capital campaigns, endowment or scholarship funds, research, special projects, publications or conferences. No matching gifts or loans.
Applications: Initial approach should be by proposal letter sent to the following address: c/o First Trust, N.A., First National Bank Building, St. Paul, MN 55101. There are no deadlines.

I.A. O'Shaughnessy Foundation, Inc.
c/o First Trust, N.A.
P.O. Box 64704
St. Paul, MN 55164
(612) 222-2323
Contact: Paul J. Kelly, Secretary-Treasurer
Geographic Giving Pattern: National with emphasis on Minnesota, Illinois, Kansas and Texas

Special Interest: Cultural programs, secondary and higher education, social services, medical research, and Roman Catholic religious organizations
Assets: $33,919,021 (Gifts received: $5,255,159)
Grant Range: $200,00–$1,000 (Grant average: $5,000–$50,000)
Limitations: No support for religious missions or individual parishes. No grants to individuals. No loans.
Applications: Grants usually initiated by directors. Send letter and proposal to contact. There are no deadlines.

The Elizabeth C. Quinlan Foundation, Inc.
1205 Foshay Tower
Minneapolis, MN 55402
(612) 333-8084
Contact: Richard A. Klein, President
Geographic Giving Pattern: Limited to Minnesota
Special Interest: Roman Catholic institutions, higher and secondary education, cultural programs, health agencies and social services
Assets: $2,150,135
Grant Range: $20,000–$100
Limitations: No grants to individuals. No loans.
Applications: Initial approach should be by letter. Submit proposals preferably in May or June; the deadline is September 1.

Gerald Rauenhorst Family Foundation
3434 Norwest Center
Minneapolis, MN 55402
(612) 333-7600
Contact: John H. Agee, Vice-President
Geographic Giving Pattern: Primarily Minnesota
Special Interest: Higher education, Roman Catholic church support and church-related institutions, and chemical dependency programs
Assets: $13,271,616 (Gifts received: $494,500)
Grant Range: $100,000–$1,000
Limitations: No grants to individuals
Applications: Contributes to pre-selected organizations only. Applications not accepted.

Margaret Rivers Fund
See entry in Interfaith

Patrick & Alice Rogers Charitable Foundation
6400 Barrie Road, No. 1504
Edina, MN 55435-2342
(612) 926-0790
Contact: Patrick W. Rogers, President
Geographic Giving Pattern: Minneapolis and St. Paul, Minnesota
Special Interest: Catholic organizations, including welfare agencies and colleges and universities
Assets: $1,140,105
Grant Range: $30,000–$25
Applications: There are no deadlines for grant proposal letters

Sexton Foundation
14973 95th Avenue North
Maple Grove, MN 55369
(612) 440-4505
Contact: Thomas D. Sexton, Vice-President
Geographic Giving Pattern: Primarily St. Cloud, Minnesota and Lewisville, Texas
Special Interest: Catholic churches and colleges
Assets: $1,620,050
Grant Range: $10,000–$1,000
Limitations: No grants to individuals
Applications: There are no deadlines for grant proposals

The Wasie Foundation
909 Foshay Tower
Minneapolis, MN 55402
(612) 332-3883
Contact: Gregg D. Sjoquist, Vice-President
Geographic Giving Pattern: Minneapolis and the St. Paul, Minnesota metropolitan area
Special Interest: Higher education, including scholarship funds at selected institutions for qualified students of Polish ancestry. Support also for Roman Catholic religious associations, health organizations, mental health and the disabled.
Assets: $11,677,969
Grant Range: $100,000–$50 (Grant average: $3,000–$5,000)
Limitations: No grants to individuals. No loans.
Applications: An application form is required. Initial approach should be by telephone. Deadlines vary.

Missouri

Enright Foundation, Inc.
7508 Main
Kansas City, MO 64114
Contact: Anna M. Cassidy, President
Geographic Giving Pattern: Primarily Missouri
Special Interest: Roman Catholic religious organizations, hospitals, child welfare and social service agencies
Assets: $3,036,872
Limitations: No grants for scholarships or awards
Applications: Contributes to pre-selected organizations only. Applications not accepted.

The Catherine Manley Gaylord Foundation
See entry in Interfaith

The McGee Foundation
4900 Main Street, Suite 717
Kansas City, MO 64112-2644
(816) 931-1515
Contact: Joseph J. McGee, Chair
Geographic Giving Pattern: Limited to the greater Kansas City, Missouri area
Special Interest: Care for the sick, education and other benevolent, charitable, religious or scientific institutions
Assets: $6,064,855
Grant Range: $50,000–$500 (Grant average: $7,209)
Limitations: No support for visual or performing arts, historic preservation, community development or rehabilitation, public information programs, united appeals or national organizations with wide support. No grants to individuals or for endowment funds, research, publications or conferences. No matching gifts or loans.
Applications: Initial approach should be by letter. There are no deadlines.

Miller-Mellor Association
708 East 47th Street
Kansas City, MO 64110
(816) 561-4307
Contact: James L. Miller, Secretary-Treasurer
Geographic Giving Pattern: Primarily Kansas City, Missouri
Special Interest: Catholic church support, higher education, cultural programs and health services

Assets: $1,813,914
Grant Range: $7,000–$13
Applications: Initial approach should be by letter or proposal. There
are no deadlines.

Orscheln Industries Foundation, Inc.
P.O. Box 280
Moberly, MO 65270
(816) 263-4900
Contact: G.A. Orscheln, President
Geographic Giving Pattern: Primarily Missouri
Special Interest: Emphasis on Roman Catholic church support and
religious organizations, community funds and higher education
Assets: $9,235,448 (Gifts received: $2,006,324)
Grant Range: $253,621–$1,000
Applications: Initial approach should be by letter

The Pendergast-Weyer Foundation
3434 West Coleman Road
Kansas City, MO 64111
(816) 561-3002
Contact: Beverly B. Pendergast, President
Geographic Giving Pattern: Limited to towns or cities in Missouri with
populations under 100,000
Special Interest: Roman Catholic church-related day care centers, pre-
schools, elementary schools, high schools and religious
organizations. A minimum of 80 percent of all grants must go to
Catholic institutions.
Assets: $3,855,358
Grant Range: $30,000–$2,000 (Grant average: $1,000–10,000)
Limitations: No support for clergymen, chanceries or church
foundations. No grants to individuals or for annual campaigns, seed
money, building funds, land acquisition, endowment funds, research,
publications or conferences. No matching gifts and no loans.
Applications: Initial approach should be made by telephone. An
application form is required and deadlines are April 10 and
September 10. The application address is as follows: Grant Selection
Committee, P.O. Box 413245, Kansas City, MO 64141. Tel. (816) 561-
6340.

Share Foundation
See entry in Interfaith

Sycamore Tree Trust
c/o A.G. Edwards Trust Co.
One North Jefferson Street, 6th Floor
St. Louis, MO 63103
(314) 289-4200
Contact: Joseph C. Morris, Associate Vice-President, A.G. Edwards
Trust Co.
Geographic Giving Pattern: Primarily Missouri
Special Interest: Roman Catholic church support and religious
associations. Support also for the arts, cultural programs, higher
education, a community fund and also some international
organizations.
Assets: $408,751
Grant Range: $40,500–$25 (Grant average: $350–$10,000)
Limitations: No grants to individuals. No support for scholarships or
fellowships. No loans.
Applications: Contributes to pre-selected organizations only.
Applications not accepted.

Vatterott Foundation
10449 St. Charles Road
St. Ann, MO 63074
Contact: The Trustees
Special Interest: Catholic churches, schools and other organizations
Assets: $974,984
Grant Range: $30,000–$160
Limitations: No stated limitations

Nebraska

Thomas D. Buckley Trust
See entry in Interfaith

Nevada

Conrad N. Hilton Foundation
100 West Liberty Street, Suite 840
Reno, NV 89501
(702) 323-4221
Contact: Donald H. Hubbs, President
Geographic Giving Pattern: National
Special Interest: Drug abuse prevention, hotel administration
education, and Catholic welfare

Assets: $492,092,546 (Gifts received: $231,630,125)
Grant Average: $5,000–$50,000
Limitations: No support for religious organizations for the benefit of their own membership. No support for medical research, the arts, the elderly, political lobbying or legislative activities. No grants to individuals or for general fund-raising events. No loans.
Applications: Initial approach should be by letter. There are no deadlines. The foundation accepts applications primarily from its specified beneficiaries.

E.L. Wiegand Foundation
Wiegand Center
165 West Liberty Street
Reno, NV 89501
(702) 333-0310
Contact: Raymond C. Avansino, Chair and President
Geographic Giving Pattern: Primarily Nevada and adjoining western states including California, Arizona, Oregon, Idaho and Utah
Special Interest: Education; health and medical research; public, civic, community and cultural affairs; emphasis on Roman Catholic institutions
Assets: $79,466,446
Grant Range: $100,000–$2,000 (Grant average: $10,000–$70,000)
Limitations: No support for organizations receiving significant support from public tax funds, organizations with beneficiaries of their own choosing, or federal, state or local government agencies or institutions. No grants to individuals or for endowment funds, fund-raising campaigns or operating funds.
Applications: An application form is required. Initial approach should be by letter. There are no deadlines.

New Jersey

The Charles Engelhard Foundation
P.O. Box 427
Far Hills, NJ 07931
(201) 766-7224
Contact: Elaine Catterall, Secretary
Geographic Giving Pattern: National
Special Interest: Emphasis on higher and secondary education, cultural, medical and religious organizations and wildlife conservation
Assets: $71,024,437

Grant Range: $1,072,500–$500 (Grant average: $1,000–$100,000)
Limitations: No grants to individuals or for building funds
Applications: Grants only to organizations known to the trustees.
Initial approach should be by proposal letter. There are no deadlines.

The Hackett Foundation, Inc.
33 Second Street
Raritan, NJ 08869
(201) 231-8252
Contact: Alice T. Hackett, Chair, Grant Committee
Geographic Giving Pattern: Primarily New Jersey, New York and
Pennsylvania
Special Interest: Emphasis on Catholic missions, also supports
Catholic health and social service agencies
Assets: $13,422,323
Grant Range: $43,131–$2,700 (Grant average: $1,000–$20,000)
Limitations: No grants to individuals or for land acquisition,
endowment funds, matching gifts, scholarships, fellowships,
research, demonstration projects, publications or conferences. No
loans.
Applications: An application form is required. Send letter and
proposal. The deadline is the 10th of each month.

The Ix Foundation
c/o Oakview Securities Corp
3300 Hudson Avenue
P.O. Box 809
Union City, NJ 07087
(201) 865-2111
Contact: The Personnel Manager
Geographic Giving Pattern: New Jersey and other areas of company
operations in New York, New York; Lexington, North Carolina; and
Charlottesville, Virginia
Special Interest: Education, Roman Catholic church support, hospitals
and community development
Assets: $1,132,877
Grant Range: $25,000–$100
Limitations: No stated limitations
Applications: An application form is required. There are no deadlines.

The John R. Kennedy Foundation, Inc.
75 Chestnut Ridge Road
Montvale, NJ 07645
(201) 391-1776

Contact: John R. Kennedy, Vice-President
Special Interest: Higher education, Roman Catholic church-related programs, social services and hospitals
Assets: $3,521,745
Grant Range: $200,000–$1,000
Limitations: No grants to individuals
Applications: Initial approach should be by letter.There are no deadlines.

Quentin J. Kennedy Foundation
22 Old Smith Road
Tenafly, NJ 07670
(201) 391-1776
Contact: Quentin J. Kennedy, President
Geographic Giving Pattern: No stated limits
Special Interest: Primarily for Catholic giving including welfare, hospitals and higher education
Assets: $5,032,628
Grant Range: $70,000–$75
Limitations: No grants to individuals
Applications: Initial approach should be by letter. There are no deadlines. Proposal letters should be sent to the contact at the following address: 75 Chestnut Ridge Road, Montvale, NJ 07645.

The James Kerney Foundation
c/o Kerney, Kuser, Drinker, et al.
100 Palmer Square, Suite 400
Princeton, NJ 08542
Contact: J. Kerney Kuser
Geographic Giving Pattern: Limited to Trenton, New Jersey and the surrounding area
Special Interest: Hospitals, youth agencies, higher education and Roman Catholic church support
Assets: $2,404,838
Grant Range: $50,000–$1,000
Limitations: No grants to individuals or for operating budgets
Applications: There are no stated deadlines

The Stefano La Sala Foundation, Inc.
One Bridge Plaza, Suite 105
Fort Lee, NJ 07024
(201) 947-9580
Contact: A. Stephen La Sala, Director
Geographic Giving Pattern: Primarily New York, New York

Special Interest: Higher and secondary education, hospitals, Roman Catholic church support and social service agencies
Assets: $2,238,658
Grant Range: $15,805–$20
Limitations: No support for private foundations. No grants to individuals.
Applications: Initial approach should be by proposal letter. There are no deadlines.

Theresa and Edward O'Toole Foundation
Eight Church Court
Closter, NJ 07624
Contact: Daniel McCarthy, Trust Officer
Geographic Giving Pattern: Primarily New York, New Jersey and Florida
Special Interest: Roman Catholic churches and welfare funds, hospitals, and higher education
Assets: $16,892,062
Grant Range: $100,000–$500
Limitations: No grants to individuals or for endowment funds, scholarships or fellowships. No loans.
Applications: Initial approach should be by letter. There are no deadlines.

Paragano Family Foundation, Inc.
899 Mountain Avenue
Springfield, NJ 07081
(201) 376-1010
Contact: Nazario Paragano, Trustee
Special Interest: Catholic churches and religious orders; minor support for hospitals, Jewish welfare and higher education
Assets: $1,528,706
Grant Range: $25,000–$1,000
Limitations: No restrictions
Applications: There is no designated procedure format. There are no deadlines.

The Harold B. and Dorothy A. Snyder Foundation
See entry in Interfaith

Frank Visceglia Foundation
300 Raritan Center Parkway
Edison, NJ 08837

Contact: Frank D. Visceglia, Manager
Special Interest: Catholic schools, churches and religious orders
Assets: $2,187,912
Grant Range: $10,000–$25
Applications: Contributes to pre-selected organizations only.
Applications not accepted.

Visceglia-Summit Associates Foundation
Raritan Plaza
Raritan Center
Edison, NJ 08818
(201) 225-2900
Contact: Diego Visceglia, President-Treasurer
Geographic Giving Pattern: Primarily Essex and Middlesex counties, New Jersey
Special Interest: Hospitals, higher education, church support and religious associations
Assets: $1,877,437
Religious Grant Range: $8,000–$100
Applications: Contributes to pre-selected organizations only.
Applications not accepted.

New York

Altman Foundation
See entry in Interfaith

The Baker Foundation
485 Washington Avenue
Pleasantville, NY 10570
(914) 747-1550
Contact: Marcus D. Baker, Treasurer
Geographic Giving Pattern: Primarily New York, New York and Los Angeles, California
Special Interest: Catholic organizations including churches, a seminary, child and other welfare agencies, and housing and homelessness
Assets: $1,652,425
Grant Range: $10,000–$500
Applications: Initial approach should be by letter

Booth Ferris Foundation
See entry in Interfaith

Brencanda Foundation
358 Fifth Avenue, Suite 1103
New York, NY 10001
(212) 736-2727
Contact: Peter S. Robinson, Executive Vice-President or Suzanne E.
Elsesser, Program Officer
Geographic Giving Pattern: National
Special Interest: Emphasis on Roman Catholic organizations and
service agencies
Assets: $1,060,547 (Gifts received: $1,825,000)
Grant Range: $149,288–$1,200 (Grant average: $5,000–$20,000)
Limitations: No support for schools, universities or stewardship. No
grants to individuals, or for scholarships, endowments or large
capital campaigns. No grants awarded outside of the U.S.
Applications: Initial approach should be by letter. Grant proposals
should be submitted by the following deadlines: January 15, April 15,
July 15 or October 15.

The Robert Brunner Foundation
c/o Capromont, Ltd.
63 Wall Street, Suite 1903
New York, NY 10005
(212) 344-0050
Geographic Giving Pattern: U.S. and Belgium
Special Interest: Catholic institutions; principally for educational and
religious organizations founded by the donor
Assets: $5,185,597
Grant Range: $128,000–$4,000
Limitations: No grants to individuals or for building funds or
endowment funds
Applications: Initial approach should be by letter

Sophia & William Casey Foundation
c/o Steven T. Rosenberg
201 Moreland Road, Suite 10
Hauppauge, NY 11788
Contact: Sophia Casey, President and Treasurer
Special Interest: A home for unwed mothers, Catholic organizations
and international affairs
Assets: $562,243

Grant Range: $50,000–$500
Limitations: No grants to individuals
Applications: Initial approach should be by letter

Coles Family Foundation
c/o Goldman, Sachs & Co.
85 Broad Street
New York, NY 10004
Contact: Michael H. Coles, President
Geographic Giving Pattern: New York
Special Interest: Catholic giving, child welfare, higher and other education, cultural programs and foreign policy
Assets: $2,470,927
Grant Range: $33,300–$25
Limitations: No grants to individuals
Applications: Applications are not accepted

Constans Culver Foundation
See entry in Interfaith

Doty Family Foundation
Goldman Sachs & Co.
85 Broad Street, Tax Department
New York, NY 10004
Contact: George E. Doty, President
Geographic Giving Pattern: Primarily New York, New York and Baltimore, Maryland
Special Interest: Primarily Catholic giving, including churches and educational organizations
Assets: $11,181,771
Grant Range: $500,000–$150
Limitations: No grants to individuals
Applications: Priority is given to charities in which Doty family members are actively involved. Applications are not accepted.

The Caleb C. and Julia W. Dula Educational and Charitable Foundation
See entry in Interfaith

Blanche T. Enders Charitable Trust
c/o Chemical Bank, Administration Service Department
30 Rockefeller Plaza
New York, NY 10112
(212) 621-2143

Contact: Barbara Strohmeier, Trust Officer, Chemical Bank
Geographic Giving Pattern: New York
Special Interest: Child welfare, social services, Catholic religious and welfare institutions, education, animal welfare, health associations and hospitals
Assets: $2,418,280
Grant Range: $15,000–$2,500
Limitations: No grants to individuals
Applications: There are no deadlines for grant proposal letters

The Catherine and Henry J. Gaisman Foundation

P.O. Box 277
Hartsdale, NY 10530-0277
Contact: Catherine V. Gaisman, President
Geographic Giving Pattern: Primarily New York
Special Interest: Hospitals and Catholic church support
Assets: $7,119,411
Grant Range: $150,000–$50
Limitations: No grants to individuals
Applications: Contributes to pre-selected organizations only. Applications not accepted.

The Goodman Family Foundation

See entry in Interfaith

William Randolph Hearst Foundation

See entry in Interfaith

Homeland Foundation, Inc.

c/o Kelley, Drye & Warren
101 Park Avenue
New York, NY 10178
(212) 808-7800
Contact: E. Lisk Wyckoff, Chair and Treasurer
Geographic Giving Pattern: International and national
Special Interest: Roman Catholic church support, including welfare organizations in the U.S. and abroad, and educational institutions
Assets: $487,805 (Gifts received: $310,000)
Grant Range: $274,886–$500
Limitations: No grants to individuals
Applications: Initial approach should be by letter. There are no deadlines.

Josephine Lawrence Hopkins Foundation
61 Broadway, Suite 2912
New York, NY 10006
Contact: Ivan Obolensky, President-Treasurer
Geographic Giving Pattern: Primarily New York
Special Interest: Emphasis on hospitals and medical research, Roman
Catholic church support, animal welfare, youth agencies, and
cultural programs
Assets: $3,499,394
Grant Range: $25,000–$1,000
Limitations: No grants to individuals. No loans.
Applications: Contributes to pre-selected organizations only.
Applications not accepted.

Hugoton Foundation
900 Park Avenue
New York, NY 10021
(212) 734-5447
Contact: Joan K. Stout, President
Geographic Giving Pattern: Primarily New York, New York and
Miami, Florida
Special Interest: Hospitals, medical research, education and some
church support
Assets: $26,920,568
Grant Range: $300,000–$1,000 (Grant average: $5,000–$25,000)
Applications: Initial approach should be by written proposal. There
are no deadlines.

The John M. and Mary A. Joyce Foundation
Seven Forest Circle
New Rochelle, NY 10804
Contact: Catherine P. Joyce, President and Treasurer
Geographic Giving Pattern: Primarily New York
Special Interest: Church support, education, hospitals and social
services
Assets: $4,586,679
Grant Range: $50,000–$1,000
Limitations: No grants to individuals
Applications: Contributes to pre-selected organizations only.
Applications not accepted.

James T. Lee Foundation, Inc.
P.O. Box 1856
New York, NY 10185

Contact: Raymond T. O'Keefe, President
Geographic Giving Pattern: New York
Special Interest: Higher and medical education, hospitals, religious associations and child welfare
Assets: $4,169,880
Grant Range: $25,000–$5,000
Limitations: No grants to individuals or for operating budgets, seed money, capital or endowment funds, publications or conferences. No loans.
Applications: Contributes to pre-selected organizations only. Applications not accepted.

The Henry Luce Foundation, Inc.
See entry in Interfaith

The Charles A. Mastronardi Charitable Foundation
c/o Morgan Guaranty Trust Co. of New York
Nine West 57th Street
New York, NY 10019
Contact: Alfred C. Turino, Executive Vice-President
Geographic Giving Pattern: Primarily New York and Florida
Special Interest: Higher education, child welfare, hospitals and Roman Catholic church support
Assets: $8,130,964
Grant Range: $60,000–$100
Limitations: No grants to individuals
Applications: Initial approach should be by letter or proposal sent to the following address: 14 Vanderenter Avenue, Port Washington, NY 10050 Tel. (516) 883-4600

The McCaddin-McQuirk Foundation, Inc.
1002 Madison Avenue
New York, NY 10021
(212) 772-9090
Contact: Robert W. Dumser, President
Geographic Giving Pattern: International
Special Interest: To foster educational opportunities for poorer students to be priests or lay teachers of the Roman Catholic Church throughout the world
Assets: $1,649,599
Grant Range: $6,000–$600
Applications: Initial approach should be by letter. Applications must be made through a bishop, rector or head of a seminary. The deadline is December 1.

James J. McCann Charitable Trust and McCann Foundation, Inc.
See entry in Interfaith

The McCarthy Charities, Inc.
P.O. Box 576
Troy, NY 12181
Contact: Peter F. McCarthy, President
Geographic Giving Pattern: Primarily the Albany Capital District, New York area
Special Interest: Roman Catholic church support and church-related education and welfare agencies. Support also for community funds, social service agencies and hospitals.
Assets: $5,104,499
Grant Range: $25,000–$100
Applications: Contributes to pre-selected organizations only. Applications not accepted.

The Michael W. McCarthy Foundation
World Financial Center, South Tower
New York, NY 10080
Contact: Michael W. McCarthy, Trustee
Special Interest: Higher education, Roman Catholic church support and religious associations
Assets: $2,269,802
Grant Range: $98,366–$225
Applications: Contributes to pre-selected organizations only. Applications not accepted.

Morania Foundation, Inc.
c/o Morgan Guaranty Trust Co.
Nine West 57th Street
New York, NY 10019
(212) 826-7190
Contact: William J. McCormack, President
Geographic Giving Pattern: International
Special Interest: Roman Catholic church-related institutions, foreign missions and welfare funds
Assets: $6,630,137
Grant Range: $150,000–$1,000
Applications: Initial approach should be by proposal. There are no deadlines.

J. Malcolm Mossman Charitable Trust
c/o Chemical Bank
30 Rockefeller Plaza
New York, NY 10112
(212) 621-2148
Contact: Barbara Strohmeier, Trust Officer, Chemical Bank
Geographic Giving Pattern: New York
Special Interest: Social service and youth agencies, education, cultural programs, health and church support with emphasis on Roman Catholic organizations
Assets: $404,966
Grant Range: $10,000–$300
Limitations: No grants to individuals
Applications: There are no deadlines for grant proposal letters

Jonathan & Shirley O'Herron Foundation
c/o Lazard Freres & Co.
One Rockefeller Plaza
New York, NY 10020-1902
Contact: Jonathan O'Herron, President
Geographic Giving Pattern: Primarily Massachusetts, Connecticut, Vermont and New York
Special Interest: Catholic churches, education, hospitals and social services
Assets: $217,280
Grant Range: $112,000–$500
Limitations: No grants to individuals
Applications: Initial approach should be by letter describing organization and its activities. There are no deadlines.

Cyril F. and Marie E. O'Neil Foundation
c/o Richards, O'Neil & Allegaert
885 Third Avenue
New York, NY 10022
(212) 207-1200
Contact: Ralph O'Neil, President
Geographic Giving Pattern: Primarily New York and Ohio
Special Interest: Higher and secondary education and Catholic church support
Assets: $4,057,187
Grant Range: $250,000–$200
Applications: Initial approach should be by letter. There are no deadlines.

The O'Sullivan Children Foundation, Inc.
355 Post Avenue
Westbury, NY 11590
(516) 334-3209
Contact: Kevin P. O'Sullivan, President
Special Interest: Catholic organizations including churches, hospitals and health associations
Assets: $5,699,900
Grant Total: $461,965
Limitations: No grants to individuals
Applications: Contributes to pre-selected organizations only. Applications not accepted.

The Vincent and Harriet Palisano Foundation
135 Huntley Road
Buffalo, NY 14215
Contact: V.M. DiAngelo
Geographic Giving Pattern: Primarily Buffalo, New York
Special Interest: Higher and secondary education (including scholarships) and Roman Catholic associations
Assets: $3,579,567
Grant Range: $50,000–$1,500
Applications: Initial approach should be by letter

The Pope Foundation
211 West 56th Street, Suite 5-E
New York, NY 10019
(212) 765-4156
Contact: Fortune Pope, Vice-President
Geographic Giving Pattern: New York City metropolitan area and Westchester County
Special Interest: Roman Catholic church support, religious associations and welfare funds, higher and secondary education and hospitals
Assets: $22,376,153
Grant Range: $201,490–$250 (Grant average: $1,000–$50,000)
Applications: Initial approach should be by letter

May Ellen and Gerald Ritter Foundation
9411 Shore Road
Brooklyn, NY 11209
Contact: Emma A. Daniels, President
Special Interest: Health agencies and Roman Catholic welfare funds
Assets: $6,928,292

Grant Range: $111,000–$50
Limitations: No grants to individuals
Applications: Initial approach should be by letter and proposal. There are no deadlines.

Santa Maria Foundation, Inc.
43 West 42nd Street
New York, NY 10036
Contact: Patrick P. Grace, Secretary
Geographic Giving Pattern: New York
Special Interest: Higher education and Roman Catholic religious organizations
Assets: $2,317,577
Grant Range: $25,000–$25
Applications: Contributes to pre-selected organizations only. Applications not accepted.

Elias Sayour Foundation, Inc.
185 Madison Avenue
New York, NY 10016-5102
(212) 686-7560
Contact: Jeanette Sayour, President
Special Interest: Roman Catholic church support, welfare funds, religious organizations and hospitals
Assets: $1,141,577
Grant Range: $7,500–$50
Applications: Initial approach should be by letter to contact at the following address: 17 Harbor Lane, Brooklyn, NY 11209 Tel. (718) 680-8378. There are no deadlines.

The Mary Jane & William J. Voute Foundation, Inc.
31 Masterton Road
Bronxville, NY 10708
Contact: William J. Voute, President and Treasurer
Geographic Giving Pattern: Primarily the New York, New York area including Westchester County
Special Interest: Catholic church support and higher education; also health and social services
Assets: $5,373 (Gifts received: $312,250)
Grant Range: $30,000–$10
Applications: Contributes to pre-selected organizations only. Applications not accepted.

The Wikstrom Foundation
c/o Norstar Trust Co.
One East Avenue
Rochester, NY 14638
(315) 424-7707
Contact: Robert J. Hughes, Norstar Trust Co.
Geographic Giving Pattern: New York and Florida
Special Interest: Cultural programs, higher education, programs for the elderly and Roman Catholic organizations, including church support
Assets: $1,703,304
Grant Average: $1,000–$20,000
Limitations: No grants to individuals. No loans.
Applications: Contributes to pre-selected organizations only. Applications not accepted.

North Carolina

The Blumenthal Foundation
See entry in Interfaith

Ohio

TheBentz Foundation
P.O. Box 18191
Columbus, OH 43218-0191
Contact: Robert T. Cull, President
Special Interest: Grants and loans primarily for Roman Catholic church support and missionary programs
Assets: $2,696,286
Grant Range: $50,000–$2,000
Limitations: No grants to individuals
Applications: Initial approach should be by letter sent to the following address: 580 South High Street, Columbus, OH 43215 Tel. (614) 221-5287. There are no deadlines.

Christopher Foundation
100 Center Street
Chardon, OH 44024
(216) 285-2242
Contact: Paul J. Dolan, Secretary
Geographic Giving Pattern: Primarily Ohio
Special Interest: Catholic organizations and churches and education

Assets: $620,979
Grant Range: $14,500–$500
Limitations: No grants to individuals
Applications: There are no deadlines for grant proposals

Clyde T. & Lyla C. Foster Foundation
c/o National City Bank
P.O. Box 5756
Cleveland, OH 44101
(216) 575-2748
Contact: Marianne Hobe
Special Interest: Catholic welfare, community projects and social services
Assets: $1,226,187
Grant Range: $50,000–$250
Applications: There are no deadlines for grant proposals

Homan Foundation
6529 Willowhollow Lane
Cincinnati, OH 45243
(606) 341-6450
Contact: John T. Collopy, Trustee
Geographic Giving Pattern: Primarily Cincinnati, Ohio
Special Interest: Roman Catholic schools and churches, other private schools, social services and hospitals
Assets: $1,338,228
Grant Range: $15,000–$50
Limitations: No grants to individuals
Applications: Initial approach should be by proposal. The deadline is November 15. The application address is as follows: P.O. Box 17350, Edgewood, KY 41017.

The Kuntz Foundation
120 West Second Street
Dayton, OH 45402
(513) 461-3870
Contact: Peter H. Kuntz, President
Geographic Giving Pattern: Primarily Ohio
Special Interest: Higher education, hospitals, Catholic church support, community funds and youth agencies
Assets: $2,572,306
Grant Range: $25,000–$100
Limitations: No grants to individuals
Applications: Initial approach should be by letter

Fred A. Lennon Foundation
29500 Solon Road
Solon, OH 44139
(216) 248-4600
Contact: John F. Fant, Assistant Secretary
Geographic Giving Pattern: Primarily Ohio
Special Interest: Higher education and Roman Catholic church support. Grants also for public policy, hospitals, cultural programs, social services and community funds.
Assets: $8,951,087 (Gifts received: $800,000)
Grant Range: $401,800–$100 (Grant average: $100–$100,000)
Applications: Initial approach should be by grant proposal. There are no deadlines.

Marian Foundation
260 Reeb Avenue
Columbus, OH 43207-1988
Contact: William Hubber, President
Geographic Giving Pattern: Primarily Columbus, Ohio
Special Interest: Catholic welfare and youth organizations
Assets: $1,002,414
Grant Range: $5,000–$600
Applications: Initial approach should be by proposal. The deadline is March 1.

The Murphy Family Foundation
See entry in Interfaith

The M.G. O'Neil Foundation
c/o Gencorp
175 Ghent Road
Akron, OH 44313
(216) 869-4412
Contact: M.G. O'Neil, President
Geographic Giving Pattern: Primarily Ohio
Special Interest: Roman Catholic organizations; some support for a community fund and social service agencies
Assets: $4,648,889
Grant Range: $11,000–$100
Limitations: No grants for conferences, seminars or special projects
Applications: There are no deadlines for grant proposals

The O'Neill Brothers Foundation
3550 Lander Road
Cleveland, OH 44122
(216) 464-2121
Contact: Robert K. Healey, President
Geographic Giving Pattern: The Cleveland, Ohio metropolitan area
Special Interest: Roman Catholic religious organizations and church support, health organizations and higher and secondary education
Assets: $635,476
Grant Range: $10,750–$25
Applications: There are no deadlines for grant proposals

Van Dorn Foundation
See entry in Interfaith

The I.J. Van Huffel Foundation
See entry in Interfaith

Oklahoma

Brown Foundation
1707 Elmhurst
Oklahoma City, OK 73120
Contact: William C. Brown or Carolyn M. Brown, Trustees
Special Interest: Catholic organizations, health associations and groups fighting hunger
Grant Total: $146,325
Grant Range: $21,000–$1,000
Applications: Contributes to pre-selected organizations only. Applications not accepted.

Warren Charite
P.O. Box 470372
Tulsa, OK 74147-0372
Contact: William K. Warren, President
Geographic Giving Pattern: Primarily Oklahoma
Special Interest: Cancer research, a hospital and some support for health associations and religion
Assets: $5,456,518
Grant Range: $50,000–$150
Applications: Initial approach should be by letter

Oregon

Clark Foundation
255 S.W. Harrison Street, GA 2
Portland, OR 97201
(503) 223-5290
Contact: Jean Ameele
Geographic Giving Pattern: Portland, Oregon
Special Interest: Emphasis on building funds for higher education and for churches and religious associations; grants also for cultural programs, youth agencies, secondary education, the environment and medical care
Assets: $66,691 (Gifts received: $551,750)
Grant Total: $492,982
Limitations: No grants to individuals or for endowment funds or research. No matching gifts and no loans.
Applications: Send letter and copy of appraisal to contact at above address. There are no deadlines.

A.J. Frank Family Foundation
P.O. Drawer 79
Mill City, OR 97360
(503) 897-2371
Contact: Douglas Highberger
Geographic Giving Pattern: Oregon
Special Interest: Roman Catholic church support and welfare funds, and secondary education
Assets: $3,244,878 (Gifts received: $856,400)
Grant Range: $10,000–$500
Limitations: No grants to individuals
Applications: Initial approach should be by letter. Deadlines are August 15 and December 15.

Maybelle Clark Macdonald Fund
405 N.W. 18th Avenue
Portland, OR 97209
Contact: Maybelle Clark Macdonald, President
Geographic Giving Pattern: Primarily Oregon
Special Interest: Local cultural programs and Roman Catholic church support
Assets: $287,550 (Gifts received: $102,212)
Grant Range: $20,000–$25

Applications: There are no deadlines for grant proposal letters. The application address is as follows: 5270-7 S.W. Landing Square Drive, Portland, OR 97201.

Pennsylvania

Bozzone Family Foundation
101 Bayberry Drive
New Kensington, PA 15068-6701
(412) 224-6776
Contact: Robert P. Bozzone, Trustee
Geographic Giving Pattern: Pennsylvania
Special Interest: Catholic organizations including churches and welfare programs
Assets: $1,814,830
Grant Range: $10,000–$500
Applications: Contributes to pre-selected organizations only. Applications not accepted.

Connelly Foundation
9300 Ashton Road
Philadelphia, PA 19136
(215) 698-5203
Contact: Josephine C. Mandeville, Vice-President
Geographic Giving Pattern: Primarily Philadelphia, Pennsylvania
Special Interest: Higher education, Christian religious institutions, including churches, schools, colleges and welfare programs, hospitals and social services
Assets: $196,355,181
Grant Range: $1,151,210–$100 (Grant average: $100–$5,000)
Limitations: No grants to individuals or for endowment funds or research. No loans.
Applications: Initial approach should be by letter. Grant proposals should be submitted preferably in the early part of the year.

The Crossroads Foundation
1082 Bower Hill Road, Suite 1
Pittsburgh, PA 15243
Contact: Edward M. Ryan, President
Geographic Giving Pattern: Primarily Pittsburgh, Pennsylvania
Special Interest: Catholic churches and welfare organizations
Assets: $202,972 (Gifts received: $100,000)
Grant Range: $98,525–$1,000

Limitations: No grants to individuals
Applications: Contributes to pre-selected organizations only. Applications not accepted.

Donahue Family Foundation, Inc.
Suite 718
Bigelow Corporate Center
Bigelow Square
Pittsburgh, PA 15219-1945
(412) 471-6420
Contact: William J. Donahue, Executive Vice-President
Geographical Giving Pattern: Southwestern Pennsylvania
Special Interest: Education, Catholic schools
Assets: $1,000,000
Limitations: No stated limits
Applications: Contributes to pre-selected organizations only. Applications not accepted.

Mary J. Donnelly Foundation
2510 Centre City Tower
Pittsburgh, PA 15222
(412) 471-5828
Contact: Thomas J. Donnelly, Trustee
Geographic Giving Pattern: Primarily Pennsylvania
Special Interest: Roman Catholic educational, welfare and religious organizations
Assets: $2,540,693
Grant Range: $100,000–$1,000 (Grant average: $10,170)
Limitations: No grants to individuals or for endowment funds. No matching gifts and no loans.
Applications: Initial approach should be by letter. There are no deadlines. Three copies of grant proposal are requested.

T. J. Kavanagh Foundation, Inc.
57 Northwood Road
Newtown Square, PA 19073-4322
(215) 356-0743
Contact: Brenda S. Brooks, C.E.O.
Geographic Giving Pattern: Primarily Pennsylvania
Special Interest: At least 55 percent of funding for Catholic church support, welfare and religious associations; support also for education including religious schools
Assets: $6,457,692

Grant Range: $10,000–$300
Limitations: No grants outside of the U.S., including Catholic organizations with missions overseas. No grants to individuals or for endowment funds, seed money, deficit financing, land acquisition, publications or scholarships. No matching gifts or loans.
Applications: Grant proposals should be submitted preferably by the end of February, July or October. The applications address is as follows: P.O. Box 609, Broomall, PA 19008.

Kate M. Kelley Foundation
c/o Hosack, Specht, Muetzel & Wood
305 Mt. Lebanon Boulevard
Pittsburgh, PA 15234
(412) 661-0134
Contact: Edward C. Ifft, Trustee
Geographic Giving Pattern: Primarily Pittsburgh, Pennsylvania
Special Interest: Roman Catholic church support and church-related education; some support for health education
Assets: $4,434,826
Grant Range: $10,000–$1,000
Applications: There are no deadlines. Proposal letter should be sent to the following address: 341 West Penn Place, Pittsburgh, PA 15224

Massey Charitable Trust
See entry in Interfaith

John McShain Charities, Inc.
540 North Seventeenth Street
Philadelphia, PA 19130
(215) 564-2322
Contact: John McShain, Foundation Director
Geographic Giving Pattern: Philadelphia, Pennsylvania
Special Interest: Higher and secondary education, Roman Catholic church support, social welfare and cultural programs
Assets: $47,775,889
Grant Range: $300,000–$10 (Grant average: $1,000–$50,000)
Limitations: No grants to individuals
Applications: Initial approach should be by letter. There are no deadlines.

The Pew Charitable Trusts
See entry in Interfaith

St. Marys Catholic Foundation
1935 State Street
St. Marys, PA 15857
(814) 781-1591
Contact: Richard J. Reuscher, Secretary-Treasurer
Geographic Giving Pattern: Primarily Erie Diocese, Pennsylvania with emphasis on the St. Marys area
Special Interest: Roman Catholic schools–all levels, and religious associations
Assets: $3,585,790 (Gifts received: $706,228)
Grant Range: $216,360–$400 (Grant average: $25,000)
Limitations: No grants to individuals or for endowment funds, scholarships or fellowships. No loans.
Applications: Contributes to pre-selected organizations only. Applications not accepted.

Texas

Abell-Hanger Foundation
See entry in Interfaith

The Burkitt Foundation
5847 San Felipe, Suite 4290
Houston, TX 77057
(713) 780-7638
Contact: Cornelius O. Ryan, President
Geographic Giving Pattern: Primarily southwestern U.S., with emphasis on Texas, New Mexico, Arizona and Louisiana
Special Interest: Private higher and secondary education, churches and religious organizations, social services with emphasis on Roman Catholic-sponsored programs
Assets: $8,854,492
Grant Range: $10,000–600 (Grant average: $2,000–$5,000)
Limitations: No grants to individuals. No support for deficit financing. No loans.
Applications: Initial approach should be by letter. Deadlines are February 15 and August 15.

Harry S. and Isabel C. Cameron Foundation
P.O. Box 2555
Houston, TX 77252-2555
(713) 652-6230
Contact: Carl W. Schumacher or Sally Braddy

Geographic Giving Pattern: Primarily Texas, especially Houston
Special Interest: Education, Roman Catholic church support, health, social services and youth agencies
Assets: $14,443,733
Grant Range: $100,000–$500 (Grant average: $100–$10,000)
Limitations: No grants to individuals or for operating support or endowment funds. No loans or matching gifts.
Applications: Initial approach should be by letter. Six copies of grant proposal are required prior to board meeting dates, which fall in April, August and December.

The James R. Dougherty, Jr., Foundation

P.O. Box 640
Beeville, TX 78104-0640
(512) 358-3560
Contact: Hugh Grove, Assistant Secretary
Geographic Giving Pattern: Texas
Special Interest: Roman Catholic church-related institutions, education, cultural programs and general charitable purposes
Assets: $8,009,748
Grant Range: $10,000–$310
Limitations: No grants to individuals. No loans.
Applications: Proposal should be sent ten days prior to board meeting. The board meets semiannually.

The John G. and Marie Stella Kenedy Memorial Foundation

1700 First City Tower II
Corpus Christi, TX 78478
(512) 887-6565
Contact: James R. McCown, General Manager
Geographic Giving Pattern: Limited to Texas
Special Interest: Ninety percent of grants issued are restricted to sectarian, primarily Roman Catholic, activities. Some support for education, arts, humanities, social services, youth and health.
Assets: $130,532,639
Grant Range: $626,500–$131 (Grant average: $5,000–$60,000)
Limitations: No grants to individuals or for operating budgets, annual fund drives, deficit financing, endowment or general funds or requests over $500,000.
Applications: An application form is required. Deadlines are January 15, April 15, July 15 and October 15.

Strake Foundation

712 Main Street, Suite 3300
Houston, TX 77002-3210
(713) 546-2400
Contact: George W. Strake, President
Geographic Giving Pattern: Primarily Texas, especially Houston
Special Interest: Roman Catholic-affiliated associations, including hospitals and educational institutions
Assets: $23,230,017
Grant Range: $100,000–$500 (Religious grant average: $1,000–$15,000)
Limitations: No grants outside of the U.S. No support for elementary schools. No grants to individuals or for deficit financing, consulting services, technical assistance or publications. No loans.
Applications: Initial approach should be by brief written proposal. The deadline is one month prior to board meetings which fall in May or June and November or December.

Virginia

Washington Forrest Foundation
See entry in Interfaith

Washington

Geneva Foundation

1250 22nd Avenue East
Seattle, WA 98112
Contact: Genevieve Albers, Trustee
Special Interest: Catholic churches and organizations, education and social services
Assets: $2,095,282
Grant Range: $30,000–$79
Limitations: No grants to individuals
Applications: Contributes to pre-selected organizations only. Applications not accepted.

The Norcliffe Fund

First Interstate Center
999 Third Avenue, Suite 1006
Seattle, WA 98104
(206) 682-4820
Contact: Theiline P. Scheumann, President

Geographic Giving Pattern: Pacific Northwest, especially Seattle,
Washington; some national and California grants
Special Interest: Cultural programs, Roman Catholic church support
and religious associations, hospitals, education and historic
preservation
Assets: $18,648,096 (Gifts received: $360,225)
Grant Range: $125,000–$25
Limitations: No grants to individuals or for deficit financing,
scholarships or fellowships. No matching gifts and no loans.
Applications: Initial approach should be by letter and grant proposal.
There are no deadlines.

Frost and Margaret Snyder Foundation
c/o Puget Sound National Bank, Trust Department
P.O. Box 11500 MS 8267
Tacoma, WA 98411-5052
(206) 593-3832
Contact: John A. Cunningham, Trust Officer, Puget Sound National
Bank
Geographic Giving Pattern: Washington
Special Interest: Roman Catholic educational and religious
associations only
Assets: $7,362,868
Grant Range: $50,000–$5,000
Limitations: No grants to individuals
Applications: Contributes to pre-selected organizations only.
Applications not accepted.

West Virginia

Sarita Kenedy East Foundation, Inc.
Suite 1300, Charleston National Plaza
P.O. Box 3969
Charleston, WV 25335
Contact: Frank Vest
Special Interest: Roman Catholic organizations
Assets: $14,776,988
Grant Range: $200,000–$100
Limitations: No grants to individuals
Applications: Contributes to pre-selected organizations only.
Applications not accepted.

Wisconsin

Carrie Foundation
One East Milwaukee Street
Janesville, WI 53545
(608) 756-4141
Contact: George K. Steil, Trustee
Special Interest: Higher education, Catholic institutions and cultural programs
Assets: $164,665
Grant Range: $60,000–$100
Limitations: No grants to individuals
Applications: There are no deadlines for grant proposal letters

William J. Cronin Foundation
c/o Management Operations, Inc.
P.O. Box 939
Janesville, WI 53547
(608) 756-3151
Contact: James P. McGuire, Trustee
Geographic Giving Pattern: Limited to Janesville, Wisconsin
Special Interest: Catholic churches and schools, social service agencies and recreation programs
Assets: $1,429,703
Grant Range: $8,100–$1,000
Limitations: No stated limitations
Applications: Initial approach should be by letter. November 1 is the deadline.

Patrick and Anna M. Cudahy Fund
See entry in Interfaith

DeRance, Inc.
7700 West Blue Mound Road
Milwaukee, WI 53213
(414) 475-7700
Contact: Paula John, Executive Vice-President
Geographic Giving Pattern: National and international
Special Interest: Roman Catholic church support, religious associations, missionary work and welfare funds in the U.S. and abroad. Support also for higher education and social development programs.
Assets: $75,060,479
Grant Range: $62,000–$10

Limitations: No grants to individuals or for endowment funds. No loans.
Applications: All U.S. organizations applying for grant aid must be listed in the *Official Catholic Directory* or submit a copy of their qualifying letter from the I.R.S. determining their tax-exempt status. Initial approach should be by proposal. There are no deadlines.

Ray and Marie Goldbach Foundation, Ltd.
c/o Marathon Cheese Corporation
304 East Street
Marathon, WI 54448
(715) 443-2211
Contact: Raymond and Marie Goldbach
Geographic Giving Pattern: Primarily Wisconsin
Special Interest: Catholic relief, churches and secondary education
Assets: $2,427,533
Grant Range: $37,000–$25
Limitations: No grants to individuals
Applications: Contributes to pre-selected organizations only. Applications not accepted.

Rose A. Monaghan Charitable Trust
2401 North Mayfair Road
Milwaukee, WI 53226
(414) 771-6450
Contact: Walter F. Schmidt
Geographic Giving Pattern: Primarily Milwaukee, Wisconsin
Special Interest: Catholic giving, welfare and religious and secondary education
Assets: $2,259,834
Grant Range: $65,000–$1,000
Limitations: No grants to individuals
Applications: Contributes to pre-selected organizations only. Applications not accepted.

U.S. Oil/Schmidt Family Foundation, Inc.
425 S. Washington Street
P.O. Box 25
Combined Locks, WI 54113
(414) 735-8267
Contact: Raymond Schmidt
Geographic Giving Pattern: Primarily Wisconsin

Special Interest: Catholic organizations and churches, also community funds, education and hospitals
Assets: $1,800,118
Grant Range: $100,000–$100
Limitations: No grants to individuals
Applications: Contributes to pre-selected organizations only. Applications are not accepted.

JEWISH FOUNDATIONS

Alabama

Fig Tree Foundation
144 Mountain Brook Park Drive
Birmingham, AL 35223
Contact: Jo Ann Myers, President
Geographic Giving Pattern: Primarily Birmingham, Alabama
Special Interest: Jewish organizations, including welfare funds
Assets: $4,283,038
Grant Range: $80,000–$18
Applications: Initial approach should be by letter. There are no deadlines.

Ronne & Donald Hess Charitable Foundation
2936 Southwood Road
Birmingham, AL 35223
Contact: Ronne Hess, President
Geographic Giving Pattern: Primarily Alabama
Special Interest: Jewish organizations, social services and performing arts groups
Assets: $3,968,628
Grant Range: $258,500–$200
Applications: Initial approach should be by letter. There are no deadlines.

California

The Ahmanson Foundation
See entry in Interfaith

Maurice Amado Foundation
3600 Wilshire Boulevard, Suite 1228
Los Angeles, CA 90020
(213) 381-3622
Contact: Aaron Oliver
Special Interest: Sephardic Jewish organizations
Assets: $17,425,794
Grant Range: $203,745–$500
Applications: Initial approach should be by letter. There are no deadlines.

Columbia Savings Charitable Foundation

8840 Wilshire Boulevard
Beverly Hills, CA 90211
Contact: Hillel S. Aronson, Vice-President
Special Interest: Jewish organizations; also higher education and
medical research
Assets: $14,988,692 (Gifts received: $7,145,000)
Grant Range: $145,000–$1,000
Applications: Initial approach should be by letter

Ben B. and Joyce E. Eisenberg Foundation

11999 San Vincente Boulevard, Suite 300
Los Angeles, CA 90049
(213) 471-4220
Contact: David J. Cohen, Vice-President
Geographic Giving Pattern: U.S. and Israel
Special Interest: Primarily Jewish welfare and Jewish giving; some
support for civic affairs and medical research
Assets: $11,450,372
Grant Range: $130,926–$25
Applications: Applications are not accepted

Isadore and Sunny Familian Family Foundation

906 Loma Vista Drive
Beverly Hills, CA 90210
(213) 272-0191
Contact: Isadore Familian, President
Geographic Giving Pattern: California
Special Interest: Jewish welfare funds and religious organizations,
higher education and cultural programs
Assets: $1,200,542 (Gifts received: $380,082)
Grant Range: $64,345–$18
Applications: Contributes to pre-selected organizations only.
Applications not accepted.

Friedman Brothers Foundation

801 East Commercial Street
Los Angeles, CA 90012
Contact: Leslie Mendelsohn, Trustee
Special Interest: Education, including religious education, and Jewish
religious and welfare organizations
Assets: $7,020,100
Grant Range: $40,000–$1,000

Applications: Initial approach should be by letter. Proposals should be sent to the following address: 184 Sherwood Place, Engelwood, NJ 07631. The deadline is October 31.

Edward & Marion Goodman Foundation
445 Bayshore Boulevard
San Francisco, CA 94124
Contact: Edward Goodman, President and Treasurer
Special Interest: Jewish giving and Jewish welfare
Assets: $3,391,121
Grant Range: $64,500–$100
Applications: Initial approach should be by letter

Allen D. Kohl Charitable Foundation, Inc.
450 North Roxbury Drive, Suite 600
Beverly Hills, CA 90210
Contact: Thomas F. Bickelhaupt, Secretary-Treasurer
Special Interest: Support for charitable causes of interest to the directors, including support for local Jewish welfare agencies
Assets: $6,078,634
Grant Range: $100,000–$100
Limitations: No grants to individuals
Applications: Contributes to pre-selected organizations only. Applications not accepted.

Hyman Levine Family Foundation
9300 Wilshire Boulevard, Suite 410
Beverly Hills, CA 90212
(213) 274-5291
Contact: Sid B. Levine, President
Special Interest: Jewish giving
Assets: $1,554,345
Grant Range: $45,680–$25
Applications: Initial approach should be by letter. There are no deadlines.

Hyman Jebb Levy Foundation
2222 South Figueroa Street
Los Angeles, CA 90007
(213) 749-9411
Contact: Hyman Levy, President and Treasurer
Geographic Giving Pattern: Primarily New York, Los Angeles, California and Israel

Special Interest: Jewish education and temple support; also social service agencies and institutions in Israel
Assets: $3,195,603
Grant Range: $20,000 –$100
Limitations: No stated limitations
Applications: Initial approach should be by letter. There are no deadlines.

Milton and Sophie Meyer Fund
c/o Wells Fargo Bank, N.A.
P.O. Box 63002
San Francisco, CA 94163
(415) 396-3895
Contact: Joseph E. Fanucci, Trust Officer, Wells Fargo Bank
Geographic Giving Pattern: Primarily San Francisco Bay area
Special Interest: Jewish charitable purposes
Assets: $3,006,972
Grant Range: $15,000–$3,500 (Grant average: $5,000–$10,000)
Limitations: No grants to individuals
Applications: Initial approach should be by letter and grant proposal. There are no deadlines.

David and Fela Shapell Foundation
9401 Wilshire Boulevard, Suite 1200
Beverly Hills, CA 90212
Contact: David Shapell, President
Geographic Giving Pattern: California, New York and Israel
Special Interest: Jewish welfare funds, temple support and religious education
Assets: $1,153,152
Grant Total: $170,250
Applications: Initial approach should be by letter

Mae and Benjamin Swig Charity Foundation
c/o The Swig Foundations
Fairmont Hotel
San Francisco, CA 94106
Contact: Nat Starr, Director
Geographic Giving Pattern: Primarily the San Francisco Bay area, California
Special Interest: Jewish welfare funds, higher and other education and the arts
Assets: $9,575,954

Grant Range: $13,500–$22
Applications: Initial approach should be by letter. There are no deadlines.

Adolph and Etta Weinberg Foundation
5355 East Airport Drive
Ontario, CA 91711
(714) 983-9766
Contact: Ray Moline, Secretary
Special Interest: Jewish religious organizations and temple support, higher education and museums
Assets: $1,366,316
Grant Range: $80,000–$45
Limitations: No grants to individuals
Applications: Two copies of grant proposals should be sent to the following address: P.O. Box 4028, Ontario, CA 91761. The deadline is June 30.

The David & Sylvia Weisz Foundation
1933 Broadway, Room 244
Los Angeles, CA 90007
Contact: Sylvia Weisz, President
Geographic Giving Pattern: Primarily California
Special Interest: Jewish welfare, cultural organizations and social services
Assets: $6,894,841
Grant Range: $200,000–$100
Applications: Initial approach should be by letter

Colorado

M.B. & Shana Glassman Foundation
3773 Cherry Creek Drive, North, No. 575
Denver, CO 80209
Contact: M.B. Glassman, President
Geographic Giving Pattern: Colorado
Special Interest: Local Jewish giving
Assets: $1,338,581
Grant Range: $40,000–$15
Applications: Initial approach should be by letter. There are no deadlines.

Connecticut

Harry E. Goldfarb Family Foundation, Inc.
c/o Blum Shapiro & Co., P.C.
231 Farmington Avenue, P.O. Box 900
Farmington, CT 06034
Contact: Harry E. Goldfarb, President
Geographic Giving Pattern: Primarily Connecticut
Special Interest: Jewish organizations, especially welfare funds; also education
Assets: $1,305,094 (Gifts received: $500,000)
Grant Range: $50,000–$25
Limitations: No grants to individuals
Applications: Contributes to pre-selected organizations only. Applications not accepted.

The Morris M. and Helen F. Messing Foundation
160 Wampus Lane
Milford, CT 06460
Contact: The Trustees
Special Interest: Jewish welfare funds, temple support, medical research and higher education
Assets: $1,971,155
Grant Range: $30,000–$500
Applications: Contributes to pre-selected organizations only. Applications are not accepted.

Delaware

Milton and Hattie Kutz Foundation
101 Garden of Eden Road
Wilmington, DE 19803
(302) 478-6200
Contact: Robert N. Kerbel, Executive Secretary
Geographic Giving Pattern: Primarily Delaware
Special Interest: Jewish social service organizations. Grants also for child welfare, social services and higher education including scholarships.
Assets: $2,329,682
Grant Total: $92,250, organizations; $44,500, individuals
Applications: Initial approach should be by letter

District of Columbia

Leo M. Bernstein Family Foundation
600 New Hampshire Avenue, N.W., Suite 1155
Washington, DC 20037
Contact: Leo M. Bernstein, President
Geographic Giving Pattern: Primarily the District of Columbia and
Strasburg, Virginia
Special Interest: Jewish religious, welfare and educational institutions
Assets: $1,178,360
Grant Range: $15,000–$50
Limitations: No stated limitations other than geographical
Applications: Initial approach should be by letter

Samuel R. Dweck Foundation
1730 M Street, Suite 907, N.W.
Washington, DC 20036
Contact: Ralph Dweck, Director
Geographic Giving Pattern: National
Special Interest: Primarily Jewish welfare funds
Assets: $4,535,970 (Gifts received: $236,500)
Grant Range: $54,224–$100
Applications: There are no deadlines for grant proposals

The Isadore and Bertha Gudelsky Family Foundation, Inc.
1503 21st Street, N.W.
Washington, DC 20036
(202) 328-0500
Contact: Philip N. Margolius, Secretary-Treasurer
Geographic Giving Pattern: The District of Columbia
Special Interest: Jewish welfare funds and temple support. Grants also
for education, hospitals and youth agencies.
Assets: $10,647,605
Grant Range: $400,000–$1,150
Limitations: No grants to individuals
Applications: Initial approach should be by letter. There are no
deadlines.

Charles I. & Mary Kaplan Foundation
1000 Connecticut Avenue, N.W., Suite 1110
Washington, DC 20036-5392
(202) 223-4636
Contact: Edward H. Kaplan, Secretary-Treasurer

Geographic Giving Pattern: Primarily the District of Columbia
Special Interest: Jewish organizations
Assets: $1,725,663 (Gifts received: $291,667)
Grant Range: $100,000–$1,000
Applications: Initial approach should be by letter

Thomas and Frances McGregor Foundation
See entry in Interfaith

Florida

The Applebaum Foundation, Inc.
11111 Biscayne Boulevard, Suite 883
North Miami, FL 33181
Contact: Leila Applebaum, President
Special Interest: Higher education, hospitals, medical research, Jewish welfare agencies, religious schools and temple support
Assets: $8,433,549
Grant Range: $195,000–$25
Limitations: No stated limitations
Applications: Initial approach should be by letter

Samuel Blank and Family Foundation
8940 N.W. 24th Terrace
Miami, FL 33172
Contact: R.J. Puck
Geographic Giving Pattern: Florida
Special Interest: Jewish welfare funds, hospitals, higher education and temple support
Assets: $5,759,822
Grant Range: $75,000–$50
Applications: There are no deadlines for grant proposals

The Leonard and Sophie Davis Foundation, Inc.
601 Clearwater Park Road
West Palm Beach, FL 33401
(407) 832-6466
Contact: Marilyn Hoadley, President
Geographic Giving Pattern: Primarily Palm Beach County, Florida and New York, New York
Special Interest: Jewish charitable, religious and educational organizations; support also for the arts, community services, health agencies and hospitals

Assets: $19,057,160 (Gifts received: $4,153,024)
Grant Range: $350,000–$100 (Grant average: $1,000–$25,000)
Limitations: No grants to individuals
Applications: Applications are not accepted

The Joe and Emily Lowe Foundation, Inc.
249 Royal Palm Way
Palm Beach, FL 33480
(407) 655-7001
Contact: Helen G. Hauben, President
Geographic Giving Pattern: Primarily the New York, New York metropolitan area and Florida
Special Interest: Jewish welfare funds, social and religious groups, the arts, museums, higher education, hospitals and health and social services
Assets: $16,533,484
Grant Range: $100,000–$250 (Grant average: $1,000–$10,000)
Limitations: No grants to individuals or for scholarships, fellowships or prizes. No loans.
Applications: Initial approach should be by letter. There are no deadlines for grant proposals.

Posnack Family Foundation of Hollywood
c/o Barnett Banks Trust Co., N.A.
P.O. Box 40200
Jacksonville, FL 32203-0200
Geographic Giving Pattern: National
Special Interest: Jewish organizations, including welfare funds and education
Assets: $6,361,344
Grant Range: $65,000–$1,000
Applications: Initial approach should be by letter

The Norman R. Rales and Ruth Rales Foundation
4000 North Federal Highway, Number 204
Boca Raton, FL 33431
Contact: Norman R. Rales, Trustee
Geographic Giving Pattern: Primarily New York and Florida
Special Interest: Jewish welfare and religious organizations, social services and health associations
Assets: $2,360,682
Grant Range: $20,000–$300
Limitations: No grants to individuals

Applications: Contributes to pre-selected organizations only. Applications not accepted.

Robert Russell Memorial Foundation
Northern Trust Bank of Florida, N.A.
700 Brickell Avenue
Miami, FL 33131-2804
Contact: Norman H. Lipoff, Trustee
Geographic Giving Pattern: Primarily Dade County, Florida
Special Interest: Jewish welfare and higher education
Assets: $13,507,789 (Gifts received: $8,315,418)
Grant Range: $130,000–$10,000
Applications: Initial approach should be by letter sent to the following address: Greenberg, Traurig, et al., 1221 Brickell Avenue, Miami, FL 33131.

Samuel M. Soref Charitable Trust
c/o London Witte & Co.
500 Cypress Creek Road West, Suite 420
Fort Lauderdale, FL 33309
Contact: Samuel M. Soref, President and Treasurer
Geographic Giving Pattern: Florida
Special Interest: Jewish welfare funds, temple support, higher education and social service agencies; some support for organizations in Israel
Assets: $11,350,944
Grant Range: $203,500–$100
Limitations: No grants to individuals
Applications: Contributes to pre-selected organizations only. Applications not accepted.

Georgia

The Davis Foundation, Inc.
One National Drive
Atlanta, GA 30336
Contact: Alfred A. Davis, President
Geographic Giving Pattern: Primarily Atlanta, Georgia
Special Interest: Jewish welfare funds and temple support, higher education, cultural programs and health services
Assets: $111,368 (Gifts received: $475,000)
Grant Range: $401,000–$95
Applications: There are no deadlines for grant proposals

Zaban Foundation, Inc.

335 Green Glen Way
Atlanta, GA 30327
Contact: Erwin Zaban, President and Treasurer
Geographic Giving Pattern: Primarily Atlanta, Georgia
Special Interest: Jewish welfare organizations and temple support
Assets: $3,320,955 (Gifts received: $202,750)
Grant Range: $186,278–$1,000
Limitations: No grants to individuals
Applications: Contributes to pre-selected organizations only.
Applications not accepted.

Illinois

The Alvin H. Baum Family Fund

See entry in Interfaith

Geifman Family Foundation, Inc.

2239 29th Street
Rock Island, IL 61201-5025
(309) 788-9531
Contact: Morris M. Geifman, President
Geographic Giving Pattern: Primarily Illinois, with some emphasis on
Rock Island
Special Interest: Primarily for Jewish organizations and temple
support
Assets: $1,516,634
Grant Range: $25,000–$50
Applications: Initial approach should be by letter. There are no
deadlines.

Nathan Manilow Foundation

754 North Milwaukee Avenue
Chicago, IL 60622
(312) 829-3655
Contact: Lewis Manilow, President
Geographic Giving Pattern: Primarily Illinois
Special Interest: Jewish welfare funds, culture and education; also
Jewish temple support and child welfare
Assets: $4,642,778
Grant Range: $50,000–$250
Applications: Initial approach should be by letter. There are no
deadlines.

Polk Brothers Foundation, Inc.
2850 North Central
Chicago, IL 60634
(312) 287-1011
Contact: Michael A. Crane, Director
Geographic Giving Pattern: Primarily Chicago, Illinois
Special Interest: Social service agencies, Jewish welfare funds and religious organizations
Assets: $45,645,546 (Gifts received: $1,967,700)
Grant Range: $20,000–$100
Applications: Initial approach should be by letter

Pritzker Foundation
c/o Jay Parker
200 West Madison, 38th Floor
Chicago, IL 60606
(312) 621-4200
Contact: Simon Zunamon, Assistant Treasurer
Special Interest: Religious welfare funds, temple support and higher education
Assets: $5,693,979 (Gifts received: $4,645,374)
Grant Range: $474,500–$25 (Grant average: $100–$25,000)
Limitations: No grants to individuals
Applications: Contributes to pre-selected organizations only. Applications not accepted.

The Retirement Research Foundation
See entry in Interfaith

Fern Goldstein Shapiro, Morris R. Shapiro, and Charles Shapiro Foundation, Inc.
330 West Diversey Parkway, Suite 1801
Chicago, IL 60657
(312) 472-1506
Contact: Fern Goldstein Shapiro, President
Geographic Giving Pattern: Primarily Chicago, Illinois
Special Interest: Jewish welfare funds and temple support; also higher education and social services
Assets: $14,789,290
Grant Range: $246,900–$100
Limitations: No grants to individuals
Applications: Contributes to pre-selected organizations only. Applications not accepted.

Indiana

The Sol and Arlene Bronstein Foundation
c/o National City Bank of Evansville
P.O. Box 868
Evansville, IN 47705-0868
(812) 425-6261
Contact: Charles Goldman
Geographic Giving Pattern: Primarily Evansville, Indiana
Special Interest: Jewish organizations, with emphasis on temple support, Jewish education and Jewish welfare funds
Assets: $4,060,514
Grant Range: $117,500–$1,000
Limitations: No support for non-Jewish-related programs. No grants for capital improvements or endowment funds.
Applications: Initial approach should be by letter. There are no deadlines.

Irwin-Sweeney-Miller Foundation
See entry in Interfaith

Louisiana

The Lupin Foundation
3715 Prytania Street, Suite 403
New Orleans, LA 70115
(504) 897-6125
Contact: Lori Wesolowski, Coordinator
Geographic Giving Pattern: Louisiana
Special Interest: Education, civic affairs, community funds, religious associations, medical research and cultural programs
Assets: $20,091,744
Grant Range: $100,000–$400
Limitations: No grants to individuals. No loans.
Applications: An application form is required. Initial approach should be by brief written proposal (not exceeding six pages).

Dorothy & Malcolm Woldenberg Foundation
2100 St. Charles Avenue, 12-H
New Orleans, LA 70130
Contact: Dorothy Woldenberg, President
Geographic Giving Pattern: Primarily Louisiana and Florida

Special Interest: Largely for Jewish welfare funds, temple support and higher and secondary educational institutions
Assets: $2,084,871 (Gifts received: $803,000)
Grant Range: $50,000–$100
Limitations: No grants to individuals
Applications: There are no deadlines for grant proposals

Maryland

Berman Charitable Trust
P.O. Box 86
Laurel, MD 20707
Contact: Dennis Berman, Trustee
Geographic Giving Pattern: National
Special Interest: Jewish organizations, including welfare funds, community centers and yeshivas
Assets: $1,721,897 (Gifts received: $973,500)
Grant Range: $30,500–$25
Limitations: No grants to individuals
Applications: Contributes to pre-selected organizations only. Applications not accepted.

Peggy & Yale Gordon Charitable Trust
Three Church Lane
Baltimore, MD 21208
(301) 484-6410
Contact: Sidney S. Sherr, Trustee
Geographic Giving Pattern: Primarily Baltimore, Maryland
Special Interest: Jewish organizations and cultural programs
Assets: $8,324,841
Grant Range: $60,382–$100
Applications: Initial approach should be by letter. There are no deadlines.

The Homer and Martha Gudelsky Family Foundation, Inc.
11900 Tech Road
Silver Spring, MD 20904
(301) 622-0100
Contact: Medda Gudelsky, Director
Geographic Giving Pattern: Maryland and Washington, D.C.
Special Interest: Higher education, local temple support and Jewish welfare funds
Assets: $18,016,834 (Gifts received: $405,449)

Grant Range: $250,000–$50
Applications: Initial approach may be by letter or grant proposal.
There are no deadlines.

Richard S. Levitt Foundation
6001 Montrose Road, Suite 600
Rockville, MD 20852
Contact: Richard Levitt, President and Treasurer
Geographic Giving Pattern: Primarily Des Moines, Iowa
Special Interest: Higher education, cultural programs, Jewish religious
and welfare organizations and social services
Assets: $4,811,515 (Gifts received: $1,467,000)
Grant Range: $100,000–$10
Limitations: No grants to individuals
Applications: Contributes to pre-selected organizations only.
Applications not accepted.

Alfred G. and Ida Mendelson Family Foundation, Inc.
8300 Pennsylvania Avenue
P.O. Box 398
Forestville, MD 20747-0398
Contact: Ida Mendelson, President
Geographic Giving Pattern: Primarily Maryland and the District of
Columbia
Special Interest: Temple support, Jewish welfare agencies and social
services
Assets: $101,019
Grant Range: $88,584–$22
Limitations: No grants to individuals
Applications: Contributes to pre-selected organizations only.
Applications not accepted.

Three Swallows Foundation
See entry in Interfaith

The Harry and Jeanette Weinberg Foundation, Inc.
5518 Baltimore National Pike
Baltimore, MD 21228
Contact: Ted Gross, Vice-President
Geographic Giving Pattern: Primarily Hawaii; Baltimore, Maryland;
and Scranton, Pennsylvania
Special Interest: Jewish welfare funds, temple support, higher
education, the homeless and the elderly

Assets: $560,117,000 (Gifts received: $137,473,000)
Grant Range: $19,330,000–$90 (Grant average: $100–$100,000)
Limitations: No grants to individuals
Applications: Contributes to pre-selected organizations only.
Applications not accepted.

Massachusetts

Joseph F. and Clara Ford Foundation
1360 Soldiers Field Road
Brighton, MA 02135
Contact: The Trustees
Geographic Giving Pattern: Primarily Massachusetts
Special Interest: Jewish concerns
Assets: $2,622,506
Grant Range: $80,000–$300
Limitations: No grants to individuals
Applications: Contributes to pre-selected organizations only.
Applications not accepted.

Israel and Matilda Goldberg Family Foundation
c/o Jomar Co.
209 West Central Street, Suite 202
Natick, MA 01760
Contact: Albert S. Goldberg or Herbert A. Goldberg, Trustees
Geographic Giving Pattern: Primarily Boston, Massachusetts
Special Interest: Jewish welfare funds and temple support
Assets: $3,024,106
Grant Range: $20,000–$10
Limitations: No grants to individuals
Applications: Contributes to pre-selected organizations only.
Applications not accepted.

Kraft Foundation
One Boston Place
Boston, MA 02108
(617) 723-3455
Contact: Robert K. Kraft, Trustee
Geographic Giving Pattern: Primarily Boston, Massachusetts
Special Interest: Primarily cultural programs, education and Jewish giving
Assets: $2,022,225 (Gifts received: $370,000)
Grant Range: $51,000–$50

Applications: Initial approach should be by letter. There are no deadlines.

Fred & Sarah Lipsky Charitable Foundation
Six Pleasant Street, Room 510
Malden, MA 02148
Contact: Benjamin L. Cline, Advisory Board Member
Geographic Giving Pattern: Primarily Massachusetts
Special Interest: Jewish welfare funds and temple support; also for education, hospitals and youth agencies
Assets: $2,122,566
Grant Range: $25,000–$100
Limitations: No grants to individuals
Applications: Contributes to pre-selected organizations only. Applications not accepted.

Sawyer Charitable Foundation
See entry in Interfaith

Michigan

Theodore and Mina Bargman Foundation
29201 Telegraph Road, Suite 500
Southfield, MI 48034
Contact: Lawrence S. Jackier, Vice-President
Geographic Giving Pattern: National and Israel
Special Interest: Emphasis on Jewish welfare funds, higher education in Israel, and temple support
Assets: $3,141,640
Grant Range: $45,000–$100
Limitations: No grants for endowment funds, scholarships or fellowships. No matching gifts and no loans.
Applications: Contributes to pre-selected organizations only. Applications not accepted.

Gerson Family Foundation, Inc.
30285 Woodside Court
Franklin, MI 48025-1439
Contact: Byron Gerson, President
Special Interest: Jewish organizations and Jewish welfare
Assets: $2,009,079
Grant Range: $131,000–$25
Applications: Initial approach should be by letter

John and Rose Herman Foundation
3001 West Big Beaver Road, Suite 404
Troy, MI 48084
(313) 649-6400
Contact: Harold S. Tobias, Secretary
Special Interest: Jewish welfare funds and temple support; some
support for education and health agencies
Assets: $2,140,566
Grant Range: $51,000–$100
Applications: Initial approach should be by letter. There are no
deadlines.

The Mendel Foundation
777 Riverview Drive
Benton Harbor, MI 49022
Contact: Eleanor Simon
Geographic Giving Pattern: Michigan
Special Interest: Jewish welfare funds, religious associations and
temple support
Assets: $3,651,087 (Gifts received: $1,000,500)
Grant Range: $100,000–$50
Applications: Initial approach should be by letter sent to the following
address: P.O. Box 688, Benton Harbor, MI 49022. There are no
deadlines.

The Meyer and Anna Prentis Family Foundation, Inc.
P.O. Box 7037
Huntington Woods, MI 48070
(313) 398-8415
Contact: Marvin A. Frenkel, Treasurer
Geographic Giving Pattern: Limited to Michigan
Special Interest: Medical research, education, the disadvantaged,
cultural programs, Jewish giving and Jewish welfare funds
Assets: $ 4,814,842
Grant Range: $3,027,840–$500
Limitations: No grants to individuals or for endowment funds,
scholarships or fellowships. No matching gifts or loans.
Applications: Initial approach should be by proposal letter. The board
meets in July and December.

The Stollman Foundation
2025 West Long Lake Road, No. 104
Troy, MI 48098-4109
(313) 643-8810

Contact: Phillip Stollman, Secretary
Geographic Giving Pattern: Primarily Michigan and New York
Special Interest: Grants for education (including religious education and higher education in Israel), temple support and Jewish welfare
Grant Total: $246,900
Applications: Initial approach should be by letter. There are no deadlines.

Samuel L. Westerman Foundation
See entry in Interfaith

Minnesota

Ted Mann Foundation
704 Hennepin Avenue, Room 202
Minneapolis, MN 55403
(612) 333-2520
Contact: Ted Mann, President
Geographic Giving Pattern: National
Special Interest: Religious and medical purposes; also education
Assets: $43,396,049 (Gifts received: $7,432,885)
Grant Range: $237,500–$200
Limitations: No grants to individuals
Applications: Contributes to pre-selected organizations only. Applications not accepted.

The Jay and Rose Phillips Family Foundation
100 Washington Square, Suite 1650
Minneapolis, MN 55401
Contact: Thomas P. Cook, Executive Director
Geographic Giving Pattern: Primarily Minnesota and the Midwest
Special Interest: Hospitals, medical research, Jewish religious organizations and welfare funds, higher education, social services and cultural programs
Assets: $56,774,301
Grant Range: $537,967–$15 (Grant average: $1,000–$36,000)
Limitations: No support for religious organizations for sectarian purposes. No grants to individuals or for endowment funds.
Applications: Initial approach should be by letter. Grant proposals should be sent to the following address: 2345 N.E. Kennedy Street, Minneapolis, MN 55413 Tel. (612) 331-6230. There are no deadlines.

Margaret Rivers Fund
See entry in Interfaith

Nebraska

Blumkin Foundation, Inc.
7001 Farnam Street
Omaha, NE 68132
Contact: Norman B. Batt, President
Geographic Giving Pattern: Nebraska
Special Interest: Jewish religious groups and welfare funds, higher education and cultural programs
Assets: $1,172,643
Grant Range: $75,000–$50
Applications: Initial approach should be by letter. There are no deadlines.

Carl Frohm Memorial Foundation
c/o FirsTier Bank Omaha
17th and Farnam Streets
Omaha, NE 68102
Contact: Donald W. Engdahl
Geographic Giving Pattern: Limited to Omaha, Nebraska
Special Interest: Jewish welfare funds and temple support
Assets: $1,512,333
Grant Range: $26,070–$1,500
Applications: Contributes to pre-selected organizations only. Applications not accepted.

The Milton S. and Corinne N. Livingston Foundation, Inc.
1125 South 103rd Street, Suite 600
Omaha, NE 68124-1071
(402) 558-1112
Contact: Yale Richards, Executive Director
Geographic Giving Pattern: Primarily Nebraska
Special Interest: Local Jewish welfare funds and temple support, higher education, culture and health services
Assets: $3,204,219
Grant Range: $100,000–$100
Limitations: No grants to individuals
Applications: Initial approach should be by proposal letter. There are no deadlines.

Nevada

Abraham and Sonia Rochlin Foundation
275 Hill Street, Suite 25
Reno, NV 89501
Contact: Larry Rochlin, President
Special Interest: Jewish religious organizations, welfare funds and higher education
Assets: $21,482,375
Grant Range: $425,000–$25 (Grant average: $3,000–$50,000)
Applications: Contributes to pre-selected organizations only. Applications not accepted.

New Jersey

Charles and Els Bendheim Foundation
One Parker Plaza
Fort Lee, NJ 07204
Contact: Charles H. Bendheim, President and Manager
Special Interest: Jewish-sponsored religious and educational institutions and Jewish welfare funds
Assets: $294,283 (Gifts received: $154,496)
Grant Range: $30,000–$10
Applications: Initial approach should be by letter

Engel Family Foundation, Inc.
48 Hook Road
Bayonne, NJ 07002
Contact: Barry Engel, Trustee
Geographic Giving Pattern: Primarily Brooklyn, New York
Special Interest: Jewish congregations and yeshivas. "Preference is given to organizations engaged in religious education."
Assets: $1,182 (Gifts received: $139,000)
Grant Range: $102,360–$1,000
Limitations: No grants to individuals
Applications: Initial approach should be by letter and clear statement of religious and charitable aims of the organization

Gindi Associates Foundation, Inc.
311 Park Avenue
Oakhurst, NJ 07755
Contact: The Trustees
Geographic Giving Pattern: No stated limits

Special Interest: Jewish religious institutions and Jewish welfare
Assets: $1,777,052
Grant Range: $170,000–$200
Applications: Contributes to pre-selected organizations only. Applications not accepted.

The Harold and Adeline Kramer Family Foundation, Inc.
85 Central Avenue
Clifton, NJ 07011-2309
(201) 546-5300
Contact: Harold Kramer, President and Manager
Special Interest: Jewish organizations, temple support, education, medical research and hospitals
Assets: $972,797
Grant Range: $25,000–$500
Limitations: No grants to individuals
Applications: Contributes to pre-selected organizations only. Applications not accepted.

The Sarah and Matthew Rosenhaus Peace Foundation, Inc.
Picatinny Road
Morristown, NJ 07960
(201) 267-6583
Contact: Irving Rosenhaus, Managing Director
Geographic Giving Pattern: Primarily New Jersey and New York
Special Interest: To promote world peace and understanding, with emphasis on medical research and health services, Jewish organizations, higher education (including theological education), and international peace organizations. Some support for social service agencies and cultural programs.
Assets: $10,516,204
Grant Range: $100,000–$200 (Grant average: $1,000–$25,000)
Limitations: No grants to individuals
Applications: Contributes to pre-selected organizations only. Applications not accepted.

The Harold B. and Dorothy A. Snyder Foundation
See entry in Interfaith

The Sutton Foundation
855 Garfield Avenue
Jersey City, NJ 07305-4497
Contact: Elie S. Sutton, President

Special Interest: Jewish welfare and other Jewish organizations including yeshivas and synagogues
Assets: $1,897,357 (Gifts received: $979,220)
Grant Total: $323,300
Applications: Initial approach should be by letter

New York

The Joseph & Rachel Ades Foundation, Inc.
240 Madison Avenue
New York, NY 10016
Contact: Joseph Ades, President
Special Interest: Jewish welfare funds, temple support, education and youth agencies
Assets: $313,109 (Gifts received: $275,000)
Grant Range: $50,000–$20 (Grant average: $550–$20,000)
Applications: Contributes to pre-selected organizations only. Applications not accepted.

AVI CHAI–A Philanthropic Foundation
509 Madison Avenue, Suite 1100
New York, NY 10022
(212) 371-5948
Contact: Bernie D. Kastner, Associate Director
Special Interest: "To encourage those of the Jewish faith towards a more traditional form of Jewish observance and lifestyle and to encourage mutual understanding and sensitivity among Jews of various backgrounds."
Assets: $21,865,107 (Gifts received: $3,054,875)
Grant Range: $87,000–$2,500
Limitations: No grants for youth programs, building projects or deficits
Applications: Solicits proposals only in the context of self-initiated projects. Applications are not accepted.

Booth Ferris Foundation
See entry in Interfaith

The Martha and Regina Brand Foundation, Inc.
521 Fifth Avenue, Room 1805
New York, NY 10175
(212) 687-3505
Contact: Marjorie D. Kogan, President

Geographic Giving Pattern: Primarily New York, New Jersey and California
Special Interest: Emphasis on Jewish welfare funds, temple support, and a theological seminary; support also for Jewish and other organizations whose general purpose relates to the betterment of parent/child relations
Assets: $1,963,229
Grant Range: $25,000–$50
Applications: Initial approach should be by letter. There are no deadlines.

The Brothers Ashkenazi Foundation
c/o Summit Rovins & Feldesman
445 Park Avenue
New York, NY 10022
Contact: Ely Ashkenazi, President
Special Interest: Jewish giving, including yeshivas and temple support
Assets: $304,603 (Gifts received: $575,000)
Grant Range: $52,000–$10
Applications: There are no deadlines for grant proposals

James J. Colt Foundation, Inc.
See entry in Interfaith

Constans Culver Foundation
See entry in Interfaith

Gerard & Ruth Daniel Foundation, Inc.
Polly Park Road
Rye, NY 10580
Contact: Gerard Daniel, President
Special Interest: Jewish welfare funds, cultural and educational organizations and temple support
Assets: $2,997,705
Grant Range: $56,400–$50
Applications: Contributes to pre-selected organizations only. Applications not accepted.

The Goodman Family Foundation
See entry in Interfaith

William Randolph Hearst Foundation
See entry in Interfaith

Hess Foundation, Inc.
1185 Avenue of the Americas
New York, NY 10036
(212) 997-8500
Contact: Leon Hess, President
Special Interest: Higher education and hospitals. Support also for performing arts organizations, synagogues and social welfare agencies.
Assets: $66,450,587 (Gifts received: $2,111,240)
Grant Range: $296,250–$1,000 (Grant average: $1,000–$100,000)
Limitations: No grants to individuals
Applications: Contributes to pre-selected organizations only. Applications not accepted.

Jesselson Foundation
1221 Avenue of the Americas
New York, NY 10020
(212) 790-5722
Contact: Ludwig Jesselson, President
Special Interest: Higher and Jewish education, welfare funds, health agencies and synagogues
Assets: $20,608,606
Grant Range: $250,000–$30 (Grant average: $100–$10,000)
Applications: Initial approach should be by letter. There are no deadlines.

The Henry Luce Foundation, Inc.
See entry in Interfaith

James J. McCann Charitable Trust and McCann Foundation, Inc.
See entry in Interfaith

Morris Morgenstern Foundation
100 Merrick Road, Room 506E
Rockville Centre, NY 11570
(516) 536-3030
Contact: Hannah Klein, Executive Director
Geographic Giving Pattern: New York, New York metropolitan area
Special Interest: Jewish welfare funds, religious institutions, (particularly synagogues), religious and secular education, health and hospitals, and youth agencies
Assets: $10,412,670

Grant Range: $320,000–$10 (Grant average: $50–$10,000)
Applications: Initial approach should be by letter. There are no deadlines.

The Reichmann Family Foundation
15 Harbor Park Drive
Port Washington, NY 11050
Contact: Charles Reichmann, President
Geographic Giving Pattern: Primarily New York
Special Interest: Jewish organizations including synagogues and yeshivas
Assets: $1,031,930 (Gifts received: $545,000)
Grant Range: $18,000–$100
Limitations: No grants to individuals
Applications: Contributes to pre-selected organizations only. Applications not accepted.

Mahir A. & Helene Reiss Foundation, Inc.
445 Park Avenue, 16th Floor
New York, NY 10022
Contact: Mahir A. Reiss, President
Special Interest: Jewish educational and religious organizations
Assets: $1,979 (Gifts received: $380,100)
Grant Range: $23,680–$100
Applications: Initial approach should be by letter

The Ridgefield Foundation
641 Lexington Avenue, 26th Floor
New York, NY 10022
(212) 750-9330
Contact: Marguerite M. Riposanu, Secretary
Geographic Giving Pattern: New York for local services; U.S. and Israel for education
Special Interest: Education, Jewish welfare funds, social service agencies and cultural programs
Assets: $4,655,934
Grant Range: $25,000–$100 (Grant average: $100–$5,000)
Limitations: No grants to individuals or for scholarships, fellowships or matching gifts. No loans. Most support is for past donees or for organizations recommended by board members.
Applications: Applications are not accepted

Joseph F. Stein Foundation, Inc.
28 Aspen Road
Scarsdale, NY 10583
(914) 725-1770
Contact: Melvin M. Stein, President
Geographic Giving Pattern: New York and Florida
Special Interest: Local Jewish welfare and social activities; some
support for higher and secondary education, including religious
education and medical research
Assets: $8,100,507
Grant Range: $211,218–$20
Limitations: No grants to individuals, including scholarships. No
matching gifts and no loans.
Applications: Initial approach should be by proposal letter

Jerome L. Stern Family Foundation, Inc.
342 Madison Avenue, Room 1912
New York, NY 10173
(212) 972-8165
Contact: Jerome L. Stern, President
Geographic Giving Pattern: New York
Special Interest: Jewish religious education, temple support and
Jewish welfare funds
Assets: $1,458,882
Grant Range: $58,250–$50
Applications: Applications are not accepted

Martin Tananbaum Foundation, Inc.
450 Seventh Avenue, Suite 1509
New York, NY 10123
(212) 687-3440
Contact: Arnold Alperstein, President
Special Interest: Jewish welfare funds, temple support, theological
education and health agencies
Assets: $1,383,739
Grant Range: $25,550–$36
Limitations: No grants to individuals or for building or endowment
funds
Applications: Initial approach should be by letter. Seven copies of
proposal letter should be submitted between October and April.

The Williams Family Philanthropic Foundation
c/o CGP Management Corporation
1200 Shames Drive
Westbury, NY 11590
Contact: Jerry Williams, President
Special Interest: Jewish organizations including religious associations, schools and welfare funds
Assets: $723,976
Grant Range: $100,000–$5
Applications: Contributes to pre-selected organizations only. Applications not accepted.

North Carolina

The Blumenthal Foundation
See entry in Interfaith

The Kaplan Family Foundation
Seven Monmouth Court
Greensboro, NC 27410-6047
Contact: Leonard J. Kaplan, President and Treasurer
Special Interest: Jewish welfare services and synagogues
Assets: $1,410,456
Grant Range: $50,000–$1,000
Limitations: No grants to individuals
Applications: Contributes to pre-selected organizations only. Applications not accepted.

Ohio

Jerome Lippman Family Foundation
P.O. Box 991
Akron, OH 44309-0991
Contact: Jerome Lippman, President
Geographic Giving Pattern: Primarily Ohio
Special Interest: Jewish organizations including welfare funds, yeshivas, temples and social services
Assets: $647,993 (Gifts received: $750,000)
Grant Range: $253,000–$60
Applications: Contributes to pre-selected organizations only. Applications not accepted.

Samuel Mendel Melton Foundation
17 South High Street, Suite 1018
Columbus, OH 43215
(614) 224-5239
Contact: Samuel M. Melton, Trustee
Special Interest: Higher education and Jewish religious educational organizations
Assets: $842,303 (Gifts received: $272,811)
Grant Range: $400,000–$25
Limitations: No grants to individuals
Applications: Initial approach should be by letter. There are no deadlines.

The Sapirstein-Stone-Weiss Foundation
10500 American Road
Cleveland, OH 44144
(216) 252-7300
Contact: Irving I. Stone, President
Geographic Giving Pattern: International and national
Special Interest: Jewish welfare funds and religious education
Assets: $17,070,939
Grant Range: $498,613–$100
Limitations: No grants to individuals or for scholarships or fellowships. No loans.
Applications: Initial approach should be by letter. Proposals should be submitted in April.

Van Dorn Foundation
See entry in Interfaith

Pennsylvania

Hyman Family Foundation
6315 Forbes Avenue
Pittsburgh, PA 15217
Contact: Yetta Elinoff, Manager
Geographic Giving Pattern: Primarily Pennsylvania
Special Interest: Jewish welfare funds, higher education and temple support
Assets: $1,423,163
Grant Range: $50,000–$36
Applications: Contributes to pre-selected organizations only. Applications not accepted.

Charles and Figa Kline Foundation
626 North Main Street
Allentown, PA 18104
(215) 437-4077
Contact: Fabian I. Fraenkel, Director
Geographic Giving Pattern: Allentown, Pennsylvania
Special Interest: Jewish welfare and community service agencies, temple support and education
Assets: $6,249,834
Grant Range: $175,000–$200
Limitations: No grants to individuals
Applications: Deadline for receipt of grant proposals is September 30

The Millstein Charitable Foundation
North Fourth Street & Gaskill Avenue
Jeannette, PA 15644
(412) 523-5531
Contact: David J. Millstein, Executive Secretary
Geographic Giving Pattern: Western Pennsylvania
Special Interest: Jewish welfare funds and temple support
Assets: $2,737,720
Grant Range: $25,000–$15
Applications: Initial approach should be by letter. There are no deadlines. Requests are reviewed as they are received.

The Pew Charitable Trusts
See entry in Interfaith

Julius L. and Libbie B. Steinsapir Family Foundation
See entry in Interfaith

Rhode Island

The Hassenfeld Foundation
1027 Newport Avenue
Pawtucket, RI 02861
(401) 726-4100
Contact: Sylvia Hassenfeld, President
Special Interest: Jewish welfare funds, higher and religious education
Assets: $2,207,715
Grant Range: $232,952–$50
Limitations: No grants to individuals
Applications: Contributes to pre-selected organizations only. Applications not accepted.

Tennessee

Belz Foundation
P.O. Box 171199
Memphis, TN 38187-1199
Contact: Jack A. Belz, Manager
Geographic Giving Pattern: Memphis, Tennessee
Special Interest: Jewish welfare funds, temple support, education and cultural programs
Assets: $5,182,801 (Gifts received: $1,170,874)
Grant Range: $223,955–$5
Limitations: No grants to individuals

Washington

Tillie and Alfred Shemanski Testamentary Trust
c/o Seattle–First National Bank
P.O. Box 3586
Seattle, WA 98124
(206) 358-3388
Contact: Rod Johnson, Vice-President, Seattle–First National Bank
Geographic Giving Pattern: Washington
Special Interest: Jewish welfare funds, temple support, higher education, health associations and hospitals, youth and child welfare agencies
Assets: $3,139,583
Grant Range: $22,766–$1,620 (Grant average: $5,100)
Applications: Initial approach should be by letter. November 30 is the deadline.

Wisconsin

Patrick and Anna M. Cudahy Fund
See entry in Interfaith

Philip Rubenstein Foundation, Inc.
400 West Boden Street
Milwaukee, WI 53207
(414) 769-1000
Contact: Philip Rubenstein, President
Special Interest: Jewish giving and Jewish welfare
Assets: $2,721,506

Grant Range: $223,867–$25
Applications: Initial approach should be by letter. There are no deadlines. The application address is as follows: 633 West Evergreen Court, Milwaukee, WI 53217.

INTERFAITH FOUNDATIONS

California

The Ahmanson Foundation
9215 Wilshire Boulevard
Beverly Hills, CA 90210
(213) 278-0770
Contact: Lee E. Walcott, Vice-President and Managing Director
Geographic Giving Pattern: Primarily southern California, with
emphasis on the Los Angeles area
Special Interest: Education, arts and humanities, medicine and health
and social welfare
Religious Preference: Protestant and Jewish
Assets: $437,995,000
Grant Range: $1,850,000–$300 (Grant average: $10,000–$25,000)
Limitations: No grants to individuals or for continuing support,
annual campaigns, deficit financing or fellowships. No loans.
Applications: Initial approach should be by letter or proposal. There
are no deadlines.

Burns-Dunphy Foundation
Hearst Building, Third & Market Streets, Suite 1200
San Francisco, CA 94103
Contact: Walter M. Gleason, President, Treasurer and Manager
Special Interest: Religious welfare, education and missionary services
Religious Preference: Roman Catholic and Protestant
Assets: $1,349,497
Grant Range: $10,000–$1,000
Applications: Initial approach should be by letter

The William and Flora Hewlett Foundation
525 Middlefield Road, Suite 200
Menlo Park, CA 94025
(415) 329-1070
Contact: Roger W. Heyns, President
Geographic Giving Pattern: Primarily California, especially the San
Francisco Bay area
Special Interest: Conflict resolution, the environment, performing arts,
education (including theological) and population
Assets: $687,664,000

Grant Average: $20,000 – $600,000
Limitations: No grants to individuals or for building funds, basic research, equipment, scholarships or fellowships. No loans.
Applications: Initial approach should be by letter. There are no deadlines.

George Frederick Jewett Foundation
One Maritime Plaza, Suite 990
San Francisco, CA 94111
(415) 421-1351
Contact: Theresa A. Mullen, Program Director
Geographic Giving Pattern: Primarily the Pacific Northwest
Special Interest: Religion and religious training; encouragement of the non-profit sector
Religious Preference: Protestant and Roman Catholic
Assets: $16,470,748
Grant Range: $25,000–$500 (Grant average: $1,000–$15,000)
Limitations: No grants to individuals or for scholarships or fellowships. No loans.
Applications: Initial approach should be by letter. Deadlines are February 15, May 15, August 15 and November 1.

Marin Community Foundation
1100 Larkspur Landing Circle, Suite 365
Larkspur, CA 94939
(415) 461-3333
Contact: Berit Ashla, Program Assistant
Geographic Giving Pattern: Marin County, California
Special Interest: To promote charitable, religious, educational, scientific, artistic and philanthropic activities.
Religious Preference: Protestant and Roman Catholic
Assets: $456,903,000 (Gifts received: $6,656,660)
Grant Average: $50,000
Limitations: No grants to individuals or for planning initiatives, research or generally for capital projects
Applications: An application form is required. Contact foundation for funding policies and application form. The deadline for religious grants is February 15.

Colorado

Kejr Foundation, Inc.

P.O. Box 264
Woodrow, CO 80757
Contact: Spencer Bower, Administrative Assistant
Geographic Giving Pattern: National
Special Interest: Interdenominational, evangelical religious programs, including radio broadcasting, church extension and missionary projects
Assets: $2,064,957
Grant Range: $19,750–$500
Applications: An application form is required. There are no deadlines. The application address is as follows: 6500 Xerxes Avenue South, Minneapolis, MN 55423. Tel. (612) 920-0574

District of Columbia

Thomas and Frances McGregor Foundation

c/o Robert Philipson & Co.
2000 L Street, N.W., Suite 609
Washington, DC 20036
Contact: Victor Krakower, Manager
Geographic Giving Pattern: The District of Columbia
Special Interest: Education, hospitals, health agencies, cultural programs and religious organizations
Religious Preference: Jewish, Roman Catholic and Protestant
Assets: $3,820,460
Grant Range: $20,000–$1,000
Applications: Initial approach should be by letter

Florida

John E. and Nellie J. Bastien Memorial Foundation

150 East Sample Road
Pompano Beach, FL 33064
Contact: The Trustees
Geographic Giving Pattern: Primarily Florida
Special Interest: Lutheran and Catholic church support; also higher education, health agencies, general welfare and youth agencies.
Religious Preference: Lutheran and Roman Catholic
Assets: $8,926,523

Grant Range: $25,000–$200
Applications: There are no deadlines for grant proposals

The Arthur Vining Davis Foundations
645 Riverside Avenue, Suite 520
Jacksonville, FL 32204
(904) 359-0670
Contact: Max Morris, Executive Director
Geographic Giving Pattern: National
Special Interest: Private higher education, hospices, medicine, public
television and graduate theological education
Religious Preference: Protestant and Roman Catholic
Assets: $114,004,000
Grant Range: $180,000–$1,100 (Grant average: $75,000–$125,000)
Limitations: No support for community chests, institutions primarily
supported by government funds or multi-year funding projects. No
grants to individuals. No loans.
Applications: Initial approach should be by letter. There are no
deadlines.

Jessie Ball duPont Religious, Charitable and Educational Fund
Enterprise Center
225 Water Street, Suite 1200
Jacksonville, FL 32202-4424
(904) 353-0890
Contact: George Penick, Executive Director
Geographical Giving Pattern: Primarily the South, especially Florida,
Delaware and Virginia
Special Interest: Higher and secondary education institutions, cultural
and historic preservation programs, social service organizations,
hospitals, health agencies, churches and church-related organizations
and youth agencies
Religious Preference: Protestant and Catholic
Assets: $138,051,073
Grant Range: $313,500–$500 (Grant average: $5,000–$100,000)
Limitations: No support for organizations other than those awarded
gifts by the donor from 1960–1964. No grants to individuals or
generally for capital campaigns.
Applications: Applicants must submit proof with initial application
that a contribution was received from the donor between 1960–1964.
An application form is required. There are no deadlines.

Georgia

Joseph B. Whitehead Foundation
1400 Peachtree Center Tower
230 Peachtree Street, N.W.
Atlanta, GA 30303
(404) 522-6755
Contact: Charles H. McTier, President
Geographic Giving Pattern: Metropolitan Atlanta, Georgia
Special Interest: Child welfare, the elderly and indigent, health, education, cultural programs and the arts
Assets: $310,191,188
Grant Range: $2,500,000–$10,000 (Grant average: $10,000 – $750,000)
Limitations: No grants to individuals or for endowment funds or operating expenses. No loans or matching gifts.
Applications: Initial approach should be by letter. Deadlines are February 1 and September 1.

Illinois

The Alvin H. Baum Family Fund
120 South LaSalle Street
Chicago, IL 60603
Contact: Ann F. Baum, President
Special Interest: Higher education, Jewish and Catholic welfare funds and local temple support
Religious Preference: Jewish and Roman Catholic
Assets: $1,948,395
Grant Range: $254,428–$25
Limitations: No grants to individuals
Applications: Applications are not accepted

The Retirement Research Foundation
1300 Higgins Road, Suite 214
Park Ridge, IL 60068
(708) 823-4133
Contact: Marilyn Hennessy, Director
Geographic Giving Pattern: National with emphasis on the Midwest and Florida
Special Interest: To improve the quality of older persons in the U.S.
Religious Preference: Protestant, Roman Catholic and Jewish
Assets: $115,713,942

Grant Average: $24,000–$25,000
Limitations: No grants to individuals or for endowment funds, construction, emergency funds, deficit financing, land acquisition, publications, conferences or annual campaigns. No loans.
Applications: Initial approach should be by letter or proposal. Three copies of proposal are required. Deadlines are February 1, May 1 and August 1.

Solo Cup Foundation
1700 Old Deerfield Road
Highland Park, IL 60035
Contact: Ronald L. Whaley, Treasurer
Geographic Giving Pattern: National
Special Interest: Higher and secondary education and Christian religious organizations
Religious Preference: Protestant and Roman Catholic
Assets: $7,771,305 (Gifts received: $7,732,473)
Grant Range: $50,000–500
Applications: There are no deadlines for grant proposals

Indiana

John A. Hillenbrand Foundation, Inc.
Highway 46 East
Batesville, IN 47006
(812) 934-7000
Contact: Daniel A. Hillenbrand, President
Geographic Giving Pattern: Primarily Batesville and Ripley County, Indiana
Special Interest: Health, social services, youth, education, civic affairs, economics and religious giving
Religious Preference: Protestant and Roman Catholic
Assets: $6,757,559
Grant Range: $30,000–1,000
Applications: There are no deadlines. Grant proposal letters should be typewritten.

Irwin-Sweeney-Miller Foundation
420 Third Street
P.O. Box 808
Columbus, IN 47202
(812) 372-0251
Contact: Sarla Kalsi, Executive Director

Geographic Giving Pattern: Primarily the Columbus, Indiana area for new funding
Special Interest: Creative programs in social justice, education, religion, the arts and improving family stability
Religious Preference: Protestant, Roman Catholic and Jewish
Assets: $1,682,765 (Gifts received: $665,861)
Grant Range: $288,715–$100 (Grant average: $1,000–$5,000)
Limitations: No grants to individuals or for deficit financing or research. No loans.
Applications: Send one copy of grant proposal with letter by March 1 or September 1.

Lilly Endowment, Inc.
2801 North Meridian Street
P.O. Box 88068
Indianapolis, IN 46208
(317) 924-5471
Contact: Craig R. Dykstra, Vice-President, Religion
Geographic Giving Pattern: National
Special Interest: National religious research centering specifically on issues facing mainstream Protestantism, historically black churches and the American Roman Catholic Church. Support also for theological seminaries, urban ministry and spiritual formation.
Religious Preference: Protestant and Roman Catholic
Assets: $3,542,397,345
Religious Grant Range: $2,000,000–$11,872
Limitations: No grants to individuals
Applications: Initial approach should be by letter, one to two pages in length. There are no deadlines.

Louisiana

Libby-Dufour Fund
321 Hibernia Bank Building, Suite 202
New Orleans, LA 70112
Contact: Eben Hardie, President
Geographic Giving Pattern: Limited to the New Orleans, Louisiana area
Special Interest: Christian charities, support for churches, church-related education and Christian welfare funds
Religious Preference: Protestant and Roman Catholic
Assets: $6,066,559
Grant Range: $50,000–$1,000

Limitations: No grants to individuals or for endowment funds, or operating budgets
Applications: There are no deadlines for grant proposals

Maryland

Three Swallows Foundation
8313 Persimmon Tree Road
Bethesda, MD 20817-2647
Contact: Ross Main, Manager
Special Interest: Social service, higher education and religious organizations
Religious Preference: Protestant and Jewish
Assets: $5,511,741
Grant Range: $59,500–$100
Limitations: No grants to individuals
Applications: Contributes to pre-selected organizations only. Applications not accepted.

Massachusetts

The Howard Johnson Foundation
P.O. Box 235
541 Main Street
South Weymouth, MA 02190
(617) 337-2201
Contact: Eugene J. Durgin, Secretary
Geographic Giving Pattern: Primarily Massachusetts, Connecticut and New York
Special Interest: Education, health and hospitals, churches and religious welfare agencies
Religious Preference: Roman Catholic and Protestant
Assets: $3,023,567
Grant Range: $25,000–$1,000
Limitations: No grants to individuals
Applications: Initial approach should be by letter. Grant proposals should be sent in the early part of the calendar year to the following address: c/o Howard B. Johnson, 720 Fifth Avenue, Suite 1304, New York, NY 10019

Sawyer Charitable Foundation
142 Berkeley Street
Boston, MA 02116
(617) 267-2441
Contact: Carol S. Parks, Executive Director
Geographic Giving Pattern: Primarily the greater New England area
Special Interest: Jewish and Roman Catholic welfare funds, community and health agencies
Religious Preference: Jewish and Roman Catholic
Assets: $4,575,049
Grant Range: $25,000–$100
Limitations: No grants to individuals or for operating budgets or building funds
Applications: Grant proposals should be sent prior to October 15.

Michigan

Samuel L. Westerman Foundation
1700 North Woodward, Suite A
Bloomfield Hills, MI 48013
(313) 642-5770
Contact: James H. LoPrete, President
Geographic Giving Pattern: Primarily Michigan
Special Interest: Hospitals and health agencies, social service and youth agencies, religious organizations and churches, higher education, and cultural programs
Religious Preference: Jewish and Presbyterian
Assets: $6,854,970
Grant Range: $50,234–$500
Limitations: No grants to individuals
Applications: Initial approach should be by letter. There are no deadlines.

Minnesota

Otto Bremer Foundation
55 East Fifth Street, Suite 700
St. Paul, MN 55101
(612) 227-8036
Contact: John Kostishack, Executive-Director
Geographic Giving Pattern: Limited to Minnesota, North Dakota, and Wisconsin, where there are Bremer Bank affiliates

Special Interest: Emphasis on rural poverty and combatting racism. Support also for post-secondary education, human services, health, religion and community affairs.
Religious Preference: Protestant and Roman Catholic
Assets: $82,496,981
Grant Range: $100,000–$85 (Grant average: $1,000–$25,000)
Limitations: No support for national health organizations. No grants to individuals, or for endowment funds, medical research or professorships.
Applications: Initial approach should be by letter or telephone. Submit proposal at least three months before funding decision is desired.

Margaret Rivers Fund
c/o First National Bank of Stillwater
213 East Chestnut Street
Stillwater, MN 55082
Contact: William Klapp, President
Geographic Giving Pattern: Primarily Minnesota
Special Interest: Hospitals, church support, youth agencies, aid to the disabled and care of the aged. Support also for cultural programs and conservation.
Religious Preference: Protestant, Roman Catholic and Jewish
Assets: $14,573,453
Grant Range: $50,000–$300
Applications: Initial approach should be by letter. There are no deadlines.

Missouri

The Catherine Manley Gaylord Foundation
314 North Broadway, Room 1230
St. Louis, MO 63102
(314) 421-0181
Contact: Donald E. Fahey, Trustee
Geographic Giving Pattern: St. Louis, Missouri metropolitan area
Special Interest: Private higher education, Protestant and Roman Catholic church support, youth and child welfare agencies, civic affairs and social services
Religious Preference: Roman Catholic and Protestant
Assets: $4,521,725
Grant Range: $40,000–$100
Limitations: No grants to individuals. No loans.
Applications: Initial approach should be by proposal letter. There are no deadlines.

Share Foundation
11901 Grandview Road
Grandview, MO 64030
(816) 966-2222
Contact: Harry J. Lloyd, President, Treasurer and Director
Special Interest: Religious organizations and church support
Religious Preference: Roman Catholic and Protestant
Assets: $13,045,066
Grant Range: $100,000–$150
Limitations: Preference is given to Christian and spiritual causes
Applications: A written proposal should be submitted for
consideration. There are no deadlines.

Nebraska

Thomas D. Buckley Trust
P.O. Box 647
Chappell, NE 69129
(308) 874-2212
Contact: Dwight E. Smith
Geographic Giving Pattern: Primarily Nebraska, particularly Chappell,
and Colorado
Special Interest: Community development programs, Christian
churches, civic affairs, hospitals and health services and education
Religious Preference: Roman Catholic and Protestant
Assets: $7,815,520
Grant Average: $500–$10,000
Limitations: No grants to individuals
Applications: An application form is required. Initial approach should
be by written proposal and request for application form. There are no
deadlines.

New Jersey

The Magowan Family Foundation, Inc.
c/o Merrill Lynch
100 Union Avenue
Cresskill, NJ 07626
Contact: Mary Ann Chapin
Geographic Giving Pattern: Primarily New York, California and Florida
Special Interest: Education, hospitals, church support and cultural
programs
Religious Preference: Episcopalian

Assets: $4,915,300
Limitations: No stated limitations
Applications: Initial approach should be by letter to the contact at the
following address: 2100 Washington Street, San Francisco, CA 94109
Tel. (415) 563-5581. There are no deadlines.

The Harold B. and Dorothy A. Snyder Foundation
P.O. Box 671
Moorestown, NJ 08057
(609) 273-9745
Contact: Audrey Snyder, Executive Director
Geographic Giving Pattern: Union County, New Jersey
Special Interest: Social service programs, scholarships for New Jersians
entering Presbyterian ministry and support for rabbinical students
studying at the Jewish Theological Seminary of America
Religious Preference: Presbyterian and Jewish
Assets: $6,779,258
Grant Range: $50,000–$200
Limitations: No capital campaigns. No grants to individuals directly.
Applications: Initial proposals should not exceed four pages. Submit
proposals preferably in the early part of the calendar year.

New York

Altman Foundation
220 East 42nd Street, Suite 411
New York, NY 10017
(212) 682-0970
Contact: John S. Burke, President
Geographic Giving Pattern: Limited to New York with emphasis on the
New York City metropolitan area
Special Interest: Education, private voluntary hospitals and health
centers, and social welfare programs for the disadvantaged
Religious Preference: Roman Catholic
Assets: $120,683,129
Grant Range: $300,000–$2,500 (Grant average: $5,000–$100,000)
Limitations: No grants to individuals
Applications: Initial approach should be by proposal letter. There are
no deadlines.

Booth Ferris Foundation
30 Broad Street
New York, NY 10004
(212) 269-3850

Contact: Robert J. Murtagh, Trustee
Geographic Giving Pattern: New York City metropolitan area for social service and cultural organizations, otherwise national
Special Interest: Private education, especially theological education, smaller colleges, and independent secondary schools. Support also for urban programs and social service agencies.
Religious Preference: Protestant, Roman Catholic and Jewish
Assets: $100,984,048
Grant Range: $250,000–$5,000 (Grant average: $15,000–$100,000)
Limitations: No support for federated campaigns, community chests, or for work with specific diseases or disabilities. No grants to individuals or for research. Generally no grants to educational institutions for scholarships, fellowships or unrestricted endowments. No loans.
Applications: Initial approach should be by proposal letter or telephone. There are no deadlines.

Frank E. Clark Charitable Trust
c/o Chemical Banking Corp.
270 Park Avenue
New York, NY 10017
(212) 270-9094
Contact: J.L. McKechnie, Vice-President, Chemical Banking Corp.
Geographic Giving Pattern: New York, New York metropolitan area
Special Interest: Income distributed to the parent body of major religious denominations for aid to needy churches. Support also for health, welfare and other charitable organizations.
Assets: $3,670,000
Grant Range: $15,750–$2,500
Applications: Initial approach should be by written proposal explaining the nature of the project. The deadline is October 31.

James J. Colt Foundation, Inc.
375 Park Avenue, Suite 3806
New York, NY 10152
(212) 371-1110
Contact: Anita C. Heard, President
Geographic Giving Pattern: New York
Special Interest: Medical education, hospitals, Jewish welfare funds, health agencies and Protestant church support
Religious Preference: Jewish and Protestant
Assets: $2,159,063
Grant Range: $25,000–$10

Applications: Initial approach should be by letter. There are no deadlines.

Constans Culver Foundation
270 Park Avenue
New York, NY 10017
(212) 270-9107
Contact: Robert Rosenthal, Vice-President, Chemical Banking Corp.
Geographic Giving Pattern: New York
Special Interest: Church support, civic and cultural organizations, higher and insurance education, the disadvantaged and housing issues
Religious Preference: Protestant, Roman Catholic and Jewish
Assets: $4,748,879
Grant Range: $22,500–$500
Limitations: No grants to individuals or for endowment funds
Applications: Submit proposal letter preferably in September.

The Caleb C. and Julia W. Dula Educational and Charitable Foundation
c/o Chemical Banking Corp.
270 Park Avenue, 21st Floor
New York, NY 10017
(212) 270-9066
Contact: Gail Fitch, Trust Officer
Special Interest: Limited to charities Dula has supported in its lifetime, with emphasis on higher and secondary education, hospitals, libraries, social service agencies, child welfare, church support, cultural programs and historic preservation
Religious Preference: Protestant and Roman Catholic
Assets: $20,800,000
Grant Range: $100,000–$1,000
Limitations: No grants to individuals. No loans.
Applications: Initial approach should be by proposal letter. There are no deadlines.

The Goodman Family Foundation
c/o Roy M. Goodman
1035 Fifth Avenue
New York, NY 10028
(212) 417-5563
Contact: Roy M. Goodman, Trustee
Geographic Giving Pattern: New York, New York

Special Interest: Higher education, Jewish welfare funds; grants also for temple and church support, social service agencies and fine arts organizations
Religious Preference: Jewish, Protestant and Roman Catholic
Assets: $2,828,146
Grant Range: $20,000–$100
Applications: Initial approach should be by letter. There are no deadlines.

William Randolph Hearst Foundation

888 Seventh Avenue, 27th Floor
New York, NY 10106-0057
(212) 586-5404
Contact: Robert M. Freshe, Jr., Executive Director
Geographic Giving Pattern: United States and its territories
Special Interest: Programs to aid poverty level and minority groups and education programs with emphasis on private secondary and higher education
Religious Preference: Protestant, Roman Catholic and Jewish
Assets: $297,000,000
Grant Range: $1,000,000–$5,000 (Grant average: $15,000–$35,000)
Limitations: No support for political purposes. No grants to individuals, or for the purchase of tickets, tables, or advertising for fundraising events.
Applications: Initial approach should be by proposal letter to contact

The Henry Luce Foundation, Inc.

111 West 50th Street, Room 3710
New York, NY 10020
(212) 489-7700
Contact: Robert E. Armstrong, Executive Director
Geographic Giving Pattern: International activities limited to East and Southeast Asia
Special Interest: Grants for specific projects in the broad areas of Asian affairs, higher education and scholarship, theology, the arts and public affairs
Religious Preference: Protestant, Roman Catholic and Jewish
Assets: $419,279,061
Grant Range: $1,000,000–$1,600 (Grant average: $25,000–$300,000)
Limitations: No support for journalism or media projects. No grants to individuals (except for Luce Scholars Program), or for endowment and/or domestic building funds, general operating support, scholarships, fellowships or annual fund drives. No loans.
Applications: Initial approach should be by proposal letter.

James J. McCann Charitable Trust and McCann Foundation, Inc.
(Also known as McCann Foundation)
35 Market Street
Poughkeepsie, NY 12601
(914) 452-3085
Contact: John J. Gartland, President
Geographic Giving Pattern: Poughkeepsie and Dutchess County, New York
Special Interest: Education, (including scholarship funds), recreation, civic projects, social services, church support, religious associations and hospitals
Religious Preference: Protestant, Roman Catholic and Jewish
Assets: $24,829,821
Grant Range: $855,000–$100
Limitations: No grants to individuals or for operating budgets, emergency or endowment funds or deficit financing. No matching gifts and no loans.
Applications: Submit letter and proposal preferably in February or August.

William M. & Miriam F. Meecham Foundation, Inc.
39 Broadway
New York, NY 10006
Geographic Giving Pattern: Primarily New York, New York
Special Interest: Catholic and Protestant churches and human services, cultural programs and higher education
Religious Preference: Roman Catholic and Protestant
Assets: $1,945,081 (Gifts received: $524,313)
Grant Range: $25,000–$16
Limitations: No grants to individuals
Applications: Contributes to pre-selected organizations only. Applications not accepted.

North Carolina

The Blumenthal Foundation
P.O. Box 34689
Charlotte, NC 28234
(704) 377-6555
Contact: Herman Blumenthal, Trustee
Geographic Giving Pattern: Primarily North Carolina, with emphasis on Charlotte

Special Interest: Higher education, Jewish welfare organizations and programs in the arts and humanities. Also supports Wildacres, a conference center in North Carolina which invites groups of a variety of religious disciplines to use its facilities.
Religious Preference: Protestant, Roman Catholic and Jewish
Assets: $19,067,751
Grant Range: $300,500–$8 (Grant average: $100–$23,000)
Limitations: No grants to individuals or for scholarships or fellowships. No loans.
Applications: Grant proposal letter should be sent 15 days prior to board meetings which fall in March, June, September and December.

Ohio

The Murphy Family Foundation
25800 Science Park Drive
Beachwood, OH 44122-5525
(216) 831-0404
Contact: Rita M. Carfagna, Secretary-Treasurer
Geographic Giving Pattern: Primarily Ohio
Special Interest: Welfare, education and Protestant and Catholic churches
Religious Preference: Protestant and Roman Catholic
Assets: $69,938 (Gifts received: $150,000)
Grant Range: $10,000–$500
Limitations: No grants to individuals
Applications: There are no deadlines for grant proposals

Van Dorn Foundation
2700 East 79th Street
Cleveland, OH 44104
(216) 361-5234
Contact: Herman R. Ceccardi, Treasurer
Geographic Giving Pattern: The greater Cleveland, Ohio area
Special Interest: Education, the performing arts and other cultural organizations, community funds and development, the disadvantaged, Catholic, Protestant and Jewish giving, wildlife preservation and health
Religious Preference: Jewish, Protestant and Roman Catholic
Assets: $8,323 (Gifts received: $200,000)
Grant Range: $90,000–$50
Applications: Initial approach should be by letter outlining usage of monies requested. There are no deadlines.

The I.J. Van Huffel Foundation
c/o Bank One, Youngstown, N.A.
106 East Market Street
Warren, OH 44481
(216) 841-7824
Contact: William Hanshaw, Vice-President, Bank One, Youngstown, N.A.
Geographic Giving Pattern: Ohio
Special Interest: Higher education, Roman Catholic and Protestant church support, hospitals and social service agencies
Religious Preference: Protestant and Roman Catholic
Assets: $1,618,595
Grant Range: $25,000–$250
Applications: Grant proposals should be sent to contact above at the following address: P.O. Box, 231, Warren, OH 44482. There are no deadlines.

Pennsylvania

Massey Charitable Trust
P.O. Box 1178
Coraopolis, PA 15108
(412) 262-5992
Contact: Walter J. Carroll, Trustee
Geographic Giving Pattern: Pittsburgh, Pennsylvania
Special Interest: Medical sciences and research, hospitals and health agencies, Protestant and Catholic church support, the arts and literacy
Religious Preference: Roman Catholic and Protestant
Assets: $24,776,928 (Gifts received: $7,998,845)
Grant Range: $100,000–100
Limitations: No stated limitations
Applications: There are no deadlines for grant proposals

The Pew Charitable Trusts
Three Parkway, Suite 501
Philadelphia, PA 19102-1305
(215) 568-3330
Contact: Joel Carpenter, Program Director for Religion
Geographic Giving Pattern: National
Special Interest: In religion, support is given to promote the development and application of Judeo-Christian values and to

encourage better understanding of how those values shape our lives and civic responsibilities. Support also to strengthen religious scholarship, foster international understanding and develop the ministry of congregations in their communities.
Religious Preference: Protestant, Jewish and Roman Catholic
Assets: $3,321,890,529
Religious *Grant Range:* $5,000,000–$20,000
Limitations: No grants to individuals or for endowment funds, deficit financing, scholarships or fellowships, except those identified or initiated by the trusts
Applications: Contact foundation for specific application procedure, guidelines and limitations in the religious program area. There are no set deadlines.

Julius L. and Libbie B. Steinsapir Family Foundation
900 Lawyers Building
Pittsburgh, PA 15219
(412) 391-2920
Contact: Samuel Horovitz, Trustee
Geographic Giving Pattern: Primarily Pennsylvania
Special Interest: Temple support, Jewish welfare funds, education and some support for Christian churches and religious orders
Religious Preference: Jewish
Assets: $1,759,780
Grant Range: $12,500–$15
Limitations: No grants to individuals
Applications: There are no deadlines for grant proposals

Texas

Abell-Hanger Foundation
303 West Wall, Room 615
Midland, TX 79701
(915) 684-6655
Contact: David L. Smith, Manager
Geographic Giving Pattern: Limited to Texas, preferably within the Permian Basin
Special Interest: Education, youth activities, cultural programs, health, the disabled and social welfare agencies; some support for religious organizations
Religious Preference: Protestant and Roman Catholic
Assets: $92,381,151
Grant Average: $10,000 – $50,000

Limitations: No grants to individuals or for scholarships or fellowships. No loans.
Applications: An application form is required. The deadlines are September 30, January 31 and May 31.

Houston Endowment, Inc.
P.O. Box 52338
Houston, TX 77052
(713) 223-4043
Contact: J.H. Creekmore, President
Geographic Giving Pattern: Primarily Texas
Special Interest: For the "support of any charitable, educational or religious undertaking"
Assets: $ 681,477,402
Grant Average: $1,000–1,000,000
Limitations: No grants to individuals or for organizational endowments. No loans.
Applications: Initial approach should be by letter. There are no deadlines.

Virginia

Washington Forrest Foundation
2300 Ninth Street South
Arlington, VA 22204
(703) 920-3688
Contact: Lindsey Peete, Executive Director
Geographic Giving Pattern: Northern Virginia
Special Interest: Arts, education, youth programs, health, religion and welfare
Religious Preference: Protestant and Roman Catholic
Assets: $6,667,270
Grant Range: $250,000–$100
Limitations: No support for public schools or colleges, national programs or foreign programs. No grants to individuals or for fellowships or multi-year pledges.
Applications: An application form is required. Contact foundation for grant proposal deadline.

Wisconsin

Patrick and Anna M. Cudahy Fund

P.O. Box 11978
Milwaukee, WI 53211
(414) 271-6020 or (708) 866-0760
Contact: Sister Judith Borchers, Executive Director
Geographic Giving Pattern: Primarily Milwaukee, Wisconsin and Chicago, Illinois; also national
Special Interest: Social service and the homeless, youth agencies and education
Religious Preference: Protestant, Roman Catholic and Jewish
Assets: $17,558,175
Grant Range: $157,200–$300 (Grant average: $5,000–$10,000)
Limitations: No grants to individulas or for endowment funds. No loans.
Applications: Initial approach should be by letter. The deadline is six weeks prior to board meetings which fall in April, June, September and December.

OTHER FOUNDATIONS

California

The Trustees of Ivan V. Koulaieff Educational Fund
651 11th Avenue
San Francisco, CA 94118
Contact: W.W. Granitow, Secretary
Geographic Giving Pattern: National, international
Special Interest:: Aid to Russian immigrants throughout the world through grants, scholarships and loans; support also for Russian Orthodox education and churches in the United States
Assets: $8,149,380
Grant Range: $33,400–$400
Applications: Initial approach should be by letter

The Stephen Philibosian Foundation
46-930 West El Dorado Drive
Indian Wells, CA 92210-8649
(619) 568-3920
Geographic Giving Pattern: Primarily California; some support for the Middle East
Special Interest:: Missionary, educational and social programs of the Armenian-American church and child welfare
Assets: $7,047,806
Grant Average: $100–$5,000
Limitations: No grants to individuals or for operating budgets, seed money, emergency funds, deficit financing, building funds, research or conferences. No loans or matching gifts.
Applications: Contributes to pre-selected organizations only. Applications not accepted.

Georgia

Thalia & Michael C. Carlos Foundation, Inc.
One National Drive, S.W.
Atlanta, GA 30336
Contact: Michael C. Carlos, President and Treasurer
Geographic Giving Pattern: Primarily Georgia
Special Interest:: Cultural programs, Greek Orthodox churches and higher education

Assets: $287,924 (Gifts received: $325,000)
Grant Range: $120,000–$100
Applications: Initial approach should be by letter

Massachusetts

Thomas Anthony Pappas Charitable Foundation, Inc.
P.O. Box 463
Belmont, MA 02178
(617) 862-2802
Contact: Charles A. Pappas, President and Treasurer
Geographic Giving Pattern: Primarily Massachusetts
Special Interest:: Higher education, hospitals, cultural programs,
Greek Orthodox church support, religious associations, and youth
and social service agencies
Assets: $15,638,813
Grant Range: $100,000–$1,000
Limitations: No grants to individuals
Applications: Grant proposal letter should be submitted preferably in
March or September. The deadline is September 30.

Michigan

India Foundation
3308 South Cedar, Suite 11
Lansing, MI 48910
Contact: Charles Haynes
Geographic Giving Pattern: National
Special Interest:: East Indian religions and charitable organizations
Assets: $1,965,097
Grant Range: $23,401–$11
Applications: Initial approach should be by letter. The deadlines are
June 30 and November 30.

Alex and Marie Manoogian Foundation
21001 Van Born Road
Taylor, MI 48180
(313) 274-7400
Contact: Alex Manoogian, President
Geographic Giving Pattern: Primarily Michigan and California
Special Interest:: Armenian welfare funds and religious institutions,
higher and secondary education and cultural programs

Assets: $45,010,251
Grant Average: $500–$25,000
Limitations: No grants for annual campaigns, deficit financing, land acquisition, publications or conferences
Applications: Contributes to pre-selected organizations only. Applications not accepted.

Mardigian Foundation
13920 East Ten Mile Road
Warren, MI 48089
(313) 778-4120
Contact: Edward S. Mardigian, President
Special Interest:: Armenian church and cultural support, religious associations and welfare funds
Assets: $4,682,442
Grant Range: $100,00–$10
Applications: Initial approach should be by letter. Telephone solicitations are not accepted. There are no deadlines.

New York

Dadourian Foundation
168 Canal Street, Suite 207
New York, NY 10013
Contact: Haig Dadourian, Secretary-Treasurer
Geographic Giving Pattern: New York, New York metropolitan area
Special Interest:: Armenian organizations, including churches and schools
Assets: $1,754,432
Grant Range: $31,305–$20
Applications: Initial approach should be by letter

United Armenian Charities, Inc.
c/o Sal Sica
168 Canal Street, Suite 207
New York, NY 10013
Contact: Dadour Dadourian, President
Geographic Giving Pattern: Primarily New York
Special Interest:: Armenian religious support, education and social services
Assets: $1,678,750
Grant Range: $32,000–$90
Applications: Initial approach should be by letter

Washington

Kawabe Memorial Fund
(Also known as Harry S. Kawabe Trust)
c/o Seattle First National Bank, Charitable Trust Administration
P.O. Box 3586
Seattle, WA 98124
(206) 358-3388
Contact: Rod K. Johnson, Vice-President, Seattle First National Bank
Geographic Giving Pattern: Primarily Seattle, Washington and Arkansas
Special Interest:: Buddhist support
Assets: $2,015,481
Grant Average: $8,000
Applications: There are no deadlines for grant proposals

APPENDIX A

The Foundation Center Cooperating Collections Network

Free Funding Information Centers

The Foundation Center is an independent national service organization established by foundations to provide an authoritative source of information on private philanthropic giving. The New York, Washington, DC, Cleveland and San Francisco reference collections operated by the Foundation Center offer a wide variety of services and comprehensive collections of information on foundations and grants. Cooperating Collections are libraries, community foundations and other nonprofit agencies that provide a core collection of Foundation Center publications and a variety of supplementary materials and services in areas useful to grant seekers.

Many of the network members have sets of private foundation information returns (IRS 990-PF) for their state or region, which are available for public use. A complete set of U.S. foundation returns can be found at the New York and Washington, DC, offices of the Foundation Center. The Cleveland and San Francisco offices contain IRS 990-PF returns for the midwestern and western states, respectively. Those Cooperating Collections marked with a bullet (•) have sets of private foundation information returns for their state or region.

Because the collections vary in their hours, materials and services, it is recommended that you call each collection in advance. To check on new locations or more current information, call toll-free: 1-800-424-9836.

Where to Go for Information on Foundation Funding

The following is a complete list of reference collections operated by the Foundation Center and cooperating collections:

Reference Collections Operated by the Foundation Center

The Foundation Center
8th Floor
79 Fifth Avenue
New York, NY 10003
212-620-4230

The Foundation Center
Room 312
312 Sutter Street
San Francisco, CA 94108
415-397-0902

The Foundation Center
1001 Connecticut Avenue, NW
Washington, DC 20036
202-331-1400

The Foundation Center
Kent H. Smith Library
1442 Hanna Building
Cleveland, OH 44115
216-861-1933

Cooperating Collections
Alabama

• Birmingham Public Library
Government Documents
2100 Park Place
Birmingham 35203
205-226-3600

Huntsville Public Library
915 Monroe Street
Huntsville 35801
205-532-5940

University of South Alabama
Library Reference Department
Mobile 36688
205-460-7025

• Auburn University at Montgomery Library
7300 University Drive
Montgomery 36117-3596
205-244-3653

Alaska
• University of Alaska
Anchorage Library
3211 Providence Drive
Anchorage 99508
907-786-1848

Juneau Public Library
292 Marine Way
Juneau 99801
907-586-5249

Arizona
• Phoenix Public Library
Business & Sciences Department
12 East McDowell Road
Phoenix 85257
602-262-4636

• Tucson Public Library
101 N. Stone Avenue
Tucson 85726-7470
602-791-4393

Arkansas
• Westark Community College Library
5210 Grand Avenue
Fort Smith 72913
501-785-7000

Central Arkansas Library System
Reference Services
700 Louisiana Street
Little Rock 72201
501-370-5950

California

Ventura County Community Foundation
Community Resource Center
1357 Del Norte Road
Camarillo 93010
805-988-0196

• Orange County Community Developmental Council
1695 W. MacArthur Boulevard
Costa Mesa 92626
714-540-9293

• California Community Foundation
Funding Information Center
606 S. Olive Street, Suite 2400
Los Angeles 90014-1526
213-413-4042

• Community Foundation for Monterey County
177 Van Buren
Monterey 93942
408-375-9712

Riverside Public Library
3581 7th Street
Riverside 92501
714-782-5201

California State Library
Reference Services, Room 301
914 Capitol Mall
Sacramento 94237-0001
916-322-4570

Nonprofit Resource Center
Sacramento Central Library
Downtown Plaza South Mall
Sacramento 95812-2036
916-449-2131

• San Diego Community Foundation
525 "B" Street, Suite 410
San Diego 92101
619-239-8815

• Nonprofit Development Center
1762 Technology Drive, Suite 225
San Jose 95110
408-452-8181

• Peninsula Community Foundation
1700 S. El Camino Real
San Mateo 94402-3049
415-358-9392

Volunteer Center Resource Library
1000 E. Santa Ana Boulevard
Santa Ana 92701
714-953-1655

• Santa Barbara Public Library
40 East Anapamu
Santa Barbara 93101-1603
805-962-7653

Santa Monica Public Library
1343 Sixth Street
Santa Monica 90401-1603
213-458-8600

Colorado
Pikes Peak Library District
20 North Cascade Avenue
Colorado Springs 80901
719-473-2080

• Denver Public Library
Sociology Division
1357 Broadway
Denver 80203
303-640-8870

Connecticut
Danbury Public Library
170 Main Street
Danbury 06810
203-797-4527

• Hartford Public Library
Reference Department
500 Main Street
Hartford 06103
203-293-6000

D.A.T.A.
70 Audubon Street
New Haven 06510
203-772-1345

Delaware

• University of Delaware
Hugh Morris Library
Newark 19717-5267
302-451-2432

Florida

Volusia County Library Center
City Island
Daytona Beach 32014-4484
904-255-3765

• Nova University
Einstein Library-Foundation Resource Collection
3301 College Avenue
Fort Lauderdale 33314
305-475-7497

Indian River Community College
Learning Resources Center
3209 Virginia Avenue
Fort Pierce 34981-5599
407-468-4757

• Jacksonville Public Libraries
Business, Science & Documents
122 North Ocean Street
Jacksonville 32206
904-630-2665

• Miami-Dade Public Library
Humanities Department
101 W. Flagler Street
Miami 33130
305-375-2665

• Orlando Public Library
Orange County Library System
101 E. Central Boulevard
Orlando 32801
407-425-4694

Selby Public Library
1001 Boulevard of the Arts
Sarasota 34236
813-951-5501

• Leon County Public Library
Funding Resource Center
1940 North Monroe Street
Tallahassee 32303
904-487-2665

Palm Beach County Community Foundation
324 Datura Street, Suite 340
West Palm Beach 33401
407-659-6800

Georgia
• Atlanta-Fulton Public Library
Foundation Collection-Ivan Allen Department
1 Margaret Mitchell Square
Atlanta 30303-1089
404-730-1900

Hawaii
• Hawaii Community Foundation
Hawaii Resource Room
222 Merchant Street
Honolulu 96813
808-537-6333
University of Hawaii

Thomas Hale Hamilton Library
2550 The Mall
Honolulu 96822
808-956-7214

Idaho

- Boise Public Library
715 S. Capitol Boulevard
Boise 83702
208-384-4024

- Caldwell Public Library
1010 Dearborn Street
Caldwell 83605
208-459-3242

Illinois

Belleville Public Library
121 East Washington Street
Belleville 62220
618-234-0441

- Donors Forum of Chicago
53 W. Jackson Boulevard, Room 430
Chicago 60604
312-431-0265

- Evanston Public Library
1703 Orrington Avenue
Evanston 60201
708-866-0305

- Sangamon State University Library
Shepherd Road
Springfield 62794-9243
217-786-6633

Indiana

- Allen County Public Library
900 Webster Street
Fort Wayne 46802
219-424-7241

Indiana University Northwest Library
3400 Broadway
Gary 46408
219-980-6582

- Indianapolis-Marion County Public Library
40 East St. Clair Street
Indianapolis 46206
317-269-1733

Iowa

• Cedar Rapids Public Library
Funding Information Center
500 First Street, SE
Cedar Rapids 52401
319-398-5123

• Southwestern Community College
Learning Resource Center
1501 W. Townline Road
Creston 50801
515-782-7081, ext. 262

• Public Library of Des Moines
100 Locust Street
Des Moines 50308
515-283-4152

Kansas

• Topeka Public Library
1515 West Tenth Street
Topeka 66604
913-233-2040

• Wichita Public Library
223 South Main
Wichita 67202
316-262-0611

Kentucky

Western Kentucky University
Helm-Cravens Library
Bowling Green 42101
502-745-6125

• Louisville Free Public Library
301 York Street
Louisville 40203
502-561-8617

Louisiana

• East Baton Rouge Parish Library
Centroplex Branch
120 St. Louis Street
Baton Rouge 70802
504-389-4960

- New Orleans Public Library
  Business and Science Division
  219 Loyola Avenue
  New Orleans 70140
  504-596-2580

- Shreve Memorial Library
  424 Texas Street
  Shreveport 71120-1523
  318-226-5894

Maine
- University of Southern Maine
  Office of Sponsored Research
  246 Deering Avenue, Room 628
  Portland 04103
  207-780-4871

Maryland
- Enoch Pratt Free Library
  Social Science and History Department
  400 Cathedral Street
  Baltimore 21201
  301-396-5320

  Carroll County Public Library
  Government and Funding Information Center
  50 E. Main Street
  Westminster 21157
  301-848-4250

Massachusetts
- Associated Grantmakers of Massachusetts
  294 Washington Street
  Suite 840
  Boston 02108
  617-426-2608

- Boston Public Library
  666 Boylston Street
  Boston 02117
  617-536-5400

Western Massachusetts Funding Resource Center
Campaign for Human Development
65 Elliot Street
Springfield 01101
413-732-3175

• Worcester Public Library
Grants Resource Center
Salem Square
Worcester 01608
508-799-1655

Michigan

• Alpena County Library
211 North First Avenue
Alpena 49707
517-356-6188

University of Michigan-Ann Arbor
209 Hatcher Graduate Library
Ann Arbor 48109-1205
313-764-1148

• Battle Creek Community Foundation
One Riverwalk Centre
34 W. Jackson Street
Battle Creek 49017
616-962-2181

• Henry Ford Centennial Library
16301 Michigan Avenue
Dearborn 48126
313-943-2330

• Wayne State University
Purdy-Kresge Library
5265 Cass Avenue
Detroit 48202
313-577-6424

• Michigan State University Libraries
Reference Library
East Lansing 48824-1048
517-353-8818

- Farmington Community Library
  32737 West 12 Mile Road
  Farmington Hills 48018
  313-553-0300

- University of Michigan-Flint Library
  Reference Department
  Flint 48502-2186
  313-762-3408

- Grand Rapids Public Library
  Business Department
  60 Library Plaza NE
  Grand Rapids 49503-3093
  616-456-3600

- Michigan Technological University Library
  1400 Townsend Drive
  Houghton 49931
  906-487-2507

- Sault Ste. Marie Area Public Schools
  Office of Compensatory Education
  460 W. Spruce Street
  Sault Ste. Marie 49783-1874
  906-635-6619

Minnesota

- Duluth Public Library
  520 W. Superior Street
  Duluth 55802
  218-723-3802

  Southwest State University Library
  Marshall 56258
  507-537-7278

- Minneapolis Public Library
  Sociology Department
  300 Nicollet Mall
  Minneapolis 55401
  612-372-6555

  Rochester Public Library
  11 First Street, SE
  Rochester 55902-3743
  507-285-8000

St. Paul Public Library
90 West Fourth Street
Saint Paul 55102
612-292-6307

Mississippi

Jackson-Hinds Library System
300 North State Street
Jackson 39201
601-968-5803

Missouri

• Clearinghouse for Midcontinent Foundations
University of Missouri Law School, Suite 1-300
52nd Street and Oak
Kansas City 64113-0680
816-235-1176

• Kansas City Public Library
311 East 12th Street
Kansas City 64106
816-221-9650

• Metropolitan Association for Philanthropy, Inc.
5585 Pershing Avenue
Suite 150
St. Louis 63112
314-361-3900

• Springfield-Greene County Library
397 East Central Street
Springfield 65801
417-866-4636

Montana

• Eastern Montana College Library
1500 N. 30th Street
Billings 59101-0298
406-657-1662

• Montana State Library
Reference Department
1515 E. 6th Avenue
Helena 59620
406-444-3004

Nebraska
• University of Nebraska
106 Love Library
14th & R Streets
Lincoln 68588-0410
402-472-2848

• W. Dale Clark Library
Social Sciences Department
215 South 15th Street
Omaha 68102
402-444-4826

Nevada
• Las Vegas-Clark County Library District
1401 East Flamingo Road
Las Vegas 89119-6160
702-733-7810

• Washoe County Library
301 South Center Street
Reno 89501
702-785-4012

New Hampshire
• New Hampshire Charitable Fund
One South Street
Concord 03302-1335
603-225-6641

• Plymouth State College
Herbert H. Lamson Library
Plymouth 03264
603-535-2258

New Jersey
Cumberland County Library
800 E. Commerce Street
Bridgeton 08302-2295
609-453-2210

The Support Center
17 Academy Street, Suite 1101
Newark 07102
201-643-5774

County College of Morris
Masten Learning Resource Center
Route 10 and Center Grove Road
Randolph 07869
201-328-5296

• New Jersey State Library
Governmental Reference
185 West State Street
Trenton 08625-0520
609-292-6220

New Mexico

Albuquerque Community Foundation
6400 Uptown Boulevard N.E.
Albuquerque 87105
505-883-6240

• New Mexico State Library
325 Don Gaspar Street
Santa Fe 97503
505-827-3824

New York

• New York State Library
Cultural Education Center
Humanities Section
Empire State Plaza
Albany 12230
518-473-4636

Suffolk Cooperative Library System
627 North Sunrise Service Road
Bellport 11713
516-286-1600

New York Public Library
Bronx Reference Center
2556 Bainbridge Avenue
Bronx 10458
212-220-6575

Brooklyn in Touch
One Hanson Place
Room 2504
Brooklyn 11243
718-230-3200

• Buffalo and Erie County Public Library
Lafayette Square
Buffalo 14202
716-858-7103

Huntington Public Library
338 Main Street
Huntington 11743
516-427-5165

Queens Borough Public Library
89-11 Merrick Boulevard
Jamaica 11432
718-990-0700

• Levittown Public Library
One Bluegrass Lane
Levittown 11756
516-731-5728

SUNY/College at Old Westbury Library
223 Store Hill Road
Old Westbury 11568
516-876-3156

Adriance Memorial Library
93 Market Street
Poughkeepsie 12601
914-485-3445

• Rochester Public Library
Business Division
115 South Avenue
Rochester 14604
716-428-7328

Staten Island Council on the Arts
One Edgewater Plaza, Room 311
Staten Island 10305
718-447-4485

• Onondaga County Public Library at the Galleries
447 S. Salina Street
Syracuse 13202-2494
315-448-4636

• White Plains Public Library
100 Martine Avenue
White Plains 10601
914-442-1480

North Carolina
• Asheville-Buncomb Technical Community College
Learning Resources Center
340 Victoria Road
Asheville 28802
704-254-1921, ext. 300

• The Duke Endowment
200 S. Tryon Street, Suite 1100
Charlotte 28202
704-376-0291

Durham County Library
300 N. Roxboro Street
Durham 27702
919-560-0100

• North Carolina State Library
109 East Jones Street
Raleigh 27611
919-733-3270

• The Winston-Salem Foundation
310 W. 4th Street, Suite 229
Winston-Salem 27101-2889
919-725-2382

North Dakota
• North Dakota State University
The Library
Fargo 58105
701-237-8886

Ohio
Stark County District Library
715 Market Avenue North
Canton 44702-1080
216-452-0665

• Public Library of Cincinnati and Hamilton County
Education Department
800 Vine Street
Cincinnati 45202-2071
513-369-6940

Columbus Metropolitan Library
96 S. Grant Avenue
Columbus 43215
614-645-2590

• Dayton and Montgomery County Public Library
Grants Information Center
215 E. Third Street
Dayton 45402-2103
513-227-9500 ext. 211

• Toledo-Lucas County Public Library
Social Science Department
325 Michigan Street
Toledo 43623-1614
419-259-5245

Ohio University-Zanesville
Community Education and Development
1425 Newark Road
Zanesville 43701
614-453-0762

Oklahoma
• Oklahoma City University Library
2501 North Blackwelder
Oklahoma City 73106
405-521-5072

• Tulsa City-County Library System
400 Civic Center
Tulsa 74103
918-596-7944

Oregon
Oregon Institute of Technology Library
3201 Campus Drive
Klamath Falls 97601-8801
503-885-1772

Pacific Non-Profit Network
Grantsmanship Resource Library
33 N. Central, Suite 211
Medford 97501
503-779-6044

• Multnomah County Library
Government Documents Room
801 S.W. Tenth Avenue
Portland 97205-2597
503-223-7201

Oregon State Library
State Library Building
Salem 97310
503-378-4277

Pennsylvania

Northampton Community College
Learning Resources Center
3835 Green Pond Road
Bethlehem 18017
215-861-5360

• Erie County Public Library
3 South Perry Square
Erie 16501
814-451-6927

Dauphin County Library System
101 Walnut Street
Harrisburg 17101
717-234-4961

Lancaster County Public Library
125 North Duke Street
Lancaster 17602
717-394-2651

• The Free Library of Philadelphia
Logan Square
Philadelphia 19103
215-686-5423

• University of Pittsburgh
Hillman Library
Pittsburgh 15260
412-648-7722

Economic Development Council of Northeastern Pennsylvania
1151 Oak Street
Pittston 18640
717-655-5581

Rhode Island

• Providence Public Library
Reference Department
150 Empire Street
Providence 02903
401-521-7722

South Carolina

• Charleston County Library
404 King Street
Charleston 29403
803-723-1645

• South Carolina State Library
Reference Department
1500 Senate Street
Columbia 29211
803-734-8666

South Dakota

• South Dakota State Library
800 Governors Drive
Pierre 57501-2294
605-773-5070
800-592-1841 (SD residents)

Sioux Falls Area Foundation
141 N. Main Avenue, Suite 500
Sioux Falls 57102-1134
605-336-7055

Tennessee

• Knoxville-Knox County Public Library
500 West Church Avenue
Knoxville 37902
615-544-5750

• Memphis & Shelby County Public Library
1850 Peabody Avenue
Memphis 38104
901-725-8877

• Public Library of Nashville and Davidson County
8th Avenue N. and Union Street
Nasville 37203
615-259-6256

Texas

• Community Foundation of Abilene
Funding Information Library
708 NCNB Building
402 Cypress
Abilene 79601
915-676-3883

Amarillo Area Foundation
700 1st National Place One
800 S. Fillmore
Amarillo 79101
806-376-4521

• Hogg Foundation for Mental Health
University of Texas
Austin 78713-7998
512-471-5041

• Corpus Christi State University Library
6300 Ocean Drive
Corpus Christi 78412
512-994-2608

• Dallas Public Library
Grants Information Service
1515 Young Street
Dallas 75201
214-670-1487

• Pan American University
Learning Resource Center
1201 W. University Drive
Edinburg 78539
512-381-3304

- El Paso Community Foundation
1616 Texas Commerce Building
El Paso 79901
915-533-4020

- Texas Christian University Library
Funding Information Center
Fort Worth 76129
817-921-7664

- Houston Public Library
Bibliographic Information Center
500 McKinney Avenue
Houston 77002
713-236-1313

Lubbock Area Foundation
502 Texas Commerce Bank Building
Lubbock 79401
806-762-8061

- Funding Information Center
507 Brooklyn
San Antonio 78215
512-227-4333

Utah
- Salt Lake City Public Library
Business and Science Department
209 East Fifth South
Salt Lake City 84111
801-363-5733

Vermont
- Vermont Department of Libraries
Reference Services
109 State Street
Montpelier 05609
802-828-3268

Virginia
- Hampton Public Library
Grants Resources Collection
4207 Victoria Boulevard
Hampton 23669
804-727-1154

- Richmond Public Library
  Business, Science & Technology
  101 East Franklin Street
  Richmond 23219
  804-780-8223

- Roanoke City Public Library System
  Central Library
  706 S. Jefferson Street
  Roanoke 24016
  703-981-2477

Washington

- Seattle Public Library
  1000 Fourth Avenue
  Seattle 98104
  206-386-4620

- Spokane Public Library
  Funding Information Center
  West 906 Main Avenue
  Spokane 99201
  509-838-3364

  Greater Wenatchee Community Foundation at the
  Wenatchee Public Library
  310 Douglas Street
  Wenatchee 98807
  509-662-5021

West Virginia

- Kanawha County Public Library
  123 Capital Street
  Charleston 25304
  304-343-4646

Wisconsin

- University of Wisconsin-Madison
  Memorial Library
  728 State Street
  Madison 53706
  608-262-3242

- Marquette University Memorial Library
  1415 West Wisconsin Avenue
  Milwaukee 53233
  414-288-1515

Wyoming

- Laramie County Community College Library
  1400 East College Drive
  Cheyenne 82007-3299
  307-778-1205

Australia

ANZ Executors & Trustees Co. Ltd.
91 William Street, 7th Floor
Melbourne VIC 3000
03-648-5764

Canada

Canadian Centre for Philanthropy
1329 Bay Street, Suite 200
Toronto, Ontario M5R 2C4
416-515-0764

England

Charities Aid Foundation
18 Doughty Street
London WC1N 2PL
71-831-7798

Japan

Foundation Center Library of Japan
Elements Shinjuku Building 3F
2-1-14 Shinjuku, Shinjuku-ku
Tokyo 160
03-350-1857

Mexico

Biblioteca Benjamin Franklin
American Embassy, USICA
Londres 16
Mexico City 6, D.F. 06600
905-211-0042

Puerto Rico
University of Puerto Rico
Ponce Technological College Library
Box 7186
Ponce 00732
809-844-8181

Universidad Del Sagrado Corazon
M.M.T. Guevarra Library
Correo Calle Loiza
Santurce 00914
809-728-1515 ext. 357

U.S. Virgin Islands
University of the Virgin Islands
Paiewonsky Library
Charlotte Amalie
St. Thomas 00802
809-776-9200

APPENDIX B

Directories of State and Local Grant Makers

Alabama (362 foundations). *Alabama Foundation Directory.* Compiled by the Public Documents Department, Birmingham Public Library, 1990. 67 p. Based primarily on 990-PF returns filed with the IRS. Main section arranged alphabetically by foundation; entries include areas of interest and officers; no sample grants. Indexes of geographic areas and major areas of interest. Available from Reference Department, Birmingham Public Library, 2100 Park Place, Birmingham, Alabama 35203. $5.00

Arizona (102 foundations). *Arizona Foundation Directory 1991-1992.* 3rd edition. Compiled by the Junior League of Phoenix, Inc. 1991. 52 p. Based on most recent 990-PF returns filed with the IRS. Lists foundations with assets over $5,000 and grants over $500. Main section arranged alphabetically by foundation entries, including purpose, restrictions, officers, sample grants. Available from the Junior League of Phoenix, P.O. Box 10377, Phoenix, AZ 85064. $15.00

Arkansas (146 grant-makers). *Guide to Arkansas Funding Sources.* 4th edition. Edited by Earl W. Anthes and Jerry Cronin. 1990. 150 p. Main section arranged alphabetically under three categories: Arkansas foundations, scholarship sources and religious funding sources. Available from Independent Community Consultants, Post Office Box 141, Hampton, Arkansas 71744. $25.00

California (800+ foundations). *Guide to California Foundations.* 8th edition. 511 p. Prepared by Carol Fanning. 1991. Based on most recent 990-PF returns filed with the IRS or records in the California Attorney General's Office; some additional data supplied by foundations completing questionnaires. Main section arranged alphabetically by foundation; entries include statement of purpose, sample grants and officers. Also section on applying for grants. Indexes of all foundations by name and county location; index of primary interest only for those foundations completing questionnaire. Price and ordering information available from Northern

California Grant-makers, 116 New Montgomery Street, Suite 742, San Francisco, CA 94108.

California *San Diego County Foundation Directory.* Compiled by the San Diego Community Foundation. 1990. Loose-leaf binder that contains duplicated copies of IRS 990-PF returns for funding sources in San Diego. Available from San Diego Community Foundation, 101 West Broadway, Suite 1120, San Diego, CA 92101. $20.00

Colorado (approximately 170 foundations). *Colorado Foundation Directory* 1990-91. 7th edition. Co-sponsored by the Junior League of Denver, the Denver Foundation and the Attorney General of Colorado. 1990. 133 p. Based on most current 990-PF returns filed with the IRS and information supplied by the foundations; entries include statement of purpose, sample grants and officers. Also sections on proposal writing, sample proposal, and sample budget form. Available from Colorado Foundation Director, Junior League of Denver, Inc., 6300 East Yale Avenue, Denver, CO 80222. Make check payable to: Colorado Foundation Directory. $12.00 including postage.

Connecticut (61+ foundations). *Directory of the Major Connecticut Foundations.* Compiled by Logos, Inc. Available from Logos Associates, 7 Park Street, Room 212, Attleboro, MA 02703. $39.95

Connecticut (1250+ foundations). *Connecticut Foundation Directory* 1990-91. 6th edition. Edited by Michael E. Burns. 1990. 573 p. Based primarily on most current 990-PF returns filed with the Connecticut Attorney General. Main section arranged alphabetically by foundation; entries include complete grants list and principal officer; no statement of purpose. Index of foundations by city and alphabetical index. Available from D.A.T.A., 70 Audubon, New Haven, CT 06510. $50.00 plus $4.00 shipping.

Connecticut (850+ foundations). *Guide to Corporate Giving in Connecticut.* Edited by Michael E. Burns. 1986. Based on information supplied by corporations. Main section arranged alphabetically by corporation; entries for most corporations include areas of interest, giving policies, geographic preference, and contact person. Indexes of corporations by town. Available from D.A.T.A., 70 Audubon, New Haven, CT 06510. $15.00 plus $3.00 shipping.

Delaware (154 foundations). *Delaware Foundations.* Produced by Delaware Community Foundation. 1990. 124 p. Based on most current 990-PF and 990-AR returns filed with the IRS, annual reports and information supplied by foundations. Main section arranged alphabetically by foundation; entries include statement of purpose and officers, grant analysis, type of recipient; no sample grants. Available from Delaware Community Foundation, Post Office Box 25207, Wilmington, DE 19899. $16.25 including postage.

District of Columbia (430 foundations). *The Directory of Foundations of the Greater Washington Area.* 1991. 178 p. Based on most current 990-PF returns filed with the IRS. Sections on large foundation, small foundations and publicly supported institutions arranged alphabetically; entries include areas of interest, officers and directors, high and low grant and five highest grants. Available from the Community Foundation of Greater Washington, Inc., 1002 Wisconsin Avenue, NW, Washington, DC 20007. $25.00 plus $3.00 postage and handling.

Florida (1,000+ foundations). *The Complete Guide to Florida Foundations.* Edited by D.B. Carlton. 3rd edition. 356 p. Based on information obtained from 990-PF returns, annual reports and survey responses. Lists foundations with assets over $2,500. Index by county, corporate foundation index and priority matrix of foundation funding. Available from Florida Funding Publications, Inc., a division of John L. Adams and Company, P.O. Box 561565, Miami, FL 33256-1565. $90.00

Florida (107 foundations). *The Directory of the Major Florida Foundations.* 1987. Lists foundations which have given away a minimum of $50,000 in the year of record, the bulk of it in Florida. Available from Logos Associates, 7 Park Street, Room 212, Attleboro, MA 02703. $39.95

Hawaii (55 foundations). *Directory of Charitable Trusts and Foundations for Hawaii's Non-Profit Organizations.* Compiled by Marcie Hanson, published by the Volunteer, Information and Referral Service with a grant from the Hawaiian Community Foundation. Lists current information on 55 Hawaiian foundations and 25 mainland foundations which have made grants of at least $5,000 to Hawaiian organizations. Available from the Volunteer, Information and Referral Service, 780 Iwilei Road, Suite 430, Honolulu, HI 96817. $20.00 plus $2.00 postage and handling.

Idaho (123 foundations). *Directory of Idaho Foundations.* 5th edition. Prepared by the Caldwell Public Library. 1990. 101 p. Based on most current 990-PF returns filed with the IRS and questionnaires. Main section arranged alphabetically by foundation; entries include area of interest, sample grants, directors and trustees, and application deadlines. Indexed by foundation name. Appendixes of grant application deadlines, and geographic orientation of foundations. Available from Caldwell Public Library, 1010 Dearborn Street, Caldwell, ID 83605-4195. $10.00 prepaid.

Illinois (approximately 54 grant-makers). *Donors Forum Members Grants List 1988.* A collection of grants of $500 or more awarded by Donors Forum members to organizations within the Chicago Metropolitan Area. Grant-makers arranged alphabetically under ten subject categories; entries include name of donee, amount of grant and whether the grant is new or a renewal of a previous grant; no address, financial data or officers. Appendix of miscellaneous grants. Available from Donors Forum of Chicago, 53 West Jackson Boulevard, Suite 430, Chicago, IL 60604. $60.00 plus postage and handling.

Illinois (493 foundations). *The Directory of Illinois Foundations.* 2nd edition. Edited by Marty Bowes. 1989. 297 p. Alphabetically arranged directory of Illinois foundations and trusts; indexes to trustees, cities, counties, areas of giving, foundations. Available from Donors Forum of Chicago, 53 West Jackson Boulevard, Suite 430, Chicago, IL 60604. $40.00

Illinois (1,976 foundations). *Illinois Foundation Directory.* Edited by Beatrice J. Capriotti and Frank J. Capriotti. 1991. 527+ p. Basted on most current 990-PF and 990-AR returns filed with the IRS plus correspondence with some foundations. Main section arranged alphabetically by foundation; entries include statement of purpose, grants and officers. Table of contents alphabetical by foundation name. Available from the Foundation Data Center, Kenmar Center, 401 Kenmar Circle, Minnetonka, MN 55343. $650.00 including one year of update service and access to a hot line, a research seminar. Update service by annual subscription, $255.00

Illinois (112 corporate foundations). *Chicago's Corporate Foundations: A Directory of Chicago Area and Illinois Corporate Foundations.* 3rd edition. Ellen Dick. 1992. A statewide alphabetical listing of corporate foundations; no sample grants. Subject index. Available from Ellen Dick, 838 Fair Oaks, Oak Park, IL, 60302. $35.00

Illinois *Members Grants List.* Donors Forum of Chicago. 1988. Lists grants of $500 or more awarded by 54 Donors Forum members to organizations within the Chicago Metropolitan Area. Available from Donors Forum of Chicago, 53 West Jackson Boulevard, Suite 430, Chicago, IL 60604. $60.00 plus $3.50 shipping and handling.

Illinois (145 foundations and corporate contributions programs). *Members and Library Partners Directory.* Donors Forum of Chicago. 1988. Provides data on Donors Forum member foundations, including principal funding areas, officers and corporate contributions programs. Available from Donors Forum of Chicago, 53 West Jackson Boulevard, Suite 430, Chicago, IL 60604. $25.00

Indiana (475 foundations, trusts, and scholarship programs). *Directory of Indiana Donors 1989-90.* Indiana Donors Alliance. 1989. 134 p. Contains profiles of active grant-making foundations, trusts, and scholarship programs. No sample grants. Indexed by grants paid, program interest, county. Available from Indiana Donors Alliance, 1500 North Delaware Street, Indianapolis, IN 46202. $15.00

Kansas (300+ foundations). *Directory of Kansas Foundations.* 2nd edition. Edited by James H. Rhodes. 1989. Based on 990-PF and 990-AR returns filed with the IRS. Fiscal date of information not provided. Main section arranged alphabetically by foundation; entries include areas of interest, sample arts grants and officers. Indexed by cities, subjects funded. Available from James Rhodes, Topeka Public Library, 1515 West 10th Street, Topeka, KS 66604. $25.000

Kentucky. See **Tennessee:** *A Guide to Funders in Central Appalachia and the Tennessee Valley.* O'Donnell, Suzanna, et al.

Louisiana (112 foundations). *Citizens' Handbook of Private Foundations in New Orleans, Louisiana.* Compiled by Joseph A. Lazaro.

1987. 146 p. Based on 1985 990-PF returns filed with the IRS. Alphabetical listing of foundations located and making grants in New Orleans. Available from Greater New Orleans Foundation, 2515 Canal Street, Suite 404, New Orleans, LA 70119. $7.00

Maine (50+ foundations). *Directory of Maine Foundations.* Compiled by the Office of Sponsored Research, University of Southern Maine. 1990. 54 p. Based on information compiled from foundations, the Foundation Center, and 990-PF returns filed with the IRS. Main section arranged alphabetically by city or town of foundation. Entries include areas of interest, sample grants and principal officer. Also sections on basic elements in a letter of inquiry, a description of IRS information returns, a sample report to funding source, and a list of recent grants. Lists Maine corporate foundations and parent corporations with plant operations in the state. Available from Office of Sponsored Research, University of Southern Maine, 96 Falmouth Street, Portland, ME 04103. $8.00

Maine (200+ corporations). *Corporate Philanthropy in New England.* Volume 3: Maine. Michael E. Burns, editor. 1987-88 edition. 105 p. Based on questionnaires and telephone interviews. Main section arranged alphabetically; entries include product, plant locations, contributions and giving interests, if available. Index of foundations by city. Available from D.A.T.A., 70 Audubon, New Haven, CT 06510. $5.00 plus $3.00 shipping.

Maryland (approximately 566 foundations). *Annual Index of Foundation Reports and Appendix. Compiled by the Office of the Attorney General.* 1990. 225 p. Based on most current 990-PF returns received by the Maryland State Attorney General's Office. Main section arranged alphabetically by foundation; entries include statement of purpose and complete list of grants and officers. Available from the Office of the Attorney General, 200 St. Paul Place, Baltimore, MD 21202. $70.00 prepaid. Make check payable to The Attorney General's Office.

Massachusetts (438 foundations). *Massachusetts Grantmakers. Prepared by Associated Grantmakers of Massachusetts.* 1990. 207 p. Based on must current 990-PF and 990-AR returns filed with the IRS, and questionnaire responses. Main section arranged alphabetically by foundation name; entries include emphasis and program areas, total grants, range, assets, trustees, contact person; no sample grants. Indexes by program areas, city; index of foundations granting support to individuals. Appendixes of smaller Massachusetts foundations, company-sponsored foundations and recently terminated foundations. Available from Associated Grantmakers of Massachusetts, Inc., 294 Washington Street, Suite 840 Boston, Massachusetts 02108. $40.00 plus $3.00 shipping and handling.

Massachusetts (100 foundations). *Private Sector Giving: Greater Worcester Area.* Prepared by the Social Service Planning Corporation. 1987. Based on most current information from 990-PF and 990-AR forms filed with the IRS and surveys. Main section arranged alphabetically by foundation; entries include financial data, trustees and grants. Indexes of foundations and areas of subject interest. Available from the Social Service Planning Corporation, 340 Main Street, Suite 329, Worcester, MA 01608. $25.00 plus $2.25 postage and handling.

Michigan (1,171 foundations). *The Michigan Foundation Directory.* 7th edition. Edited by Jeri L. Fischer. Prepared by the Council of Michigan Foundations and the Michigan League for Human Services. 1990. 282 p. Based on information compiled from foundations, the Foundation Center, and most recent 990-PF returns filed with the IRS. Identifies the 534 largest foundations in the state (those with assets of $200,000 and/or grant-making of $25,000), 84 special purpose foundations, 471 smaller foundations, 66 corporate giving programs and/or foundations, and 16 public foundations. Available from Michigan League for Human Services, 300 North Washington Square, Suite 401, Lansing, MI 48933. $25.00

Michigan (350 foundations). *The Directory of the Major Michigan Foundations.* 2nd edition. 1989. In-depth information for over 350 corporate and private foundations, based on IRS financial data and the most current annual reports. Available from Logos Associates, 7 Park Street, Room 212, Attleboro, MA 02703. $39.95

Minnesota (650+ grantmakers). *Guide to Minnesota Foundations and Corporate Giving Programs, 1992-92.* 6th edition. Edited by Jacqueline Reis. 1991. 240 p. Based primarily on most current IRS

990-PF returns and a survey of grantmakers. Main section arranged alphabetically by foundation name; entries include program interests, officers and directors, assets, total grants, number of grants, range, and sample grants. Some entries include geographic orientation, types of organizations funded, and types of support. Indexes of foundations, types of organizations funded by specific grantmakers, and grantmakers by size. Available from Minnesota Council on Foundations, 425 Peavey Building, Minneapolis, MN 55402. $30.00 plus $1.50 postage, $2.10 sales tax if applicable.

Minnesota (700 foundations). *Minnesota Foundation Directory.* Edited by Beatrice J. Capriotti and Frank J. Capriotti. 1985. Based on most current 990-PF and 990-AR returns filed with the IRS. Main section arranged alphabetically by foundation; entries include statement of purpose, sample grants and officers. Indexes of donors, administrators and trustees, and banks and trust companies as corporate trustees. Available from Foundation Data Center, Kenmar Center, 401 Kenmar Circle, Minnetonka, MN 55343. $450.00 (Includes research training seminar, one year's updating and access to hotline information). Update service by annual subscription, $225.00

Minnesota (60 major foundations). *Minnesota Foundations Sourcebook.* Compiled by Minnesota Council of Nonprofits. 1989. 120 p. Provides detailed information on the grant-making activities of 60 major Minnesota foundations (private and corporate). Available from Minnesota Council of Non Profits, 2700 University Avenue West, St. Paul, MN 55114. $25.00

Mississippi. See **Tennessee:** *A Guide to Funders in Central Appalachia and the Tennessee Valley.* Suzanna O'Donnell, et al.

Missouri (919 foundations). *The Directory of Missouri Foundations.* 3rd edition. Compiled and edited by Wilda H. Swift. 1990. 132 p. Based on 990-PF returns and questionnaires of the foundations. Profiles large (annual grants $15,000+), community, and small foundations. Indexed alphabetically and by cities. Available from Swift Associates, 110 Orchard Avenue, St. Louis, MO 63119. $30.00 plus $3.50 postage and handling.

Missouri (394 foundations and trusts). *The Directory of Greater Kansas City Foundations.* Edited by Linda Hood Talbott, Clearinghouse for Midcontinent Foundations. 1991. 162 p. Profiles foundations and trusts in the eight-county Greater Kansas City (Missouri) metropolitan area. Available from Clearinghouse for Midcontinent Foundations, P.O. Box 22680, Kansas City, MO 64113-0680. $55.00 plus $3.00 postage and handling.

Montana (65 Montana and 20 Wyoming foundations). *The Montana and Wyoming Foundations Directory.* 5th edition. Edited by Kendal McRae and Kim Pederson. 1990. Based on 990-PF and 990-AR returns filed with the IRS, the National Data Book, and information supplied by the foundations. Main section arranged alphabetically by foundation; entries include areas of interest and contact person; no sample grants. Indexes of foundation names and areas of interest. Available from Grants Assistance Center, Eastern Montana College Library, 1500 North 30th Street, Billings, MT 59101. $10.00, including postage.

Nebraska (approximately 158 foundations). *Nebraska Foundation Directory.* Compiled by the Junior League of Omaha. 1989. 32 p. Based on most recent 990-PF and 990-AR returns filed with the IRS. Main section arranged alphabetically by foundation; entries include statement of purpose and officers. No sample grants or indexes. Available from Junior League of Omaha, 11915 Pierce Plaza, Omaha, NE 68144. $10.00

Nevada (82 foundations). *Nevada Foundation Directory.* 2nd edition. Compiled by Vlasta Honsa and Mark L. Stackpole. 1989. 132 p. Based on most current 990-PF forms filed with the IRS and interviews with foundations. Main section arranged alphabetically by foundation; entries include contact person, financial data, funding interests and sample grants. Section on 42 national foundations that fund Nevada projects. Index of fields of interest and index of foundation location. Available from Nevada Foundation Directory, Las Vegas-Clark County Library District, 1401 East Flamingo Road, Las Vegas, NV 89119. $15.00 plus $2.00 postage and handling.

New Hampshire (approximately 400 foundations). *Directory of Charitable Funds in New Hampshire: For General Charitable Purposes* *and Scholarship Aid.* 4th edition. 1988. 83 p. Based on records in the New Hampshire Attorney General's office. Updated with cumulative, annual supplement published in June. Main section arranged alphabetically by foundation; entries include statement of purpose and officers; no sample grants. Geographical index and index of purpose. Available from the Office of the Attorney General, Division of Charitable Trusts, 25 Capitol Street, Concord, NH 03301-6397. $5.00. Annual supplement which includes changes, deletions, and additions available from same address. Make checks payable to State of N.H.

New Hampshire (275 corporate giving programs). *Corporate Philanthropy in New England: New Hampshire.* Volume 2. Edited by Michael E. Burns. 1987. 159 p. Based on information supplied by corporations. Main section arranged alphabetically by corporation; entries for most corporations include areas of interest, giving policies, geographic preference and contact person. Indexes of corporations by town. Available from D.A.T.A., 70 Audubon, New Haven, CT 06510. $5.00 plus $3.00 shipping.

New Jersey (360 foundations). *The Mitchell Guide to Foundations, Corporations, and Their Managers, New Jersey.* Edited by Wendy P. Littman. 1990. Based primarily on 990-PF returns filed with the IRS and information supplied by the foundations. Main section arranged alphabetically by foundation; entries include sample grants and officers; no statement of purpose. Also sections on corporations. Indexes of foundations and corporations by county and by managers. Available from Wendy P. Littman, P.O. Box 613, Belle Mead, NJ 08502. $125.00

New Jersey (approximately 110 foundations). *The Directory of the Major New Jersey Foundations.* 2nd edition. Prepared by Logos Associates, 1988. 83 p. Based on financial information. Arranged alphabetically by foundation; entries include contact person, activities, officers and directors, geographic limitations, financial data, and sample grants. No indexes. Available from Logos Associates, 7 Park Street, Room 212, Attleboro, MA 02703. $39.95

New Mexico (295 foundations). *New Mexico Funding Directory.* 2nd edition. Edited by Denise A. Wallen. 1990. 139 p. Alphabetical listing of foundations with officers, statement of purpose, sample grants. Indexed by subject. Available from Office of Research Administration, University of New Mexico, Scholes Hall, Room 102, Albuquerque, NM 87131. $15.00 prepaid.

New York (90 foundations and 100 corporations). *The Mitchell Guide to Foundations, Corporations and Their Managers: Central New York, Including Binghamton, Corning, Elmira, Geneva, Ithaca, Oswego, Syracuse, Utica.* 2nd edition. Edited by Rowland L. Mitchell, Jr. 1987. 80 p. Based on 990-PF returns filed with the IRS. Main sections arranged alphabetically by foundation and by corporation; entries include managers, financial data, and sample grants. Alphabetical indexes of foundations and corporations and index to managers. Available from The Mitchell Guide, Rowland L. Mitchell, Box 172, Scarsdale, NY 10583. $30.00

New York (180 foundations and 130 corporations). *The Mitchell Guide to Foundations, Corporations and Their Managers: Long Island, Including Nassau and Suffolk Counties.* 2nd edition. Edited by Rowland L. Mitchell, Jr. 1987. 116 p. $30.00

New York (60 foundations and 40 corporations). *The Mitchell Guide to Foundations, Corporations and Their Managers: Upper Hudson Valley, Including Capital Area, Glens Falls, Newburgh, Plattsburgh, Poughkeepsie, Schenectady.* 2nd edition. Edited by Rowland L. Mitchell, Jr. 1987. 45 p. $30.00

New York (214 foundations and 75 corporations). *The Mitchell Guide to Foundations, Corporations and Their Managers: Westchester, Including Putnam, Rockland and Orange Counties.* 2nd edition. Edited by Rowland L. Mitchell, Jr. 1987. 126 p. $30.00

New York (130 foundations and 90 corporations). *The Mitchell Guide to Foundations, Corporations and Their Managers: Western New York, Including Buffalo, Jamestown, Niagara Falls, Rochester.* 2nd edition. Edited by Rowland L. Mitchell, Jr. 1987. 106 p. $30.00

New York (2,183 foundations and 557 corporations). *The Mitchell Guide to Foundations, Corporations, and Their Managers: New York City.* Edited by Rowland L. Mitchell, Jr. 644 p. $150.00

New York (4,000 foundations). *New York State Foundations: A Comprehensive Directory.* 2nd edition. Published by the Foundation Center. 1991. 799 p. Comprehensive directory of independent, company-sponsored, and community foundations that are currently active in New York State and that have awarded grants of $1 or more in the latest fiscal year. Supplemental grant lists for over 800 entries. Index of 300 grantmakers outside of New York that fund groups in the state. Available from the Foundation Center, 79 Fifth Avenue, Dept. RE, New York, NY 10003-3050. $150.00 plus $4.50 shipping.

North Carolina (700 foundations). *North Carolina Giving: The Directory of the State's Foundations.* Compiled by Anita Gunn Shirley. 1990. 862 p. Based on information from 990-PF returns filed with North Carolina Attorney General's office and the IRS. Indexed by subject, county, alphabetically by foundation. Main sections list large, medium and small foundations alphabetically. Available from Capital Consortium, Inc. P.O. Box 2918, Raleigh, NC 27690-0204. $99.00

Ohio (1,800 foundations). *Charitable Foundations Directory of Ohio.* 9th edition. 1990. 115 p. Based on records in the Ohio Attorney General's office and returns filed with the IRS. Main section arranged alphabetically by foundation; entries include statement of purpose and contact person; no sample grants. Indexes of foundation by county location and purpose. Available from Charitable Foundations Directory, Attorney General's Office, 30 East Broad Street, 15th Floor, Columbus, OH 43266-0410. $7.50. Make check payable to 1990 Charitable Foundations Directory of Ohio.

Ohio (38 foundations). *Guide to Charitable Foundations in the Greater Akron Area.* 3rd edition. Prepared by Grants Department. 1986. 45 p. Based on United Way files, the Charitable Foundations Directory of Ohio, 990-PF and 990-AR returns filed with the IRS, and information supplied by foundations. Main section arranged alphabetically by foundation; entries include statement of purpose, sample grants and officers. Also section on proposal writing. Appendixes include indexes of assets, grants, and officers and trustees. Available from Grants Department, United Way of Summit County, P.O. Box 1260, 90 North Prospect Street, Akron, OH 44304. $8.00

Oklahoma (approximately 181 foundations). *The Directory of Oklahoma Foundations*. 3rd edition. Compiled and edited by Mary Deane Streich. 1990. 112 p. Basic information on Oklahoma foundations from the latest IRS 990 forms on file at the Oklahoma Attorney General's office. Available from Foundation Research Project, P.O. Box 1146, Oklahoma City, OK 73101-1146. $20.00 prepaid.

Oregon (350 foundations). *The Guide to Oregon Foundations*. Compiled by Craig Mcpherson. 1987. 241 p. Based on 990-PF and 990-AR forms filed with the Oregon Attorney General's Charitable Trust Division and information supplied by the foundations. Available from United Way of the Columbia-Williamette, 718 West Burnside, Portland, OR 97209. $20.00. Make checks payable UWCW/Guide.

Pennsylvania (over 2,300 foundations). *Directory of Pennsylvania Foundations*. 4th edition. Compiled by S. Damon Kletzien. 1990. 384 p. Based on 990-PF and 990-AR returns filed with the IRS and information supplied by foundations. Main section arranged alphabetically within geographic regions; profile entries include statement of purpose, grants of $100 or larger, application guidelines, and officers of foundations meeting criteria of assets exceeding $75,000 or awarding grants totaling $4,000 or more. For foundations under criteria, entries include foundation name, address and status code only. Appendixes on approaching foundations, program planning and proposal writing, and broadening the foundation search. Available from Triadvocates Press, P.O. Box 336, Springfield, PA 19064. $54.95 including postage and tax.

Rhode Island (250 corporations). *Corporate Philanthropy in Rhode Island*. 2nd edition. Edited by Michael E. Burns. 1989. 76 p. Based on questionnaires and interviews, profiles charitable contributions of Rhode Island corporations. Available from D.A.T.A., 70 Audubon, New Haven, CT 06510. $16.95 plus $3.00 shipping.

South Carolina (196 foundations). *South Carolina Foundation Directory*. 3rd edition. Edited by Guynell Williams. 1987. 255 p. Based on 990-PF returns filed with the IRS. Main section arranged alphabetically by foundation; entries include areas of interest, principal officer, assets, total grants, number of grants, range and geographic limitations. Indexes of foundations by city and field on interest. Available from South Carolina State Library, P.O. Box 11469, Columbia, SC 29211. Send $10.00 check payable to the South Carolina State Library.

South Dakota (300 grant-making institutions). *The South Dakota Grant Directory*. Compiled by the South Dakota State Library. 1989. 93 p. Information on grant-making institutions in South Dakota; also lists major foundations located outside the state that have funded projects in South Dakota. Available from the South Dakota State Library, 800 Governors Drive, Pierre, SD 57501-2294. Free

Tennessee (493 funders). *A Guide to Funders in Central Appalachia and the Tennessee Valley*. Edited by Suzanna O'Donnell and Kim Klein. 1988. 225 p. Lists nearly 500 funders that give grants in the geographical region that includes northern Alabama, northern Georgia, eastern Kentucky, western North Carolina, southeastern Virginia, and the entire states of Mississippi, Tennessee, and West Virginia. Available from Appalachian Community Fund, 517 Union Street, Knoxville, TN 37902. $35.00 plus $3.00 postage.

Tennessee (58 foundations, 21 corporations). *Tennessee Directory of Foundations and Corporate Philanthropy*. 3rd edition. Published by the City of Memphis, Bureau of Intergovernmental Management. 1985. Based on 990-PF and 990-AR returns filed with the IRS and questionnaires. Two main sections arranged alphabetically by foundation and alphabetically by corporation; entries include contact person, contact procedure, fields of interest, geographic limitations, financial data, officers and trustees and sample grants. Indexes of foundations and corporations by name, fields of interest and geographic area of giving. Appendixes of foundations giving less than $10,000 a year and major corporations in Tennessee which employ more than 300 persons. Available from City of Memphis, Bureau of Intergovernmental Management, 125 North Mid-America Mall, Room 508, Memphis, TN 38103.

Texas (1,545 foundations). *Directory of Texas Foundations*. 11th edition. Edited by Mary Elizabeth Webb. 1990. 179 p. Main section alphabetical listings of large and small foundations. Indexes by areas of giving, city, trustees and officers, foundation name. Available from Funding Information Center, 507 Brooklyn, San Antonio, TX 78215. $119.00

Texas (approximately 147 foundations). *Directory of Tarrant County Foundations.* 4th edition. Compiled by Dorothy Blackwell and Catherine Rhodes. 1989. 163 p. Based on 990-PF forms filed with the IRS and foundation questionnaires. Main section arranged alphabetically by foundation; entries include financial data, background and program interest, officers and trustees, types of support and geographic focus. Indexes of foundations, trustees and officers, types of support and fields of interest. Appendices of foundations by asset amount and foundations by total grants. Available from Funding Information Center, Texas Christian University Library, Fort Worth, TX 76129. $30.00

Texas (73 major foundations). *The Directory of the Major Texas Foundations.* Compiled by Logos Associates. 1986. Full profiles of foundations making grants above $400,000 in Texas. Available from Logos Associates, 7 Park Street, Room 212, Attleboro, MA 02703. $39.95

Texas *Directory of Dallas County Foundations.* 3rd edition. Compiled by Ed Walton and David Wilkinson. 1990. Information on all private foundations in Dallas County. Available from Dallas Public Library, Grants Information Service, Government Publications Division, 1515 Young Street, Dallas, TX 75201. $30.00 Make checks payable to Dallas Public Library.

Vermont (80 foundations). *Vermont Directory of Foundations.* 3rd edition. Edited by Christine Graham. 1990. 57 p. Based on IRS 990-PF forms and information from foundation personnel, profiles of foundations incorporated in the state. Also lists 27 foundations incorporated outside of Vermont that have demonstrated an interest in funding Vermont nonprofits. Available from CPG Enterprises, Box 199, Shaftsbury, VT 05262. $25.00 plus $2.50 postage.

Vermont (over 125 corporate giving programs). *Corporate Philanthropy in New England: Vermont.* Vol. 4. Edited by Michael E. Burns. 1987. Available from D.A.T.A., 70 Audubon, New Haven, CT 06510. $5.00 plus $3.00 shipping.

Virginia (approximately 500 foundations). *Virginia Foundations.* Published by the Grants Resource Library of Hampton, Virginia. 1991. 200+ p. Based on 990-PF and 990-AR returns filed with the IRS. Main section arranged alphabetically by foundation; entries include officers and directors, assets, total grants and areas of interest. Index by foundation name, areas of interest. Available from Grants Resource Library, 4207 Victoria Boulevard, Hampton Public Library, Hampton, VA 23669-4243. $25.00

Virginia. See **Tennessee:** *A Guide to Funders in Central Appalachia and the Tennessee Valley.* O'Donnell, Suzanna, et al.

Washington (approximately 400 organizations). *Charitable Trust Directory.* Compiled by the Office of the Attorney General. 1991. Based on the 1991 records in the Washington Attorney General's office. Includes information on all charitable organizations and trusts reporting to Attorney General under the Washington Charitable Trust Act. Main section arranged alphabetically by organization; entries include statement of purpose and officers. No sample grants or indexes. Price and order information available from Sandy Sternberg, Office of the Attorney General, Charitable Trust Division, P.O. Box 40106, Olympia, WA 98504-0106.

West Virginia (over 62 foundations). *West Virginia Foundation Directory.* 2nd edition. 106 p. 1987. Based on 990-PF and 990-AR returns filed with the IRS. Main section arranged alphabetically by foundation; entries include sample grants and officers; no statement of purpose. Also a section on inactive or terminated foundations. Index of counties and cities. Available from the Kanawha County Public Library, 123 Capitol Street, Charleston, WV 25301. $7.50

Wisconsin (775 foundations). *Foundations in Wisconsin: A Directory.* 10th edition. Compiled by Susan H. Hopwood. 1990. 216 p. Based on 990-PF and 990-AR returns filed with the IRS. Main section arranged alphabetically by foundation; entries include areas of interest and officers; sample grants. Also sections listing inactive foundations, terminated foundations, and operating foundations. Indexes of areas of interest, counties and foundation managers. Available from The Foundation Collection, Marquette

University Memorial Library, 1415 West Wisconsin Avenue, Milwaukee, WI 53233. $25.00

Wyoming (70 foundations). *Wyoming Foundations Directory.* Based on 990-PF and 990-AR returns filed with the IRS and a survey of the foundations. Main section arranged alphabetically by foundation; entries include statement of purpose and contact person when available. Also sections on foundations based out-of-state that award grants to Wyoming and a list of foundations awarding educational loans and scholarships. Index of foundations. 5th edition available from Laramie County Community College Library, 1400 East College Drive, Cheyenne, WY 82007 in 1992.

Wyoming See **Montana**: *The Montana and Wyoming Foundation Directory.* McRae, Kendal, et al.

APPENDIX C

Other Sources of Information

Annual Register of Grant Support. Marquis Who's Who, 4300 West 62nd Street, Indianapolis, IN 46206. Lists grant programs supported by foundation, government agencies, corporations, etc. Updated annually.

Aubin, Pierre, and George Cotter. *Agencies for Development Assistance: Sources of Support for Small Church Sponsored Projects in Developing Countries.* 4th ed. New York: Mission Project Service, 1991.

Burns, Michael E., ed. *Religious Philanthropy in New England: A Sourcebook.* Hartford, CT: D.A.T.A., 1987.

Butler, Francis J., ed. *Funding Churches in the Future: A Symposium on Financial Support and Development in the Catholic Church.* Washington, D.C.: FADICA, Inc., 1988.

Catalog of Federal Domestic Assistance. Executive Office of the President (OMB), Washington, DC 20503. For sale by Supt. of Documents, U.S. Government Printing Office, Washington, DC 20402. Marvelously indexed, kept up-to-date by loose-leaf additions throughout the year. (This book is helpful to those religious organizations seeking public funding for educational and/or social service purposes).

Council on Foundations. *The Philanthropy of Organized Religion.* Washington: Council on Foundations, 1985.

Foundation 500. Douglas M. Lawson Association, 39 East 51st Street, New York, NY 10022. Categorizes 500 largest foundations by general subject areas, amount of giving and giving patterns. Updated yearly.

Foundation Reporter. Taft Group, 835 Penobscot Building, Detroit, MI 48226 or call 1-800-877-TAFT. Includes 550 major American foundations, board members described, lists of grants paid, and description of purposes. There are nine regional publications and one national publication. Updated annually.

Fund Raiser's Guide to Religious Philanthropy. Taft Group, 835 Penobscot Building, Detroit, MI 48226 or call 1-800-877-TAFT. Details 390 foundation and corporate giving programs interested in religious philanthropy. Updated

Independent Sector. *Giving and Volunteering in the United States: Findings from a National Survey.* Washington, D.C., 1990.

National Fraternal Congress of America. *Statistics of Fraternal Benefit Societies.* Napperville, IL: 1991.

National Guide to Funding in Religion. Gives details of 2,800 foundations and corporate direct giving programs which have a history of funding churches, missionary societies, religious welfare, religious education programs and religiously affiliated organizations. This book is available through the Foundation Center at 79 Fifth Avenue, Dept. CE, New York, New York 10003-3050 or call 1-800-424-9836. $125.00.

Pierson, John. "Double Identity: Several Churches and Synagogues Operate Grantmaking Programs Exactly like Private Foundations." *Foundation News* 25 (September-October 1984): 44-50.

Reckard, Edgar C. "The Philanthropy of Organized Religion: What It Is, What It Does, and How It Relates to the Work Being Done by Private Foundations and Corporate Grantmakers." *Foundation News* 25 (September-October 1984): 18-9.

Robinson, Anthony L. *Foundations That Support Roman Catholic Activities.* Washington: Campaign for Human Development U.S. Catholic Conference, 1984.

The Taft Corporate Giving Directory. Taft Group, 835 Penobscot Building, Detroit, MI 48226 or call 1-800-877-TAFT. Includes 550 major companies and their corporate giving programs. Lists sales, profits and Fortune rank of company; contact information; how much is awarded annually; types of support; and, geographic giving patterns.

Where America's Large Foundations Make Their Grants. Public Service Materials Center, 355 Lexington Avenue, New York, NY 10017. Updated yearly.

Zehring, John William. *You Can Run a Capital Campaign: Raising Funds for Special Purposes. A Step-by-Step Guide for Church Leaders. Called to Serve.* Nashville, TE: Abingdon Press, 1989.